published by Duke University Press

W9-DGE-719

**positions** east asia cultures critique

volume 13   number 1   spring 2005

**Against Preemptive War**

# Contents

## Editors' Introduction

Jorge Luis Borges provided one of the canniest images of the relation between empire and representation. In "On Exactitude in Science," he wrote of an empire whose ambition to map the entire world in all its detail and variations led it to gradually increase the scope and complexity of its maps. Its "Cartographers Guild struck a map of the Empire whose size was that of the Empire, and which coincided point for point with it."[1] Thus, in its bid for full and complete representation, the map moved closer and closer to coinciding with the territory to be mapped. Quite literally, the map promised (or threatened) complete coverage. Yet "the Following Generations, who were not so fond of the Study of Cartography as their Forebears had been, saw that that vast Map was Useless" (ibid.). Thus the next generations "delivered it up to the Inclemencies of Sun and Winters" (ibid.). Borges leaves us with an image of the map slowly wearing away, stretched and torn and tattered over its lands, inhabited by Animals and Beggars.

*positions* 13:1 © 2005 by Duke University Press

Borges's Map of Empire recalls an ideal of representation that, in retrospect, we associate with Cold War intelligence and academic disciplines centered on nations, areas, and regions; it was about mapping and knowing the enemy, point for point, as it were—and the ally as well, for one never knows when an ally might prove detrimental. Cold War strategic knowledge embraced point-for-point knowledge of peoples and of the history, psychology, and culture of potential enemies, that is, of whoever happened to play the role of "the rest" to the West. It involved constant fuss about detailed intelligence and in-depth coverage, about filling gaps and mapping the world. There was a sense that in time one might gather sufficient intelligence to know the world and consequently to predict and forestall the outbreak of hostilities. After all, professors were there to provide knowledge about every imaginable culture and territory in the world, while journalists reported on location and undercover operatives blended like chameleons into any possible environment, all apprising the West of what the rest were really doing.

Of course, with his image of the imperial map rotting over its territory, Borges exposed an ideal whose full absurdity and naïveté only appears now, in retrospect. Borges's story thus provides a useful point of departure for assessing the current situation.

With the benefit of hindsight, Borges appears to have produced a humorous assessment not of Empire in general but of the mapping of knowledge of the Cold War era. Today, however, the older ideal of empire based on point-for-point knowledge and detailed intelligence lies in tatters. For various reasons, and often with good reason, many still adhere to associated ideals of thorough and detailed knowledge, not to shore up empire but to challenge it where it works, in the hopes of besting the empire at its own game. Nonetheless, the situation has changed from that of the Wilsonian world and its Cold War aftermath, and not simply because the following generations have not been so fond of the prior mapping, as in the Borges fable. Nor is it simply that those responsible for intelligence have become lazy or stupid or simply overtaxed. As the appearance of a crisis in intelligence surrounding 9/11 makes clear, something has fundamentally transformed. As Fred Kaplan argues in his assessment of the 9/11 reports, "The failure was not one of imagination but rather of incentives."[2] No one in a position of power felt compelled to respond to reports.

Similarly, we might cite what appears to be a complete lack of concern about accuracy. We must, of course, hold the Bush regime (and prior regimes) accountable for deliberate deception about the weapons of mass destruction in Iraq, and for continuing to lie about links between al Qaeda and Saddam Hussein. Nevertheless, we need to acknowledge the Bush regime's great success in treating strategic intelligence and "older" forms of imperial knowledge with such contempt. Is it not because they see older forms of knowledge rotting over the territory? In this respect, we cannot be content to think of this new contempt for intelligence wholly in terms of a repression of truth or a will to deceive on the part of a president, or an administration, or both. This is not to say that the current regime has not done its best to put its spin on events, even punishing those whose reports do not agree with its agenda. Rather we wish to signal that fidelity to an older code of intelligence will not necessarily save the day or explain the unreasonable effectiveness of the Bush regime at crucial junctures.

There is a tendency to see the current political crisis in terms of repression and deception. For instance, with the belated apologies of various newspapers for their biased and inaccurate coverage of the buildup to the American invasion of Iraq, we are invited to conclude that the decision for invasion came about through a repression of truth. We are encouraged to focus on the president and the administration's will to deceive. While there was, and is, mass media deception (and the documentary *Outfoxed: Rupert Murdoch's War on Journalism* [dir. Robert Greenwald, 2004] is instructive here), we must still acknowledge that the deception leading to invasion was an exceedingly thin and poor deception. How did it hold sway, then? With so many both within North America and around the world telling a very different story and with people of intelligence and integrity resigning from important positions in the media, we can only conclude that the American press is very easy to deceive. Or maybe it is willing to be deceived. As for the unitary "people" whom members of the media continually summon up to justify their part in the deception, it is difficult to speak of them. But we suspect, from the swell of underreported or unreported protests and demonstrations over the past three years, that there are all kinds of people who see through governmental attempts at media deception. How can one not feel tremendous gratitude to those who have struggled to speak accurately and frankly, and, if necessary, critically and polemically, and to march and demonstrate? In comparison, belated regrets and retractions from the media appear rather disingenuous, even as the media's confirmation of inaccuracy proves chilling.

A problem persists, one evident in the lack of motivation for accurate intelligence. It has recently become not only possible but also apparently desirable to speak of the United States as an empire (usually as a sort of "wake-up-and-smell-the-coffee" admonition to Americans to take stock of their status in the world). Whereas only a few years ago, to suggest that America was an empire brought down the wrath of the media establishment (witness the attacks on Gore Vidal for daring to bring the words *America* and *empire* together), we are now asked openly to think in terms of a difference between "old" empire and "new" empire. Jonathan Schell, for instance, wrote aptly before the 2004 presidential election, "A Kerry administration would undoubtedly try to return us to our older forms of imperial creep. The question is: Could it do so? Or rather, has the world so changed in the brief but wrenching interim that imperial policy in any form will prove bankrupt?"[3] In other words, a profound transformation has occurred. Suddenly, the American empire is completely visible, and we are asked not only to think in terms of American empire, but also in terms of a transformation from an older to a newer formation of empire.

A significant strand of reflection in recent theory, commentary, and study dealing with the problem of empire posits a radical break between an older formation of power, knowledge, and sovereignty and the new formation. In view of the problems of totalization presented by theories of radical rupture or total break, however, we will speak here of a transformation in empire. Indeed, as a point of departure for the various contributions to this volume, we would like to signal, somewhat schematically, a series of transformations that crop up in the current literature on empire, with an emphasis on ideological and operative recodings:

| | |
|---|---|
| Keynesian capitalism | crony capitalism |
| development | marketization |
| World Trade Organization | bilateral, regional trade |
| Cold War | hegemonic unilateralism |
| multilateralism | coalition of the willing |

| | |
|---|---|
| democracy vs. totalitarianism | civilization vs. barbarism |
| evil empire | axis of evil |
| threat of communist aggression | threat of terrorism |
| the Berlin Wall | counterinsurgency |
| Communist subversion | terrorist infiltration |
| nuclear deterrence | strategic preemption |
| peripheral ground war | mobile, high-tech war |

In understanding such transformations, Borges's image of the rotten, tattered Map of Empire provides some insight. It allows us to think about both the continuities and discontinuities that inform the current transformation toward a doctrine of preemptive war.

Today, we see not so much a lack of interest in mapping reality as contempt for reality. We also see contempt for attempts to map, represent, and even simulate reality, which translates into contempt for multilateral alliances, nuclear deterrence, and war on the ground. It is as if we can see at once both the ground and the impossibility of the older imperial project of mapping it. It is as if transparent tape or a thin coat of clear varnish had been layered onto the tattered map, allowing us to see the territory and its maps, and inviting us to accept a promise that these different realities will magically hold together. We are asked to put our faith in the adhesive and tensile strength of an exceedingly thin and transparent layer. We are asked to believe in it, not in spite of the visibility of the underlying inconsistencies and contradictions. Rather, we are exhorted to trust because the thin but powerful veneer allows us to see contradictions so plainly. The current contempt for reality, and for older means of representing it, appears to rely on this new transparent layer that promises to bring older modalities together into whatever new formation that we think desirable. It is as if we are offered a chance to create the world, not the opportunity to represent it.

It is this sense of powerful, almost unbearable clarity (yet entirely without intelligence) that allows for the belief that the world can now be fashioned anew. It is this sense that also justifies the logic of preemption. (See the U.S. National Security Policy, September 17, 2002.) The ability to see contradictions and cohesiveness at once imparts a sense that we can fight the future, and that the future is now.

Surely new technologies, new media, and new economies are crucial, ideologically and materially, to the emergence of this conceit that the world is now to be made anew. In fact, if the thin yet strong veneer were given a name, it might be new technologies or new media. Saying this, we don't wish to betray the genuine promise of these new media and technologies. After all, the Internet has been crucial to efforts to resist and challenge the current regime. Rather, we wish to highlight the relation between contradictions and a movement of noncontradiction at this moment of imperial transformation. One might think of this by way of the new corporate structures of weather reporting.

It is not unusual, for instance, to look out the window at rain while listening to a weather report garnered from patterns tracked via global satellite (collected through corporate structures rather than local weather stations) that announces sunshine. Of course, in such situations, we know that the report is mistaken. Yet, even if we have little faith in weather prediction generally, such counterfactual reports continue to circulate, mapping us into larger patterns in such a way that we may actually come to think that they are true, but in a different way from the weather before our eyes. We may even watch and listen to them ever more anxiously, struggling to comprehend blatant contradictions. This is where new technologies promise to hold contradictions together, not by overcoming or sublating them, but simply by holding them in clearly visible patchwork assemblies, as if bound with a fine film of transparent substance, which imparts a sense of command and control. Harry Harootunian's essay in this volume discusses one possible ideological response to this emergence of a space of noncontradiction. He writes of a situation in which all the contradictions are transparent, in which there is no evidence of cohesiveness. Yet we claim or believe that there is cohesiveness, in another way, at another level. He styles this stance of "I know very well but ... " as fascism. With fascism comes the sense that a space of noncontradiction can be physically realized, bound, and controlled, if only by worshipping it into transcendence.

Another example appears in Chalmers Johnson's *Sorrows of Empire*. He writes, "Overseas bases, of which the Defense Department acknowledges some 725, come within the scope of peacetime standing army and constitute a permanent claim on the nation's resources while being almost invariably inadequate for actually fighting a war."[4] Although recently the Bush regime has stepped up its efforts to increase the arsenal in Taiwan and to transform bases in Japan into command centers (to broaden their purposes beyond protection in East Asia to include military intervention in far-off wars), Johnson argues persuasively that "the American network of bases is a sign not of military preparedness but of militarism, the inescapable companion of imperialism."[5]

This culture of American militarism—a culture of masculine strength and bravado at a time when, ironically, physical strength has never been less important for American troops—was well in evidence at the Republican convention with all its hysteria over "girlie men." Can there be anything more absurd than a man who made his career with his body, with breasts to rival Dolly Parton's, who shows signs of extensive cosmetic surgery, speaking of girlie men? No wonder Jacques Lacan said that the display of virility appears feminine.[6] Again, the contradictions are completely transparent, even embarrassingly so. Accounts of the ironies and flat contradictions explicit in Cheney, Bush, and cronies talking of girlie men are already out there, quotable, on the Web. The point is, the new networks of American militarism do not care about reality or its representation. That's something for girlie men, or maybe women (whose reality does not register at all in this formation).

The transparency of contradictions has become crucial to the functioning of the new formation of American empire. Obviously, signs of inherent dysfunction and imminent failure abound. Many of the essays in this volume delve into these signs of dysfunction and failure, calling attention to reality and the importance of representing it accurately. We see in such essays not a simple extension of an older formation, a return to the older maps of reality (and thus belated reaction). Rather, they inscribe resistance to complete rupture with the past, to all those declarations of utter discontinuity that capitulate to the new empire. Other contributions to this volume strive to move beyond the politics of reality and its representation. In other words, they analyze the nonrepresentational forces to which the new imperial formation would lay claim. These essays attempt to shift the current transformation in new directions.

In brief, if the current situation is not to be unitary and monolithic, resistance must take diverse forms—as different as a "return" to reality and the accuracy of representation, and a push beyond the bind of representation. That is the aim of this collection, drawing responses against preemptive war from a variety of perspectives. The goal is not merely to multiply perspectives and to generate endless analysis, but to address the very difficult task of making visible the ways in which American imperialism and militarism operates preemptively. How do we put an end to preemptive war? How do we end this war waged against the future, against what might come to pass rather than against what actually is?

Tani Barlow, Yukiko Hanawa, Thomas LaMarre, and Donald Lowe

## Notes

1   Jorge Luis Borges, "On Exactitude in Science," in *Collected Fictions*, trans. Andrew Hurley (London: Penguin, 1998), 325. Jean Baudrillard also cites Borges's fable "On Exactitude in Science" to open his account of simulation (*Simulations* [New York: Semiotext(e), 1983], 1), but we evoke it not to speak of simulation (that is, a desperate attempt to produce the real in its absence), but rather to highlight the current regime's contempt for reality and its representation, which is accompanied by a delight in sustaining contradictory positions.

2   Fred Kaplan, "Show Me the Money: The 9/11 Commission's Report Is Superb, but Will It Change Anything?," *Slate*, July 22, 2004. www.slate.msn.com/id/2104208/.

3   Tom Engelhardt, "Tomgram: Jonathan Schell on the Empire that Fell before It Rose," August 21, 2004, tomdispatch.com. See also www.americanempireproject.com.

4   Chalmers Johnson, *The Sorrows of Empire: Militarism, Secrecy, and the End of the Republic* (New York: Metropolitan Books, 2004), 24.

5   Ibid., 25.

6   Jacques Lacan, "La signification du phallus," in *Écrits*, vol. 2 (Paris: Éditions du Seuil, 1971), 115.

# Preemptive Manhunt: A New Partisanship

Alberto Moreiras

"You idiot!" said the turtle. "Now you will die too! How could you do this?"
"My nature," shrugged the scorpion.

We are familiar with press descriptions of some of the search operations
carried out by Task Force 121 and other special forces (including the Pak-
istani Quick Reaction Force) to track down Saddam Hussein, Osama Bin
Laden, Mullah Muhammad Omar, Ayman al-Zawahiri, and other leaders
of Al-Qaeda, the Taliban, and the Baathist Party.[1] All of the aforementioned
are, or were, leaders of countries or partisan factions with which the United
States is formally at war. Their capture can be thought of as a necessity of
war in the traditional sense. But we are less familiar with what, according
to Seymour Hersh, Pentagon advisers are calling *preemptive manhunting*,[2]
a term they use to characterize a specific kind of operation entrusted to
those forces. *Manhunt* is a term that Donald Rumsfeld apparently uses to

*positions* 13:1 © 2005 by Duke University Press

designate the kind of military policy commensurate to the task of ending the Iraqi insurgency and other terrorist threats. Hersh quotes "an American who has advised the civilian authority in Baghdad" as saying, "The only way we can win is to go unconventional. We're going to have to play their game. Guerrilla versus guerrilla. Terrorism versus terrorism. We've got to scare the Iraqis into submission."[3] Preemptive manhunting would seem to refer to an unconventional, guerrilla, or partisan style of warfare deployed by regular combatants in the allied coalition.

Hersh compares this new policy of targeted assassination to the Vietnam War's Phoenix Program, through which at least twenty thousand "targets" under suspicion of being Vietcong collaborators were liquidated. But the Phoenix Program was not preemptive in nature (although it may actually have been so in many cases). What seems new now is the Bush administration's use of special forces to engage in preemptive strikes against guerrilla operations months after the conventional war was declared over.[4] There is an important precedent, however: the notorious and highly effective Israeli Mist'aravin commando units, which specialize in the assassination or capture of "potential suicide bombers along with many of the people who recruit and train them."[5] American Special Forces seem to be following the Israeli model. A recent report in the *Guardian Weekly*, after mentioning that urban warfare specialists from the Israeli Defense Forces had been training U.S. forces at Fort Bragg, NC, states that "U.S. special forces teams are already behind the lines inside Syria attempting to kill foreign jihadists before they cross the border, and a group focused on the 'neutralization' of guerrilla leaders is being set up."[6]

We are in murky waters. Even if the clear (but covert) mission of these forces is to search out and destroy potential insurgents in the Baathist party and in other militant Iraqi or extra-Iraqi sectors, it is not clear that we should be content to call these missions assassinations. "When the Special Forces target the Baathists," a former intelligence official said, "it's technically not assassination—it's normal combat operations."[7] Or, one could say, perhaps a preemptive assassination is not an assassination at all, since everything depends on the political valence of the term *preemptive*. We are in American science-fiction author Philip K. Dick territory, about which more will be said later.

In his book *Partisan Theory*, Carl Schmitt, after stating that partisan theory had become "the key to recognizing political reality"[8] (he was writing in 1962), devotes a few pages to the French general Raoul Salan, the head of the OAS during the Algerian rebellion against French colonial rule. In Salan, Schmitt says, "an existential conflict is exposed that is decisive for the partisan problem, one that arises when a conventional combat soldier must endure not only occasional but constant war with a fundamentally revolutionary and irregular fighting enemy."[9] Under Salan, the OAS "carried out premeditated terrorist actions against the Algerian enemy as well as the civil population in Algiers and the population of France itself. The premeditation involved methods of the so-called psychological warfare of modern mass terror."[10] Salan abandoned his role as a conventional combat soldier to engage in extralegal activities that, to his mind, furthered the cause of the French state. The paradox of a powerful colonial power seeming unable to contain the Algerian insurgency precipitated him, Schmitt tells us, into full participation in an *Irrsinnslogik*, or logic of unreason, "that embittered a courageous and intelligent man and drove him to the search for a countermeasure."[11] Countermeasures of the kind Salan espoused are not yet a part of U.S. policy, but Hersh's account, as well as other reports, would seem to indicate that a number of U.S. government officials are pushing for policy changes that would move in the direction of a direct incorporation of partisan tactics into regular combat activities—even though this time they would not be considered part of a logic of unreason, but rather rationalized into a practice of war as absolute enmity.

I am interested in exploring the notion of absolute enmity as a revision of the concept of the political, which for me must no longer be circumscribed by the Schmittian friend-enemy division.[12] It is not my intention to pass moral judgment on the particular kind of military logic deployed by the Bush administration. This military logic will rather be taken in what follows as a symptom of the political configuration of our times.

In his classic *Political Philosophy of Hobbes*, Leo Strauss notes that "the two fundamental innovations which are to be attributed to Hobbes, the subordination of law to right and the recognition of the full significance of the idea of sovereignty, are closely connected."[13] Sovereign power, in modern times, must be conceived of not as reason but as will, since the claim of sovereign right takes precedence over its lawfulness. Hence the fact that in modern politics there is a primacy of "foreign policy," as the legislator "carries out his legislation . . . with an eye to war, that is, to the assertion of the State against external conditions."[14] The fight against external conditions can be justified through fear of violent death: the state fears its demise at the hands of its enemies. Or it can be justified through a pursuit of power, which a monistic metaphysics would have to consider preemptive in nature: the pursuit of power in the enlargement of the state and its sovereign claims to domination would then be an apotropaic intensification of the means to ward off violent death, making it less likely, or infinitely deferrable. This is the ostensible reason offered by the Bush administration to justify its military policy—including selective unilateralism—after September 11, 2001. But Strauss's contribution was precisely to point out the indecisiveness of Hobbes's monism:

> The idea of civilization presupposes that man, by virtue of his intelligence, can place himself outside nature, can rebel against nature. This dualism is transparent all the way through Hobbes' philosophy, not least in the antithesis of *status naturalis* and *status civilis*. The antithesis of nature and human will is hidden by the monist (materialist-deterministic) metaphysic, which Hobbes *teaches*, which he found himself forced to adopt simply because he saw no other possibility of escaping the "substantialist" conception of mind, and therefore "the kingdom of darkness."[15]

Striving for power, insofar as it embodies a surreptitious return of the kingdom of darkness, no longer constitutes a moral basis for the political: the fear of death does not totally regulate it. An excess sets in, has always already set in, and this excess undoes not just the moral containment of the will to power but also the determination of the political as contained by the friend-enemy division.

If Hobbes establishes the horizon of the political in the negation of the state of nature and the elaboration of a philosophy of culture, or of the *status civilis*, there can be no transcendence of the liberal horizon except through a deconstruction of the cultural. Carl Schmitt's description or determination of the political as the field of division between friend and enemy does not touch on the otherwise necessary reinscription of the political into the cultural as the properly sovereign sphere in the liberal horizon (which can, of course, be defined as the dominant horizon of modernity). Schmitt says that the friend-enemy split is relational and always reactive in the face of an existential negation whose truth is war.[16] But to think of war as the *ultima ratio* of the political erases the question as to the sufficient reason for war itself. Under what conditions does war occur? If the Hobbesian war of all against all marks the state of nature, then, by definition, war between friends and enemies is a conflict that is structurally mediated by the cultural. If the cultural mediates the political, then, *pace* Schmitt, the political is not the ultimate instance of constitution of sovereignty: the political is not the field of decision if the decision must appeal, in every case, and in order to produce itself as decision, to the transpolitical dimension of the cultural. Schmitt was wrong in positing the friend-enemy distinction "independently of other antitheses"[17] because, in Hobbesian terms, this distinction is only possible on the basis of the vanquishing of the state of nature by the state of culture.

In politics, sovereignty exists in the relational form of a sovereignty without sovereignty, that is, a sovereignty that is absolutely limited by the possibility of violent death. For Schmitt, "in the orientation toward the possible extreme case of an actual battle against a real enemy, the political entity is essential, and it is the decisive entity for the friend-enemy grouping; and in this (and not in any kind of absolutist sense), it is sovereign. Otherwise the political entity is nonexistent."[18] Relational sovereignty has been the basis of the interstate system of world regulation throughout modernity. But sovereignty without sovereignty finds its absolutization in the positing of humanity as the only possible political subject, which is for Schmitt the tendential goal of liberalism: "Humanity according to natural law and liberal-individualistic doctrines is a universal, i.e., all-embracing, social ideal, a system of relations between individuals. This materializes only when the real possibility of war is precluded and every friend and enemy grouping becomes impossible. In this universal society there would no longer be nations in the form of political entities, no class struggles, and no enemy groupings."[19] There would only be humanity, conceived as one. This unique subject of humanity—this unique human subject, the apotheosis of the liberal worldview—forms the sufficient reason of absolute sovereignty for modernity. In humanity as subject or in the subject of humanity, modern sovereignty enters into full sovereignty.

Sovereignty enters sovereignty when the cultural has absolutely invaded the state of nature—when the war of all against all is subsumed into the neutral war of a humanity that has become full subject, with neither enemies nor friends, which is for our world metonymically symbolized in the triumph of liberal capitalism and the demise of the Soviet bloc circa 1989. Politics then becomes a relationless relation, a condition called by some "the end of history."[20] Under this condition, to think of the political as a relationless relation is, on the one hand, to think of a "beyond the subject" as the condition of possibility of the abyssal relation of the subject with itself, now become absolute in the form of empty totality. But it is also, and simultaneously, to think of a "beyond the cultural," since culture is the liminal realm of relational sovereignty whose political end is the end of the political as friend-enemy field. To think of beyond absolute sovereignty as the truth of history in accomplished globalization and to think of beyond relational sovereignty as the truth of the political today is to think of the enigmatic remainder for a new partisanship.[21]

This enigmatic remainder, the obscure leftover in the constitution of the full subject of liberal humanity, in the context of the division of the political field between friends and enemies, occupies the nonplace of the nonfriend—that which does not enter into the sovereign relation, but in relation to which any sovereign relation becomes possible. In the context of the division between absolute and relational sovereignty (this division is the founding relation of the principle of hegemony in modernity), the enigmatic remainder occupies the nonplace of subalternity—that is, that which can only experience the hegemonic articulation as domination, and which is therefore beyond hegemony. This thinking of the neutral and obscure war beyond the war might be capable, perhaps, of restoring the political against the political understood as the contemporary dispensation of sovereignty.

In the war beyond the war that the coalition's special forces are now waging against pro-Iraqi insurgents, partisan theory becomes crucial. As Schmitt puts it, "in the diabolical circle of terror and counter-terror the attack on partisans is often a mirror-image of partisan battle itself. The old saw attributed to a command of Napoleon's General Lefevre on 12 September 1813 remains valid: you have to fight like a partisan wherever there are partisans—*il faut operer en partisan partout ou il y a des partisans.*"[22]

And the consequences remain incalculable, as the partisans, and then the counterpartisans, themselves now partisans, become the true heroes of the war, of any war. In generalized partisanship, no rules obtain, except the rules of force. This was formalized for the first time in history, says Schmitt, in the Prussian edict on the Territorial Reserves of April 1813, which was itself based on the 1808 Spanish *Reglamento de partidas y cuadrillas*:

> Every Prussian is charged to obey no order from the enemy, but to harm him with whatever means are at hand. Even if the enemy is trying to establish public order no one is supposed to obey, because obedience facilitates his military operations. It is explicitly stated that the "excesses of the unbridled rabble" are less damaging than the state of affairs in which the enemy can dispose freely of all his troops. . . . War is justified as a defensive necessity that "sanctifies every means," even the unleashing of total civil disorder.[23]

In the total resistance of the partisan, and then, by implication, in the total resistance against the partisan, a "striking transformation" in "the concept of the political" occurs, and the partisan becomes "a figure of the world-spirit."[24] It is not by chance that the partisan becomes a Hegelian figure of world history precisely in the resistance against the postrevolutionary Napoleonic armies. The modern partisan (and there is *no* nonmodern partisan, Schmitt tells us) is the embodiment of what Jacques Rancière calls the part of no-part, that is, it is the embodiment of the enigmatic remainder of the full (liberal) subject of humanity.[25]

But the striking transformation that Schmitt has in mind affects the constitution of enmity as "absolute enmity," not yet overcoming the concept of the political as exhausted in and by the friend-enemy division: "In comparison with a war of absolute enmity, the limited war of classical European international law, proceeding by recognized rules, is little more than a duel between cavaliers seeking satisfaction. . . . The war of absolute enmity knows no limits" as it calls "the whole edifice of political and social order into question."[26] Absolute enmity is a radical disavowal of commonality as it promotes "a new kind of warfare whose sense and purpose [is] the destruction of the existing social order."[27] Against the partisan's commitment to destruction, the counterpartisan's commitment can only be to destroy the destructor. But the counterpartisan is not yet the partisan insofar as the counterpartisan wills the preservation of an order, even if the order to be preserved is precarious and has been gained at the price of a previous destruction, even if it is just the order of an occupation.

Let us assume that the occupation is preemptive, that it wards off the possibility of violent death for the occupying power and for the social order for which it stands. A corollary would be that such an occupation is moral insofar as no excessive striving for power determines it. It is then strictly defensive, and even tellurian, in that its fundamental dimension is the protection of home territory against its enemy. But a tellurian defense of the homeland bespeaks limited enmity. There is an inherent excessive dimension to preemption when preemption seeks to destroy the foundations of the potential enemy order in its home territory. Preemptive excess is the conversion of limited enmity into absolute enmity; as such it is guided by what Schmitt called "the absolutism of an abstract righteousness"[28] and is no longer tellurian.[29]

Schmitt develops his partisan theory within the horizon of the Cold War. The communists, after Lenin, are partisans because they identified the class enemy as absolute enemy. "The irregularity of class struggle calls not just the military line but the whole edifice of political and social order into question. In the Russian professional revolutionary, Lenin, this new reality was raised to philosophical awareness. The association of philosophy with the partisan . . . unleashed new, explosive forces. It produced nothing less than the demolition of the whole Eurocentric world."[30]

Stalin and Mao Zedong radicalized communist partisanship by linking the tellurian element of patriotic self-defense with the abstract righteousness of international communist revolution. In particular, Mao's struggle was able to join various enmities (racial enmity, internecine enmity, colonial enmity, class enmity) into a radical theoretical consciousness of absolute enmity that nevertheless could not hide an inner contradiction: the confusion of "an undifferentiated, global-universal, absolute world-enemy, the Marxist class enemy, with a territorially specific, actual enemy of the Chinese-Asiatic defense against capitalist colonialism" (47). It is that contradiction or confusion, at the same time constitutive of and detected by partisan theory, that makes partisan theory "the key to recognizing political reality," in 1963 or throughout the Cold War (49). But we are no longer in the Cold War. The contradiction must be redescribed, at the price of a new transformation in the concept of the political.

Schmitt could not anticipate developments beyond the politics of his own time. Nevertheless, he ventures a question that seems to prefigure the events of September 11: "What if the human type that went into the partisan adapted to its new technical-industrial environment, learned how to make use of the new means, and developed a new, adapted sort of partisan—call him the industrial partisan?" (66). This question already forms beyond the constraints of the political in the Cold War, in that it assumes the resolution of the contradiction between the terranean or tellurian residual partisanship of the communist fighter and her or his engagement in abstract righteousness: within the constellation that Schmitt's question opens to view, and in his terms, abstract righteousness, as the disembodied embodiment of the radical victory of culture over nature, has won, promoted by communism, but not in its favor. The inner contradiction of communist partisanship plays itself out in the voiding of its tellurian element as it announces necessarily postcommunist times:

> The autochthonous defenders of home and earth, who died *pro aris et focis*, the national and patriotic heroes who went into the woods, all elemental, telluric force in reaction to foreign invasion: it has all come under an international and transnational central control that provides assistance and support but only in the interest of its own quite distinctive aggressive international purposes. It protects, or abandons, accordingly. At this point the partisan ceases to be essentially defensive. He becomes a manipulated cog in the wheel of revolutionary aggression. He is stirred up, and swindled of everything he was fighting for, everything the telluric character, the source of his legitimacy as an irregular partisan, was rooted in. (60)

Without legitimacy, postcommunist, the new abstract righteousness is precariously dependent on a legality that does not yet exist. And yet, "to settle on an enemy for oneself means assuming responsibility for a new legality, if one does not wish to follow the determinations of the existing legal regime" (68). The new legality is then a posited "third party" that could have been constituted by the Soviet government during the Cold War or could be constituted in the present by a new—if, today, still phantom—order of regularity. But the order of regularity is essential to the partisan if he or she is not to sink into abyssal criminality. "The interested third party [plays] an essential function in connecting the partisan to an order of regularity so that he [remains] within the purview of the political. The basis of the political is not enmity per se, but the distinction of friend and enemy, it presupposes both friend and enemy" (73). There can be no politics, for Schmitt, unless the new partisan is sustained in her or his struggle by a legality, present or potential, that would then be constitutive of friendship. The notion of friendship is thus tied by Schmitt to legality, since legitimacy is no longer a given ("the bitter alternative between legality and legitimacy is a direct consequence of the French revolution") (69).

So where can partisan theory be taken today? To the extent that coalition special forces are secure in their friendship and in their legality, even when it is a new legality without foundation in the 1949 Geneva Conventions, coalition special forces must be defined as counterpartisan. As counterpartisan, they are partisan, not least in their definition of the opposing forces as absolute enemy. The other partisans, the enemy, are the absolute enemy, hence their present or potential order of regularity must be totally destroyed. The phrase *preemptive manhunting* arises from an ideological position that recognizes no valid order of friendship to the enemy: they are securely condemned to an impossible and, as it were, postlapsarian state of nature from which they are not to emerge into a *status civilis* or cultural order of any kind. Schmitt concludes his *Partisan Theory* with the following reflection:

> The ultimate danger lies then not so much in the living presence of instruments of annihilation and human evil. It consists in the inevitability of a moral impulse. Men who turn these means against others see themselves obliged to annihilate their victims and objects, even morally obliged. They have to consider the other side as entirely criminal and inhuman, as totally worthless. Otherwise they are themselves criminal and inhuman. The logic of value and its obverse, worthlessness, unfolds its annihilating consequences, compelling ever deeper discriminations, criminalizations, and devaluations, to the point of annihilating all of unworthy life. (75)

Thus, "we're going to have to play their game," indeed. The danger of a Hobbesian politics of power not checked by the condition of fear—that is, the excessive dimension of preemption, which results in a tendentiously unchecked striving for power, and for absolute power against an absolute enemy—destroys the political game as a game within the state of culture, within the borders of the friend-enemy division. Even Schmitt, who remains thoroughly committed to a consideration of the political in terms of friendship and enmity, must admit that "enmity [could become] so terrifying that it will perhaps no longer be possible to speak of the enemy or of enmity and both words will have to be esteemed and damned before the work of annihilation can begin" (75). A new partisanship emerges, the partisanship of absolute counter-partisanship, which nevertheless must open a new possibility for politics.[31]

In Don De Lillo's *Cosmopolis*, a novel that allegorizes what one could call our actually existing civilization, the protagonist, Eric Packer, witnesses an antiglobalization anarchist action and reflects that those actors come from within, arise from civilization itself, and sum up its very condition of existence. War, even the neutral and obscure war beyond the war, is a fantasy inherent to the civilizing process, a self-civilizing melodrama. In any war, an outside has been previously subjected to an apparatus of capture. War is only possible when the exteriority of the enemy has vanished as such. As a consequence, every war is a civil war. Civilizations exist, and Samuel Huntington is right to that extent, but that affirmation already reveals that civilizations are not what they used to be.[32] There are civilizations in the strict measure in which they cease to be: they can only be recognized through their loss as such. Modernity is nothing but the process of absolute reduction of civilizations, not to one civilization, but rather to what we could call a civilizational trace, or a constellation of such traces. If it was thought that within modernity such a vast process of capture and subjection of the world could incarnate into a "concrete universal"—Charles V's *monarchia universalis*, Catholic union, communism, or Pax Americana—then within postmodernity there would be the abandonment of such a notion in favor of the notion of civilizational trace, the acknowledgement that there can only be *distance* regarding any civilizational process, and the knowledge that any civilizational process, such as war, a given war, is only *distance* regarding any possible civilizational project. This is nothing but a repetition of the Nietzschean intuition: if you abandon the notion of an outside, you end up losing the possibility of interiority. What remains is a neutral and indifferent space, a space without place, an impossible claustrophobia that is the site of the trace and the site of the infinite circulation of the trace. In De Lillo's novel, two men enter a coffee shop holding rats by their tails. "Then the men flung the rats, stilling the room. . . . The animals tail-whipped through the air, hitting and rebounding off assorted surfaces and skimming tabletops on their backs, momentum-driven, two lurid furballs running up the walls, emitting a mewl and squeak, and the men ran too, taking their shout out to the street with them, their slogan or warning or incantation."[33] The rats' vectors—their panic displacement through the café space—allegorize the movement of the trace in our world.[34]

Huntington's "clash of civilizations" is an ideological displacement conditioned by the crisis of sovereignty in the nation-state. Huntington seeks to reterritorialize the national-popular as civilizational subject in order to turn the latter into the chosen hero of the history of the future. But if there is a crisis of sovereignty of the national-popular subject, it is because the national-popular subject never was in the first place more than an ideological configuration of power. If the national-popular subject was what Louis Althusser could call an instance of melodramatic consciousness ("false consciousness of a real situation"), the civilizational subject is a fortiori an instance of melodramatic consciousness and concealment of real situations.[35] One can talk about the desired formation of civilizational or continental subjects and be in favor of pan-Europeanisms, pan-Latin Americanisms, or pan-Asianisms with the purpose of arresting the power of the American *hegemon*, in a sort of Leninist Huntingtonianism, as John Beverley has put it.[36] But if this idea is proposed as a purely political tactic—that is, as a prescription for a new biopolitical manipulation of the political, as a sort of self-engineering of subjects—the very voluntarism of the proposal destroys its viability: subjects do not form themselves freely, as we have known at least since Althusser.[37] If the Leninist-Huntingtonian idea offers itself as the conceptual anticipation of a spontaneous development, if it is therefore asserted that the world moves of its own accord toward the formation of firmly reterritorialized subjects under continental or civilizational guises (this is, of course, Huntington's position, although his interest is to preserve the power of the *hegemon* rather than contain it), then one suspects that what is prophesied as liberating is pure reactionary force and a potential new night of the world. That we must spontaneously be subject to that which we are and we ought to be, that we must make civilizational or continental militancy our business, that we must configure our political identity on the basis of historico-cultural determinations—all of that is the very name of oppression, first self-oppression, and then oppression of others. We should fight against that nightmare rather than advise it as a cure against actually existing antagonisms.

Actually existing antagonisms are class antagonisms between the rich and the poor. They are not civilizational antagonisms, although in every case the civilizational trace translates into the violence of political economy. It has been years since Hisham Sharabi proposed the term "neopatriarchy" to refer to Islamic postmodernity.[38] Neopatriarchy, as well as Muslim fundamentalism, is in itself reaction and distance. Neither neopatriarchy nor Muslim fundamentalism are signs of an alternative or other civilization, but rather both are traces of the modern reduction of civilizations, the political and geopolitical result of a loss of place in the space that Felipe Martínez Marzoa calls the "unlimited continuum" of modernity.[39] Because the continuum is unlimited, it has no outside, and therefore no inside. There is only a claustrophobic exacerbation in the open, in regard to which the terrorist violence of September 11, and other instances of terrorism, are symptomatic torsions. Al-Qaeda, the Taliban, Saddam Hussein's regime needed to be bellically rather than politically destroyed, not because they were over there, beyond the borders of Western civilization or of civilization in general, nor because they were threatening to destroy or destabilize the latter, but rather because there is no longer an "over there, beyond," and this makes claustrophobic panic—the rats in the coffee shop—intolerable. Such panic is universal. War becomes indistinguishable from the capacity to unleash it, since it is neutral and total, *potentia* has become *actus*, *dynamis* has become *energeia*.

For Carl Schmitt the need to protect oneself against the enemy is total and requires no further justification, because the enemy is he or she who threatens your existence. The need for self-defense is absolute and structures the political, even when the political manifests itself as the field of relational

mediations or negotiations between enemies. When the enemy deploys its
annihilating force, war becomes explicit. Before that, war is implicit, potential, since we are always under the threat of the enemy. Is it possible to
contemplate the possibility of an enemy-less humanity? Only if we could
simultaneously consider the possibility of a total absence of friendship, since
there are only friends to the extent that there are—or that there may be—
enemies. Liberalism's promise is precisely the promise of the antipolitical
constitution of a full subject of humanity; this is also communism's promise,
since communism, for Schmitt and others, is a historical extension of liberalism. The unlimited continuum of modern temporality closes on itself by way
of the riftless constitution of a unique subject—*the* subject. Humanity enters its final time, the unimaginable end term of every politics of friendship,
which is also the end of politics *tout court*.

Is the end of politics the final redemption of humanity in perpetual peace?
We live in transitional times. War is today diffused as neutral war, since the
enemy—now merely residual, only abject, only inhuman, no longer enemy
of my friends, but the enemy of humanity as a whole—must be destroyed
absolutely. The figure of the enemy is hyperreal, since *potentia* is *actus* and
*dynamis* is *energeia*. Political antagonisms are no longer recognized primarily as antagonisms between friends and enemies, but rather as antagonisms
between the friendless subject of humanity and the obscene and abject forces
that refuse their incorporation into it—the rats in the coffee shop. We live
in the twilight or at the dawn of perpetual peace, the historical moment
of maximum intensification of hatred for the enemy—the negation of its
human character, its conversion into bare life, to use the Benjaminian expression Giorgio Agamben has made his, or into unworthy life, in Schmitt's
formulation.[40] Such is the "inevitability of [our] moral impulse."

Dick's short story "The Minority Report" is indeed as good a spur as any
to make us reflect on the paradoxes of preemption: "The assertion that this
man [this state] will commit a crime is paradoxical. The very act of possessing
this data renders it spurious."[41] In the story, which was recently made into a
film, John Allison Anderton, the Precrime unit founder and director, faces
a Senate-appointed assistant, Ed Witwer, who will most likely become his
successor. "Precrime" is of course a police unit that works preemptively, on
the basis of information provided by the so-called precog mutants, that is,

individuals able to foresee the future. Precrime has "boldly and successfully abolished the postcrime punitive system of jails and fines," which "was never much of a deterrent" (72). Precog mutants can read the future and see who needs to be taken in prior to his or her (inevitable) commission of a crime. Precrime methodology, Anderton understands, incorporates a "basic legalistic drawback": the individuals apprehended "have broken no law" (72) (but they surely will; but, then again, they have not). The result is a society with "no major crimes" but with "a detention camp full of would-be criminals" (72). No doubt in Dick's story this ever-present background of the criminal camp is the very source of the story's political engagement, its political unconscious. The story is, in fact, silently written from the perspective of one of the camp inhabitants—what Anderton will become at the story's end.

But at the beginning, as Anderton shows Witwer the functioning of the analytical machinery, a card pops up, and Anderton realizes its content: "John A. Anderton was going to kill a man—and within the next week" (75). What to do? Has the card been planted? Is it all a conspiracy? Is he being framed for the sake of an obscure dictatorial design on the part of the Senate, the Army, the Police? He has twenty-four hours to find out before he is arrested.

As he prepares to escape, he is kidnapped by men at the service of the man Anderton is supposed to kill, General Kaplan, who wishes to know why Anderton would want to kill him before turning him over to Witwer, the new authority. The radio blares out an interdiction against Anderton. The conspirators have not wasted any time. But Anderton must confront the thought that even the possibility of a successful conspiracy against him destroys the legitimacy of the Precrime system: if one person can be framed, many can. It is at this point that a new set of actors, seemingly related to the resistance against the regime, kidnap Anderton from the kidnappers, confirm that there is indeed a frame-up going on, and give him false papers and money for him to go into hiding "until [he's] proved [his] point" (83). They also give him an enigmatic message: "The existence of a majority logically implies a corresponding minority" (84).

The resistance's message is not ostensibly a reference to the Schmittian friend-enemy division, but rather to the theory of multiple futures, according to which "if only one time-path existed, precognitive information would be of no importance, since no possibility would exist, in possessing this information, of altering the future" (85). Precrime works following a statistical logic: two of the three precog mutants must be in agreement, which necessarily implies the disagreement of the third. Anderton, then, "had to see the minority report" (85).

With the help of a former associate, Anderton visits Jerry, the idiot precog mutant who produced the minority report, and hacks the relevant data. According to the minority report, for Anderton "the preview of the murder had cancelled out the murder; prophylaxis had occurred simply in his being informed. Already, a new time-path had been created. But Jerry was outvoted" (88). Anderton now has the proof that the majority report was rendered obsolete by the fact that the minority report had already incorporated it into its own account. But didn't Witwer know that?

Perhaps General Kaplan, his life no longer threatened, will help Anderton—on the condition that everybody understands that, if the minority report is not a fake, then the two majority reports are not fakes either. There has been no conspiracy. Witwer simply followed something like the inevitability of a moral impulse: "He believes in Precrime. He wants the system to continue" (90). Another dilemma presents itself: if Witwer is really innocent, if there has been no bad faith, if everything in Anderton's case is unique because it is dependent on his own privileged access to the analytical machinery, then no other flukes will occur, and the system is worth preserving. Anderton's wife points out that going to Kaplan will surely destroy the system, for Kaplan will go public with his information. Anderton must choose between going to Kaplan to help himself or going to Witwer to preserve the system. He chooses to help himself, but the resistance warns him that Kaplan and Witwer work together. Anderton's wife disagrees. She must be killed, since she is, the resistance insists, working for the conspirators. Anderton saves her and discovers that Fleming, the partisan, was actually working for military intelligence, and for Kaplan, against Witwer, a so-far unwitting counterpartisan. Anderton realizes that Kaplan wants to destroy the system on behalf of the army and against the police and political order. Now, since Anderton won't kill him, as the minority report states, Kaplan can prove the system wrong whether Anderton is imprisoned or not. "Heads or tails—he wins" (94).

Is there a way out? To discover it, Anderton must study the two majority reports. He does, and finds a solution: "I'm going to have to fulfill the majority reports. I'm going to have to kill Kaplan. That's the only way we can keep them from discrediting us" (96). But, Witwer says, "the majority report has been superseded" (96). Is the minority report incorrect? "'No,' Anderton said, 'it's absolutely correct. But I'm going to murder Kaplan anyhow'" (96). And he does, immediately on Kaplan's realization of his fate.

The truth is, there were three minority reports, although the first and the third coincided in their final prophecy that Anderton would murder Kaplan, thus constituting the majority. If the second report started a different time-path on the basis of the knowledge Anderton acquired about the prophesied deed, the third report inaugurated a third time-path, based on knowledge of that knowledge. The truth came out aporetically, through an accumulation of errors that could have continued as such, through further reports, changing thus the very content of the truth. Could this ever happen again? Are we imprisoning potentially innocent individuals? Does the system need to be overhauled? It could happen, Anderton says, but only to the person in a position to know of knowledge, and of knowledge of knowledge, that is, it could happen to the next police commissioner. "'Better keep your eyes open,' [Anderton] informed young Witwer. 'It might happen to you at any time.'" (102).

Kaplan had understood at the last minute before his death what was about to happen to him because he made the logical inference: "There can be no valid knowledge of the future. As soon as precognitive information is obtained, it cancels itself out" (99). Preemption is therefore absurd. But, by the same token, any preemptive system, by eradicating alternative time-paths, proves itself right every time, insofar as it limits itself to eradicating those time-paths that would preempt preemption itself. It is all a mere question of the administration of knowledge, of an impossible intelligence whose only condition, whose sufficient and therefore necessary reason, is always already self-fulfilling, absolute enmity.

The new partisanship is the partisanship of the full subject of humanity, of full sovereignty, exercised against the actual and potential inhabitants of the camp. Whoever engages in it, acting from hegemonic power or against it, in the void aspiration to a new legality without legitimacy, has already given up the friend-enemy division for the sake of a relationless relation—which is the more accurate political formation of our time. Unilateralism necessarily prevails through the full hypostasis of political subjectivity, long announced by modernity. Against it, a conception of political practice beyond subjectivity is not only possible but necessary. For, after all, the nonfriend, the nonenemy, or the nonsubject, in the full anonymity of the fear of death, is not just the outside of any preemptive political system—that is, of any political system that articulates itself on the basis of the anticipation of the destruction of its enemy—but also the conditionless condition of any system, and thus the effective, and effectively unrecognized, ground of all politics.

Absolute sovereignty occurs through the infinite production of new enemies, new outlaws, new groupings, even if the new enemy, beyond absolute enmity, has entered the realm of the posthuman. There are still friends and enemies, but in absolute sovereignty, in the historical dispensation of actually existing globalization, the friend-enemy division is insufficient to capture the specificity of the political. Thus, a politics of the nonsubject, of the enigmatic remainder, committed to the redemption of the part of no-part, is no longer primarily a politics of friendship, which is another name for a politics of hegemony. How is a political act imaginable whose primary determination must be to move beyond philocentrism, beyond community, beyond translation, and not against an enemy, but rather into the region of nonmilitancy whence all militancies and all partisanships arise? Not for neutrality, not for pacifism, but against all factual partisanships of enmity, which are also preemptive partisanships of friendship.

## Notes

1   See, for instance, Eric Schmitt, "Finding Hussein Took Skill and Plenty of Legwork," *New York Times*, December 16, 2003.

2   Seymour M. Hersh, "Moving Targets: A Vietnam-Style Mission in Iraq," *New Yorker*, December 15, 2003, 50.

3   Ibid., 49–50.

4   For the official formulation of the doctrine of preemptive strike, see "The National Security Strategy of the United States of America," www.whitehouse.gov/nsc/nss.html, secs. III and V.

5   Hersh, "Moving Targets," 52.

6 Julian Borger, "Israel Hired to Train U.S. Killer Team for Iraq Ops," *Guardian Weekly*, December 11–December 17, 2003, 1.

7 Hersh, "Moving Targets," 55.

8 Carl Schmitt, "*Partisan Theory*: Intervention on the Concept of the Political," trans. A. Clint Goodson, *Centennial Review*, forthcoming.

9 Ibid., 50.

10 Ibid., 51.

11 Ibid., 54.

12 As developed in the 1932 essay "The Concept of the Political" in Carl Schmitt, *The Concept of the Political*, trans. George Schwab (Chicago: University of Chicago Press, 1996). The friend-enemy division is identified by Schmitt as the specifically political division: "The inherently objective nature and autonomy of the political becomes evident by virtue of its being able to treat, distinguish, and comprehend the friend-enemy antithesis independently of other antitheses" (27). The 1962 lectures on partisan theory are subtitled "Interventions on the Concept of the Political" and are therefore to be read as a supplement to the 1932 essay. See Schmitt, *Partisan Theory*, 1.

13 Leo Strauss, *The Political Philosophy of Hobbes: Its Basis and Its Genesis*, trans. Elsa M. Sinclair (Chicago: University of Chicago Press, 1963), 158.

14 Ibid., 162.

15 Ibid., 168.

16 "The friend, enemy, and combat concepts receive their real meaning precisely because they refer to the real possibility of physical killing. War follows from enmity. War is the existential negation of the enemy. It is the most extreme consequence of enmity. It does not have to be common, normal, something ideal, or desirable. But it must nevertheless remain a real possibility for as long as the concept of the enemy remains valid." Schmitt, *Concept of the Political*, 33.

17 Ibid., 27.

18 Ibid., 39.

19 Ibid., 55.

20 I refer, of course, to Fukuyama's book, which has had many disciples, avowed or not. Francis Fukuyama, *The End of History and the Last Man* (New York: Free Press, 1992).

21 For a fuller treatment of these questions, some of whose formulations I have partially repeated here, see Alberto Moreiras, "A Thinking Relationship: The End of Subalternity. Notes on Hegemony, Contingency, Universality. Contemporary Dialogues on the Left," *South Atlantic Quarterly* 101 (2002): 97–131.

22 Schmitt, *Partisan Theory*, 10.

23 Ibid., 34.

24 Ibid., 38, 37.

25 Jacques Rancière, *Disagreement. Politics and Philosophy*, trans. Julie Rose (Minneapolis: University of Minnesota Press, 1999). For Rancière, "just as the people are not really the people but

actually the poor, the poor themselves are not really the poor. They are merely the reign of a lack of position, the effectivity of the initial disjunction that bears the empty name of freedom, the improper property, entitlement to dispute. They are themselves in advance the warped conjunction of what is proper to them that is not really proper to them and of the common that is not really common. They are simply the constitutive wrong or torsion of politics as such. The party of the poor embodies nothing other than politics itself as the setting-up of a part of those who have no part. Symmetrically, the party of the rich embodies nothing other than the antipolitical. From Athens in the fifth century B.C. up until our own governments, the party of the rich has only ever said one thing, which is most precisely the negation of politics: there is no part of those who have no part" (13–14). For Rancière, therefore, partisan theory is also the key to all politics. The part of those who have no part, that part that is not, is always the enigmatic remainder, the radical outside of any possible subject of or for humanity, and therefore the very possibility of a politics beyond the subject—a politics of the nonsubject, which is, perhaps even for Rancière, the only possible formulation of politics proper.

26  Schmitt, *Partisan Theory*, 42.

27  Ibid., 58.

28  Ibid., 16.

29  Of course, the very phrase "absolutism of an abstract righteousness" introduces the immense problem of the proper relation of morality to politics. For Schmitt, the friend-enemy division is independent of the good-bad or the good-evil division, which seems to imply a radical autonomy between morality and politics. Schmitt's concept of the political—"nothing is more alien than the possibility of morality"—is discussed by Oscar Cabezas in "On Schmitt's *The Concept of the Political*" (unpublished manuscript). However, to the extent that the friend-enemy grouping projects at least one "abstract righteousness," if not two or more, the very political division gets entangled back into moral issues. Even if the friend is defined as he who must stand with me in the face of a common fear of violent death at the hands of someone else, it would seem that actions resulting from that common fear are both moral and political, in double register (and moral also in the sense that they may exceed morality, or break the rules or boundaries of morality). This note is meant to open up the problem, not to solve it.

30  Schmitt, *Partisan Theory*, 42.

31  Schmitt had already foreseen, in the 1932 essay, the possibility that the accomplishment of a liberal closure of the world might prompt a new dispensation of the political, in terms that one cannot avoid associating with the present situation: "War is condemned but executions, sanctions, punitive expeditions, pacifications, protection of treaties, international police, and measures to assure peace remain. The adversary is thus no longer called an enemy but a disturber of peace and is thereby designated to be an outlaw of humanity. A war waged to protect or expand economic power must, with the aid of propaganda, turn into a crusade and into the last war of humanity. This is implicit in the polarity of ethics and economics, a polarity astonishingly systematic and consistent. But this allegedly nonpolitical and apparently even antipolitical system serves existing or newly emerging friend-and-enemy groupings and

cannot escape the logic of the political" (*Concept of the Political*, 79). My goal throughout this essay is not to deny the importance of the friend-enemy determination of the political, but rather to show that there can be a beyond of the friend-enemy division, not in an antipolitical or postpolitical sense, but in an alternative political sense.

32  I am referring to Huntington's notion of "clash of civilizations," which not only presupposes civilizations but hypostasizes them into the real site of politics today: "The most important countries in the world come overwhelmingly from different civilizations. The local conflicts most likely to escalate into broader wars are those between groups and states from different civilizations. The predominant patterns of political and economic development differ from civilization to civilization. The key issues on the international agenda involve differences among civilizations. Power is shifting from the long predominant West to non-Western civilizations. Global politics has become multipolar and multicivilizational." Samuel P. Huntington, *The Clash of Civilizations and the Remaking of World Order* (New York: Simon and Schuster, 1996), 29.

33  Don De Lillo, *Cosmopolis* (New York: Scribner, 2003), 75.

34  The importance of the rat episode for a novel announcing that "a specter is haunting the world—the specter of capitalism" (96) is reinforced by the novel's epigraph, a quotation from Zbigniew Herbert: "A rat became the unit of currency" (n.p.).

35  Regarding melodramatic consciousness, Althusser says about the characters of a certain play: "These unfortunates live their misery within the arguments of a religious and moral conscience; in borrowed finery. In it they disguise their problems and even their condition. In this sense, melodrama is a foreign consciousness as a veneer on a real condition. The dialectic of the melodramatic consciousness is only possible at this price: this consciousness must be borrowed from outside (from the world of alibis, sublimation and lies of bourgeois morality), and it must still be lived as the consciousness of a condition (that of the poor) even though this condition is radically foreign to the consciousness." Louis Althusser, "The 'Piccolo Teatro': Bertolazzi and Brecht. Notes on a Materialist Theatre," in *For Marx*, trans. Ben Brewster (London: Verso, 1965), 139–40.

36  Beverley employed that formulation during a session at a panel at the Latin American Studies Association meeting in Dallas, April 2003.

37  Louis Althusser, "Ideology and Ideological State Apparatuses. (Notes Towards an Investigation)," in *Lenin and Philosophy and Other Essays*, trans. Ben Brewster (New York: Monthly Review Press, 1971), 127–86. In the face of so many attempts at making "the subject" into the very possibility of political resistance—which has become, particularly in the United States, a veritable plague of contemporary thinking, if it can be called thinking—one could do worse than return to Althusser's old essay on ideology. There we learn—and nobody to my knowledge has discredited this, although many ignore it—that "the category of the subject . . . is the constitutive category of all ideology" and "the category of the subject is only constitutive of all ideology insofar as all ideology has the function (which defines it) of 'constituting' concrete individuals as subjects" ("Ideology and Ideological State Apparatuses," 171). A discourse

"which tries to break with ideology" (173) is necessarily a discourse that abandons "the subject" as the site of emancipation—and denounces it as an ideological notion whose function is, precisely, subjection.

38 Hisham Sharabi, *Neopatriarchy: A Theory of Distorted Change in Arab Society* (New York: Oxford University Press, 1988). Neopatriarchy is "an entropic social formation characterized by its transitory nature and by specific kinds of underdevelopment and non-modernity—visible in its economy and class structure as well as its political, social, and cultural organization" (4); "the most advanced and functional aspect of the neopatriarchal state . . . is its internal security apparatus, the *mukhabarat*. A two-state system prevails in all neopatriarchal regimes, a military-bureaucratic structure alongside a secret police structure, and the latter dominates everyday life, serving as the ultimate regulator of civil and political existence" (7). Sharabi's crucial thesis is that the horrors of neopatriarchy are not at all systemic to Islamic societies, but rather are themselves historically produced as a reaction to capitalist modernity: "Modernization in this context is for the most part only a mechanism promoting underdevelopment and social entropy, which in turn produce and reproduce the hybrid, traditional, and semi-rational structures and consciousness typical of patriarchal society" (7).

39 Felipe Martínez Marzoa, *Heidegger y su tiempo* (*Heidegger and His Time*) (Madrid: Akal, 1999). Martínez Marzoa states, "In the sphere where the exigency of totality obtains, a sphere that we have provisionally agreed to call 'the modern,' the presence of things that is taken as ordinary and . . . normative in a prephilosophical sense is defined through the postulate of compatibility with . . . the unlimited continuum" (12). The unlimited continuum defines ontology in modernity. I must refer to the entirety of Martínez Marzoa's book, which is a careful working out of the implications of that idea.

40 For an extended definition and clarification of bare life as the life that can be killed without murder or sacrifice, see Giorgio Agamben, *Homo Sacer: Sovereign Power and Bare Life*, trans. Daniel Heller-Roazen (Stanford: Stanford University Press, 1998). For Agamben, bare life is constitutive of contemporary biopolitics, hence of politics today.

41 Philip K. Dick, "The Minority Report," in *The Minority Report and Other Classic Stories* (New York: Citadel, 2002), 99.

# Fear (The Spectrum Said)

Brian Massumi

> That momentary paralysis of the spirit, of the tongue and limbs, that profound agitation descending to the core of one's being, that dispossession of self we call *intimidation.* . . . It is a *nascent social state* that occurs whenever we pass from one society to another. —Gabriel Tarde

> The future will be better tomorrow. —attributed to George W. Bush

In March 2002, with much pomp, the Bush administration's new Department of Homeland Security introduced its color-coded terror alert system: green, "low"; blue, "guarded"; yellow, "elevated"; orange, "high"; red, "severe." The nation has danced ever since between yellow and orange. Life has restlessly settled, to all appearances permanently, on the redward end of the spectrum, the blue-greens of tranquility a thing of the past. "Safe" doesn't even merit a hue. Safe, it would seem, has fallen off the spectrum of perception. Insecurity, the spectrum says, is the new normal.[1]

*positions* 13:1 © 2005 by Duke University Press

The alert system was introduced to calibrate the public's anxiety. In the aftermath of 9/11, the public's fearfulness had tended to swing out of control in response to dramatic, but maddeningly vague, government warnings of an impending follow-up attack. The alert system was designed to modulate that fear. It could raise it a pitch, then lower it before it became too intense, or even worse, before habituation dampened response. Timing was everything. Less fear itself than fear fatigue became an issue of public concern. Affective modulation of the populace was now an official, central function of an increasingly time-sensitive government.

The self-defensive reflex-response to perceptual cues that the system was designed to train into the population wirelessly jacked central government functioning directly into each individual's nervous system. The whole population became a networked jumpiness, a distributed neuronal network registering en masse quantum shifts in the nation's global state of discomfiture in rhythm with leaps between color levels. Across the geographical and social differentials dividing them, the population fell into affective attunement. That the shifts registered en masse did not necessarily mean that people began to act similarly, as in social imitation of each other, or of a model proposed for each and all. "Imitation renders form; attunement renders feeling."[2] Jacked into the same modulation of feeling, bodies reacted in unison without necessarily acting alike. Their responses could, and did, take many forms. What they shared was the central nervousness. How it translated somatically varied body by body.

There was simply nothing to identify with or imitate. The alerts presented no form, ideological or ideational and, remaining vague as to the source, nature, and location of the threat, bore precious little content. They were signals without signification. All they distinctly offered was an "activation contour": a variation in intensity of feeling over time.[3] They addressed not subjects' cognition, but rather bodies' irritability. Perceptual cues were being used to activate direct bodily responsiveness rather than reproduce a form or transmit definite content.

Each body's reaction would be determined largely by its already-acquired patterns of response. The color alerts addressed bodies at the level of their dispositions toward action. The system was not in any direct way a subjective positioning device. It was a body-aimed dispositional trigger mechanism.

Bodies would be triggered into actions over the exact nature of which the governmental emission of the perceptual cue had little direct control. Individuals would inevitably express their attunement to the affective modulation in their own unique ways. It was in a second moment, through the diversity of the resultant actions thus triggered, that each would position him- or herself subjectively in relation to others. Any moment of reflection that might come would come after, in discussion or retrospective review. The system addressed the population immediately, at a presubjective level: at the level of bodily predisposition or tendency—action in its nascent state. A color shift would trip each body's tendencies into an unfolding through which its predispositions would regain determinate form in particular actions attuned to a changed situation. Each body's individuality performed itself, reflexively (that is to say, nonreflectively) in an immediate nervous response. The mode under which the system operated was cued directness of self-expression, in bodily action. It was less a communication than an assisted germination of potentials for action whose outcome could not be accurately determined in advance—but whose variable determination could be determined to occur, on hue.

The system was designed to make visible the government's much advertised commitment to fighting the "war" on terrorism it had so dramatically declared in the days following 9/11. The collapse of the World Trade Center towers had glued the populace to the TV screen with an intensity not seen since the assassination of President Kennedy in the medium's early days, and in its recent history comparable only to the Gulf War show. In a time of crisis, television was once again providing a perceptual focal point for the spontaneous mass coordination of affect, in a convincing rebuttal of the widespread wisdom that as a medium it was falling into obsolescence as a consequence of the Internet's meteoric rise in the late 1990s. Any ground television may have lost to the Web as an information source and as the pivot point for family entertainment was recouped in its resurgent role as the privileged channel for collective affect modulation, in real time, at socially critical turning points. Television had become the *event* medium. The terror alert system sought to piggyback on television as social event-medium, capturing the spontaneity with which it regained that role. To capture spontaneity is to convert it into something it is not: a habitual function. The alert system was part of the habituation of the viewing population to affect modulation as a governmental-media function.

This taming of television's affective role accomplished a number of further conversions. For one, it yoked governmentality to television in a way that gave the exercise of power a properly perceptual mode of operation. Government gained signal access to the nervous systems and somatic expressions of the populace in a way that allowed it to bypass the discursive mediations on which it traditionally depended and to regularly produce effects with a directness never before seen. Without proof, without persuasion, at the limit even without argument, government image production could trigger (re)action. But what public government function gained in immediacy of effect it lost in uniformity of result. If skillfully played, the system could reliably determine people to action, but the nature of the trigger, or inducer, as an activation contour lacking definite content or imitable form meant that it could not accurately determine *what* actions would be signaled forth. In a sense, this was an admission of political reality: the social environment within which government now operated was of such complexity that it made a mirage of any idea that there could be a one-to-one correlation between official speech or image production and the form and content of response. The social and cultural diversity of the population, and the disengagement from government on the part of many of its segments, would ensure that any initiative relying on a linear cause-effect relationship between, on the one hand, proof, persuasion, and argument and, on the other, the form of a resultant action—if in fact there was to be any—was bound to fail, or to succeed only in isolated cases. The contradiction-friendly pluralism of American politicians' public address is evidence that this has long been recognized in practice (the fact, for example, that a George W. Bush will address car workers in his down-home, Texas-transplant drawl as a man of the people looking out for the struggling families of Middle America, then tell a fund-raising dinner that his "base" is the "haves and have-mores"[4]). Addressing bodies from the dispositional angle of their affectivity, instead of addressing subjects from the positional angle of their ideations, shunts government function away from the mediations of adherence or belief and toward direct *activation*. What else is a state of alert? Orienting for the indeterminacy of pure activation assumes that the nature of the actual responses elicited will be finally determined by off-screen co-factors that are beyond politicians' ken, and not for lack of effort but because they are highly contingent and therefore highly changeable. The establishment of the alert system as a linchpin in the government's antiterror campaign is an implicit recognition that the production of political effects, if they are to be direct and widespread, must unfold in a manner that is nonlinear and co-causal; that is to say, complex. The perceptual mode of power set in place by the yoking of governmentality to television in this affective way couples governmental functioning with the contingency native to complex systems, where input does not necessarily equal output, because all manner of detourings, dampenings, amplifications, or interference patterns may occur in the playing out of the signal. With affect, perceptually addressed, chance becomes politically operational. A political uncertainty principle is *pragmatically* established. It practically acknowledges that the systemic environment within which power mechanisms function is metastable, meaning provisionally stable but excitable, in a state of balance but ready to jog.[5]

The necessity for a pragmatics of uncertainty to which the color system alerts us is related to a change in the nature of the object of power. The formlessness and contentlessness of its exercise in no way means that power no longer has an object. It means that the object of power is correspondingly formless and contentless: post 9/11, governmentality has molded itself to *threat*. A threat is unknowable. If it were known in its specifics, it wouldn't be a threat. It would be a situation—as when they say on television police shows, "we have a situation"—and a situation can be handled. A threat is only a threat if it retains an indeterminacy. If it has a form, it is not a substantial form, but a time form: a futurity. The threat as such is nothing *yet*—just a looming. It is a form of futurity yet has the capacity to fill the present without presenting itself. Its future looming casts a present shadow, and that shadow is *fear*. Threat is the future cause of a change in the present. A future cause is not actually a cause; it is a virtual cause, or quasicause. Threat is a futurity with a virtual power to affect the present quasicausally. When a governmental mechanism makes threat its business, it is taking this virtuality as its object and adopting quasicausality as its mode of operation. That quasicausal operation goes by the name of security. It expresses itself in signs of alert.

Since its object is virtual, the only actual leverage the security operation can have is on threat's back-cast presence, its pre-effect of fear. Threat, understood as a quasicause, would qualify philosophically as a species of final cause. One of the reasons that its causality is quasi is that there is a paradoxical reciprocity between it and its effect. There is a kind of simultaneity between the quasicause and its effect, even though they belong to different times. Threat is the cause of fear in the sense that it triggers and conditions fear's occurrence, but without the fear it effects, the threat would have no handle on actual existence, remaining purely virtual. The causality is bidirectional, operating immediately on both poles, in a kind of time-slip through which a futurity is made directly present in an effective expression that brings it into the present without it ceasing to be a futurity. Although they are in different tenses, present and future, and in different ontological modes, actual and virtual, fear and threat are of a piece: they are indissociable dimensions of the same event. The event, in its holding both tenses together in its own immediacy, is *transtemporal*. Since its transtemporality holds a passage between the virtual and the actual, it is a *process*—a real transformation that is effected in an interval smaller than the smallest perceivable, in an instantaneous looping between presence and futurity. Since it is in that smaller-than-smallest of intervals, it is perhaps best characterized as *infra-temporal* rather than transtemporal.

As William James famously argued, fear strikes the body and compels it to action before it registers consciously. When it registers, it is as a realization growing from the bodily action already under way: we don't run because we feel afraid, we feel afraid because we run.[6] He means "consciously afraid." We have already begun to experience fear nonconsiously, wrapped in action, before it unfurls from it and is felt as itself, in its distinction from the action with which it arose. *Activation* is a better word than action, because fear can be, and often is, paralyzing. When it is, in the place of action there is agitation, a poising for action, the taut incipiency of action that may fail to take definitive form. Where a specific action does unfold, its onset still will have been in an indistinction with affect, in that vague feeling-acting-coming-on, in a durationless moment of suspense in the time slip of threat. It will have been a shock to the system, whose immediacy disconnects the body from the ongoing flow of its activities while already poising it for a restart.

Fear at this level of pure activation in the time slip of threat is the *intensity* of the experience and not yet a content of it. Threat strikes the nervous system with a directness forbidding any separation between the responsiveness of the body and its environment. The nervous system is wired directly to the onset of the danger. *The reality of the situation is that activation*. If an action triggers, the activation follows, prolonging the situation along a line of flight. The fear follows down the line, gathering into itself the momentum of the run, using that accumulation to fuel each successive footfall, moving the activation through a series of steps. The fear snowballs, as the reaction runs its course. The fear is a dynamic ingathering of action assuring the continuity of its serial unfolding and moving the reality of the situation, which is its activation, down the line of fright.[7] *The experience is in the fear*, in its ingathering of action, rather than the fear being the content of an experience. At the starting line, the affect of fear and the action of the body are in a state of indistinction. As the action unfolds, they begin to diverge. The action is linear, step-by-step, and dissipative, it exhausts itself. It runs its course along the line of flight. The affective intensity, on the other hand, is cumulative. It snowballs as the action unfolds, and when the running stops, it keeps on rolling. Its rolling on after the running unwraps it from the action. It comes out into itself. It is only now, past action's stop-point, that it registers as a *feeling* of fear as distinct from its acting out. What registers distinctly with that feeling is the reality of the situation—which was and remains fundamentally affective in nature. The reality of the situation is its affective *quality*—its being an unfolding of fear, as opposed to anger, boredom, or love.

To say that at this level the experience is in the fear, rather than the fear being the content of an experience, is to say that its momentum-gathering, action-driving, reality-registering operation is *not phenomenal*. It is the in-which of experience; in other words, experience's *immanence*. But on the stop-beat, the experience comes out, into itself, registering its quality. Its unfolding then continues, along other lines. For it is only with the luxury of the pause that the body can begin to distinguish the details of the situation, previously lost to shock. It can look around, seeking to identify clearly the cause of the alarm, and take in the surroundings in case further action is necessary. It begins to *perceive*—to divide the situation into component parts, each with a location relative to the others and each with a recognizable constancy of form.

Objects in spatial configuration begin to appear, distinguishing themselves from the fear in which they were enveloped. This enables *reflection*. What just happened is placed under retrospective review and mapped as an objective environment. The location of the threat is sought by following the line of flight in reverse. The cause of the fright is scanned for among the objects in the environment. Directions of further flight or objects that can serve for self-defense are inventoried. These perceptions and reflections are gathered up in *recollection*, where their intensity will ultimately fade. It is at this point, in this second ingathering toward lowered intensity, in the stop-beat of action, that the fear, and its situation, and the reality of that situation, become a content of experience.

The unfolding reality of *that fearful feeling* has become the *feeling of that fear* enfolded in perception.[8] The perception has been wrapped in reflection, and the reflection, in turn, has been taken up in memory. In recollection, the affective unfolding has folded back in, at a different level, in a different mode, after passing a threshold marked by the exhaustion of the action with which the feeling grew. The threshold is a conversion point, on a number of counts. It is where the nonphenomenal in-which of experience turns phenomenal, passing into the content of experience, its immanence translated into an interiority. At the stop-beat, the affective quality of the event comes out in its purity from action, but as it does, it becomes quantifiable. It had been, in its indistinction with action, the totality of the situation. The situation has now branched, the affect separating from the exhausted action by virtue of its continuing. The situation further divides into a *collection* of perceived objects, then again into reflections distinct from the perception, and *re*collections of some or all of those components. The fear that came out in its affective purity at the stop-beat is retrospectively but one of a number of ingredients of the experience. It is a countable component of an experience. That experience, which began as the dynamic unity of feeling in action, is now a collection of particular elements. The whole has become divisible, and what the experience was globally now counts in it as one of its parts. As a content of experience, this fear becomes comparable to other fear incidents in other recollected situations. It can now be counted as a greater or lesser fright. Where once it was intensity, it now has magnitude. It still qualifies the situation, but its quality is now quantifiable, in two ways: it counts as a one among a number, and it can be assigned a relative magnitude. In intensity, it could only be *lived through* the body. As bodily lived it was unrefusable, a direct and immediate activation. It was *compelling*, and its compelling was one with the propelling of an action. Now it has taken its place as one content of the experience among others. It can be approached inactively as from the outside. It can be set alongside the other components and compared to them. As a quality, it still retains a certain ungraspability. Thus the objects to whose perception it led, whose appearance, as it happened, was a differentiation of the fear, now seem more solid and dependable than it. Retrospectively, they take on a larger share of the recognized reality of the event. The emotion is sidelined as the event's merely subjective content. Yet another branching has occurred, between the subjective and the objective. This bifurcation structures recollection.

If the event is recounted, the narrative will place the objective unfolding of the occurrence on a parallel track with its subjective registering, as if this duality were operative from the onset of the event, rather than an artifact of its self-differentiating unfolding. The personal history of the narrating body will have to negotiate this duality, presenting a public face allied with the content, defined as objective, in contradistinction to the subjective content, defined as private. The private content may not be recounted, or may be edited for reasons of tact or to avoid embarrassment. The emotional content may then waver and even start to break away from its anchoring to the objective narrative. The two-track narrative of the event may lose its parallelism. Unanchored, the vivacity of the emotional content diminishes, to the point where the emotion can be second-guessed: "I wasn't really scared—just startled." The emotion pales, as if it could be separated even as it happened from the immediacy of bodily response, and as if the subject of the experience could choose to have it or to pass it up. To treat the emotion as separable in this way from the activation-event from which it affectively sprang is to place it on the level of representation. It is to treat it, fundamentally and from the start, as a subjective content: basically, an idea. Reduced to the mere idea of itself, it becomes reasonable to suppose that a private subject, in representing it to itself, could hold it and the aleatory outside of its arising as well as the body in live-wire connection with that outside, at a rational, manageable distance. It makes it seem comfortably controllable.

A startle without a scare, however, is like a grin without a cat. The separation between direct activation and controlled ideation, or affect in its bodily dimension and emotion as rationalizable subjective content, is a reflective wonderland that does not work this side of the mirror. James is quick to make the discomfiting point. "Where an ideal emotion seems to precede [or occur independently of] the bodily symptoms, it is often nothing but a representation of the symptoms themselves. One who has already fainted at the sight of blood may witness the preparations for a surgical operation with uncontrollable heart sinking and anxiety. He anticipates certain feelings, and the anticipation precipitates their arrival."[9] What he calls a representation here is clearly a *re*-presentation: the heart-sinking *is* the anticipation of the emotion, in the same way that he argues that in a case like running in fear, "our feeling of bodily changes as they occur *is* the emotion" in its initial phase of emergence.[10] Anticipation is similarly a triggering of changes in the body. That affective reactivation of the body then develops unrefusably into a reemergence of the fear. What we sloppily think of as the idea of an emotion, or the emotion as an idea, is in fact the anticipatory repetition of an affective event, precipitated by the encounter between the body's irritability and a sign. In the surgical example, the blood functions as a sign of fear. Like a red alert, it directly activates the body. But the context obviates the need to run. You are in a condition to react to the blood precisely because you're not the one under anesthesia on the operating table. This is also a reason why actually running away would be somewhat off the point. The particular nature of the context inhibits the acting out of the movement. The activation of the body, however, was *already* that movement in incipient form. The failure of the movement actually to express itself does not prevent the development of the emotion proper, which should rightly phase in, on pause, after the action's actualization. Here, the body gives pause in advance, due to contextual constraints. In this context, the emergence of the emotion *preempts* action. Actual action has been short-circuited. It is *in*-acted: it remains enveloped in its own activated potential. The development of the emotion is now bound entirely to potential action. It can regenerate itself without the detour through actual movement: it can be *en*acted through in-action.

Part of the affective training that the Bush color alert system assures is the engraining in the bodies of the populace of anticipatory affective response to signs of fear even in contexts where one is clearly in no present danger. This significantly extends the purview of threat. An alert about a suspected bombing plan against San Francisco's Golden Gate Bridge (one of the early alert episodes) can have direct repercussions in Atlanta. As a plus, the enaction of the affective event in inaction has obvious political control benefits.

The purview of threat is extended in another way as well. When an emotion becomes enactable in anticipation of itself, independent of action, it becomes *its own threat*. It becomes its own virtual cause. "I am told of a case of morbid terror, of which the subject confessed that what possessed her seemed, more than anything, to be *the fear of fear itself*."[11] When fear becomes the quasicause of itself, it can bypass even more readily any limitation to contexts where a fearful action is actually called on and, in so doing, bypass more regularly the necessity to cycle through an unfolding of phases. The phases telescope into each other, in a short circuit of the affective process. The affective event rolls ever more tightly around the time slip of threat, as fear becomes its own pre-effect. "We see plainly how the emotion both begins and ends with what we call its effects."[12] Fear, the emotion, has revirtualized. Its emergence as an end effect has threateningly looped back to the beginning as its cause. This marks another turning point. Now, fear can potentially self-cause even in the absence of an external sign to trigger it. This makes it all the more uncontainable, so much so that it "possesses" the subject. It wraps its time-slip so compellingly around experience that it becomes experience's affective surround. Without ceasing to be an emotion, it has become the affective surround of existence, its in-which. Self-caused and all-around: at once the ground and background of the experience it now tends to take over. Call an emotion that has revirtualized in this way, to become self-caused ground and enveloping background of overtaken existence, an *affective tone* or *mood* (as equally distinct from action, vitality affect, pure affect, and emotion proper).

Fear's intoning revirtualization does not mean that it will never again feature narratively as a contained emotion. Efforts to contain it will in fact have to be doubled in order to mitigate the subject's possession by it. But it is a vicious circle. The more successful the efforts, the more the subject's existence is wed to the process. Having fear as a subjective content against the background of fear revirtual becomes *a way of life*. However many times fear is contained, it will always also exceed the containment because its capacity to self-regenerate will continue to loom and that looming will define the surrounding mood. Any particular fear clearly featured as an emotional life content will stand out against that comparatively vague or generic affective background from which it emerged. It will be clearly redundant: wherever it actually occurs as emotion, it will already have been as affective tone. Everywhere, fear double-features: as vaguely and clearly featured; as generic and particular; as ground of existence for itself as a way of life. Fear, in its quasicausal relation to itself, has become redundantly self-sufficient—an autonomous force of existence. It has become *ontogenetic*.[13]

This autonomization of fear is a next natural step from its preemption of action in the sign-response short circuit. Its development is conditioned by the independence that preemption enables from actual contexts of fear. When fear itself is frightening, its capacity to self-cause means that it can even trigger in the absence of any of its external signs. Politically, fear's autonomization risks undoing the control gained in that phase: fear can now *run away with itself*. It has the capacity to be self-propelling. This ups the ante of unpredictability. Where fear unleashed can lead is any alert emitter's guess. While the signs of danger may no longer be necessary for the triggering of the affective event of fear, their repetition and multiplication seeds the conditions for their own overcoming. They prepare the (back)ground.

It is only superficially that self-propelling fear can forego sign action. According to Peirce, "every thought beyond immediate perception *is* a sign."[14] When fear is of fear itself, the retriggering of its affective process hinges on a thought-sign. This triggering still entails bodily activation. "There is some reason to think that, corresponding to every feeling within us, some motion takes place in our bodies. This property of the thought-sign, since it has *no rational dependence upon the meaning of the sign*, may be compared to what I have called the *material quality* of the sign; but it differs from the latter inasmuch as *it is not essentially necessary that it should be felt* in order that there should be any thought-sign."[15]

Consider that the only way to regain control over one's possession by fear once it has become self-propelling is to not feel it. "Put a stopper on the gush," as James indelicately puts it. In a word, suppress it. We are all taught how as children. "When we teach our children to repress their emotions, it is not that they may *feel* more."[16] The emotion doesn't build up volcanically because fear as self-propellingly in need of being controlled is not a sulphurous content but a revirtual cause. It has no substance to build up (only efficacity to intensify). So it is not that they may feel more, "quite the reverse. It is that they may *think* more" (ibid.). To suppress emotion is to produce more thought-signs, in an even tighter short-circuit. Now it is not only actual action but the feeling itself that is bypassed. The bodily activation continues necessarily to occur. But there is no "more" of it to build up either. It is not quantitative. By Peirce's reckoning, it is a material *quality* of the body (a mode of its irritability). It may pass *unfelt*. The thought-sign is now intensively coupled with an incalculably qualitative unfeeling on which it has "no rational dependence." Fear is coming to revolve more and more tightly around the logical vanishing point of an unexperience where matter and quality are one. This vanishing point lies at the very limit of the phenomenal. Fear's passage to this limit carries its virtualization close to as far as it can go. Fear's quasicausality can cycle in the shortest possible circuit, with the fewest actual requisites or intervening phases, between the qualitative-material unconscious and the thought-sign. This intensifies its efficacity, reinforcing the autonomy of its ontogenetic powers.

What Peirce means when he says that there is no rational dependence on the meaning of the sign is that "there is nothing in the content of the thought which explains why it should arise only on occasion of . . . determining thoughts."[17] In other words, there is no need for the thought-sign of fear to have any rational connection to contexts in which thoughts logically relating to it might occur. "If there is such a relation of reason, if the thought is essentially limited in its application to these objects [objects with which it is logically connected by context], then the thought comprehends a thought other than itself." Without a relation of reason determining it, the thought may still occur, but when it does, it comprehends only itself. Fear has *self-abstracted*. It has become exclusively self-comprehending. It has become the autonomous thought of itself. It can now boldly go wherever thought can reach. And thought can reach wherever *attention* goes. Unfelt bodily motion (what Peirce calls "sensation") and attention are, he says, "the sole constituents" of thought. "Attention is the power by which thought at one time is connected with and made to relate to thought at another time . . . it is the *pure demonstrative application* of a thought-sign." In the case of a thought determined by and comprehending only itself, the thought to which attention demonstratively links it at one time as to another is—itself. In thought, fear becomes intensively self-relating, independent to the extreme of actual context, or even other thoughts. It demonstratively signs itself.

This implies that *techniques of attention* applied against the background of the affective tone of fear revirtual may purely and demonstratively regenerate thought-signs of it, along with the unfeeling of its corresponding bodily activation. Fear has attained a summit of virtualization, almost fully autonomized (contingent only on the vagaries of attention) and abstracted from its actions, contexts, external signs, logical content or meaning, and, last but not least, its own feeling.

We have now entered the wonderland world where the startle can come without the scare: body activation without the feeling James insists that it *is*. We have passed to the other side of the affective mirror where fear "reflects" only its own Cheshire-cat-like occurrence, at the phenomenal vanishing point, where it is without.

Fear can now operate as the nonphenomenal background of existence, or outside in-which of experience, in its role as the affective tone or generic context for a way of life. It can also still be contained, featuring as a particular life's phenomenal content. In addition, it can function purely self-demonstratively, as a self-sufficient thought process unencumbered by the bodily activation still necessarily accompanying it. Which of these modes, or which combination of them, will be in operation at any given point will depend on the regime of external signs in play, the nature of the contexts through which they multiply, the acquired skills of suppression impressed on the bodies populating those contexts, and the techniques of attention in operation (for example, as associated with the media, in particular as they disseminate themselves more widely and finely through the social field, assisted by miniaturization and digitization).

In this journey through fear, we have cycled, more than once, from virtual cause to virtual cause, the degree of virtuality increasing at each loop. In a first loop, we saw a self-differentiating unfolding into a variety of modes: from activation to feeling-in-action, from feeling-in-action to pure expression of affect, from pure expression of affect to branchings into perception, reflection, and recollection, then on to affective containment. The process then continued, looping back into itself, through and in excess of its own containment. It attached itself to signs, then to thought-signs. At each cycle, its quasicausal powers expanded. Its modes of expansion emerged sequentially, as phases of a continuing process. But beyond the threshold of affective suspense in the first loop, the emergence of the modes was additive. The branching was onto levels of operation that were in cooperation, potentially working with or in some cases on each other. Although the phases emerge sequentially, they operate conjointly to form a complex, multilayered formation. The overall process is at once additive and distributive.

If the different phasings unfolded from the initial activation, their full variety must have already been in it, in their incipiency—in *potential*. The intensity of that activation was the immanence of their potential. Rather than layered in a structure, they were immediately, virtually, co-occurring. In the feeling-in-action of the first run, they were all coursing together, in a state of actual indistinction from each other. They were actively fused, in dynamic superposition. This means that in any reactivation of the event by a virtual cause, the variety of modes become re-fused. They roll back into one another in shared potential. They *dephase* or dedifferentiate, then phase back out or re-unfold.[18] Another occasion of experience self-differentiates into an unfolding variety. Experience regenerates itself. The strike of another actual threat will initiate a reemergence. But, given fear's emergent self-reflective capacity to be its own beginning and end, or to be the threat of itself, so, too, may any sign of the threat's potential effect (as in the sight of blood). A thought-sign may also initiate a recurrence, even if it is not logically the thought-sign of a threat or a fear (given the thought-sign's independence from its rational determinants). Once fear has become the ground of existence, every change can regenerate its experience under one or a combination of its species. Every shift in attention against the background mood of fear may carry the ontogenetic charge of an alert triggering a regeneration of experience and its variation (what Benjamin termed "shock").

George Bush's color alert system is designed to exploit and foster the varieties of fear while expanding on their ontogenetic powers. It assumes the full spectrum of fear, up to and including its becoming-autonomous as a regenerative ground of existence, in action and in-action, in feeling and without it with thought. This refocusing of government sign-action on complex affective modulation is a tactic of incalculable power. It allies the politics of communication with powers capable of "possessing" the individual at the level at which its experience reemerges (*dis*possessing it of its own genesis). In other words, affective modulation operates co-optively at what Gilbert Simondon calls the "pre-individual" level. By *pre-individual* he does not mean "within the individual" but rather "at the limit between the subject and the world, at the limit between the individual and collective."[19] That limit is the body activatable—the bodily irritability that is the generic "material quality" of human life.

For "action and emotion to be in resonance with each other" in the affectively self-regenerating ways just described "there must be a superior individual that encompasses them: this individuation is that *of the collective*."[20] When an individual life overflows its containment in private narrative and representation—as each life tends affectively to do—the living runs straight to the limit of the collective. There it irritably rejoins the potential from which it arose, toward a next iteration of its many-phased ontogenesis. "The subject can coincide with itself only in the individuation of the collective." This is because that limit is where the phases fold into each other toward a next deployment. It is there, in that immanence, that a life coincides with its affective potential. For better or for worse.

The alert system is a tool for modulating collective individuation. Through the mass media, it addresses itself to the population from the angle of its potential to reindividuate differentially. The system recenters government sign action on Gabriel Tarde's nascent social state of intimidation in order to induce its collective individuation to pass from one form of society to another. All for the better, Bush says. The future, he promises, will be better tomorrow. America will be a stronger and safer place.

But tomorrow's future is here today, as virtual cause. And America is neither stronger nor safer than it was yesterday. If anything, it is more precarious than ever because the form under which the promise of tomorrow is here today is ever-present threat. This hinges its actualization on nonlinear and quasicausal operations that no one can fully control, but which, on the contrary, are capable of possessing each and every one, at the level of his or her bodily potential to be individually what will have collectively become.

The outcome is anything but certain. All that is certain is that fear itself will continue becoming—the way of life. The grounding and surrounding fear that the system helps develop tends toward an autonomy that makes it an ontogenetic force to be reckoned with. That reckoning must include the irrational, self-propelling mode of fear-based collective individuation we call fascism. Although there is nothing in the content of any thought that explains why it *should* arise, the passage to a society of that kind is a potential that cannot be excluded. The Bush administration's fear in-action is a tactic as enormously reckless as it is politically powerful.

Confusingly, it is likely that it can only be fought on the same affective, ontogenetic ground on which it itself operates.

## Notes

1  "The future will be better tomorrow" is one of the many "Bushisms" circulating in the press and on the Internet. This one appears to be apocryphal. It seems actually to belong to Dan Quayle, vice president under George Bush Sr. As regularly attributed to George W. Bush, however, it squarely belongs to his corpus. For an interactive time line of alert levels since the inception of the system through March 2004, see www.cnn.com/SPECIALS/2004/fighting.terror.

2  Daniel N. Stern, *The Interpersonal World of the Infant* (New York: Basic Books, 1985), 142.

3  On the concept of the activation contour, see Stern, *The Interpersonal World*, 57–59.

4  George W. Bush addressing the Al Smith Memorial Dinner, New York, October 19, 2000. This scene is memorably included in Michael Moore's film *Fahrenheit 9/11*.

5  On metastability, see Gilbert Simondon, *L'individu et sa genèse physico-biologique* (Grenoble: Million, 1995), 72–73, 204–5; and *L'individuation psychique et collective* (Paris: Aubier, 1989), 49, 230–31.

6  "Our natural way of thinking about these coarser emotions is that the mental perception of some fact excites the mental affection called the emotion, and that this latter state of mind gives rise to the bodily expression. My theory, on the contrary, is that *the bodily changes follow directly the perception of the exciting fact, and that our feeling of the same changes as they occur IS the emotion*. Common-sense says, we lose our fortune, are sorry and weep; we meet a bear, are frightened and run; we are insulted by a rival, are angry and strike. The hypothesis here to be defended says that this order of sequence is incorrect, that one mental state is not immediately induced by the other, that the bodily manifestations must first be interposed between, and that the more rational statement is that we feel sorry because we cry, angry because we strike, afraid because we tremble, and not that we cry, strike, or tremble, because we are sorry, angry, or fearful. . . . it makes us realize more deeply than ever how much our mental life is knit

up with our corporeal frame, in the strictest sense of the term." William James, *Principles of Psychology*, vol. 2 (New York: Dover, 1950), 449–50, 467.

7   On affect as "the primary ground for the continuity of nature," see Alfred North Whitehead, *Adventures of Ideas* (New York: Free Press, 1938), 183–84; and Brian Massumi, *Parables for the Virtual* (Durham, NC: Duke University Press, 2002), 208–18.

8   This formula was suggested by Whitehead's theorization of "the sensa as qualifications of affective tone." The experience, he writes, "starts as that smelly feeling, and is developed by mentality into the feeling of that smell." This applies as well to the "affective tones" we call "moods," which must be considered "direct perceptions . . . on equal terms with the other sensa." In other words, philosophically, the theory of affect and emotion and the theory of perception strictly coincide. The concept of affective tone will be discussed later in this article. Whitehead, *Adventures of Ideas*, 246.

9   William James, "What is an Emotion?" in *Essays in Psychology*, vol. 13 of *The Works of William James* (Cambridge, MA: Harvard University Press, 1983), 177.

10   James, "What is an Emotion?" 170.

11   James, "What is an Emotion?" 177.

12   Ibid.

13   On fear as ground of existence and way of life, see Brian Massumi, "Everywhere You Want to Be: Introduction to Fear," in *The Politics of Everyday Fear*, ed. Massumi (Minneapolis: University of Minnesota Press, 1993), 3–38.

14   C. S. Peirce, "Pragmatism," in *The Essential Peirce: Selected Philosophical Writings*, vol. 2 (Bloomington: Indiana University Press, 1998), 402. (Emphasis added.)

15   Ibid. (Emphasis added.)

16   James, "What is an Emotion?" 179.

17   All quotations in this paragraph are from C. S. Peirce, "Some Consequences of the Four Incapacities," in *The Essential Peirce*, vol. 1 (Bloomington: Indiana University Press, 1992), 44–46.

18   On dephasing, see Simondon, *L'individu et sa genèse physico-biologique*, 232, 234–35.

19   Simondon, *L'individuation psychique et collective*, 109.

20   All quotations in this paragraph are from Simondon, *L'individuation psychique et collective*, 108.

## Canada Park: Two Family Albums

Freda Guttman

In June 1967, the Palestinian villages of Beit Nuba, 'Imwas (Emmaus), and Yalu were occupied, bulldozed, and totally demolished by Israel on the orders of Yitzhak Rabin; these acts have been rightly described as war crimes.[1] Approximately twelve thousand people were driven away from their homes, many of them trucked to the River Jordan, others sent wandering in the desert without food or water. The inhumanity of dispossession and the brutality that goes with it are difficult to describe. The process of the destruction of these villages was hidden from the rest of the world, and a process of rewriting history ensued. Today, at the site of the ruins of these villages, stands the infamy called Canada Park, built with Canadian, tax-deductible dollars.

In 1991, during a trip to Israel and Palestine, a friend took me to Canada Park, and there I saw my parents' names listed as donors of trees. It wasn't that I didn't know that my parents gave money for trees for the park, because

*positions* 13:1 © 2005 by Duke University Press

just about every Canadian Jew did; but, in a shock of recognition, the experience clarified thoughts I had about layers of complicity. The existence of Canada Park confirmed for me in a most compelling way that history cannot be denied; that this truth challenges us ethically. My parents, like most Canadian Jews, did not know that they had helped build a park that was created to conceal a war crime—the ethnic cleansing of the inhabitants of three Palestinian villages, which were then destroyed. Nonetheless, my family and I are implicated in various degrees of complicity. My country, Canada, considers the occupation of Palestinian lands illegal, yet the payment for the trees is tax deductible for Canadian citizens because the Jewish National Fund of Canada, through which the trees are bought, has charitable status in Canada. Several Canadian activist groups are working to have the JNF's charitable status revoked.

The artwork I did on Canada Park was an installation titled *Canada Park: Two Family Albums*. It consisted of four digitized wall images of 'Imwas, one before it was destroyed, and then three others in 1968, 1978, and 1988, as it gradually became Canada Park. All were photographed from the same vantage point. In front of these images, two family photograph albums were placed on stands—one of my parents' trip to Israel, which included a visit to Canada Park, the other a faux album that I made of portraits of Palestinians who had lived in the area that is now the park.

**Note**

1   For about information about 'Imwas, Yalu, and Beit Nuba, see www.palestineremembered .com/al-Ramla/Imwas/index.html.

'Imwas before 1967

To Ramallah
Boys School
Church
Main Mosque
Girls School
Main Rd Leading To Ramallah
Coffe House
Main Upper Cemetery
Abu 'Ubayda's Shrine

'Imwas 1968

Church Used To Be Here
To Ramallah & Beit Seirah
Boys School was here
Main Mosque was here
Old Road
Coffee House was here
Girls School was here
To Latrun Junction
The Cemetery. Shrine Of Abu Uabydah is the only surviving structure

'Imwas 1988

Church Used To
Be Here

Old Roard To
Ramallah

New Road

Boys School
Was Here

Main Mosque
Used To Be Here

Coffee House
Used To Be Here

To Latrun Junction

Girls School
Used To Be Here

The Old Cemetery
And The Shrine Of Abu 'Ubaydah
Is the Only Surviving stucture

# Midnight's Gate

Bei Dao

Knowledge of death is the only key that can open midnight's gate. —Bei Dao

At 3:30 p.m. on March 24, 2002, Air France flight 1992 came to a stop on the parking apron of Tel Aviv International Airport. We took a shuttle to the entrance to the border inspection area and crowded together in line. An official from the Israeli foreign affairs office unexpectedly burst in, collected our passports, disappeared, and then reappeared; we filed out behind him through a special exit. I had just breathed a sigh of relief when I was stopped by an official-looking young man who was clearly a plainclothes police officer. He said that for security purposes, I had to answer some questions. The purpose of my trip? I mumbled that I was a member of the International Parliament of Writers delegation. He heard "delegation" as "interrogation." What? International Writers' Interrogation? His ears pricked up. No, not interrogation, I hurriedly waved my hand to call over our secretary general,

Christian Salmon. But Salmon spoke only French, and the three of us grew more confused as we tried to communicate, unable to figure out just who was interrogating whom. Fortunately, the representative of the French consulate in Israel—who had come to pick us up—made a timely appearance and finally broke the standoff. The plainclothes policeman, tapping two fingers to his temple, said goodbye to us in French.

There were eight members of the International Parliament of Writers delegation; they came from eight countries on four continents and included the chairman of the International Parliament of Writers, American novelist Russell Banks; South African poet Breyten Breytenbach; Italian novelist Vincenzo Consolo; Spanish novelist Juan Goytisolo; the secretary general of the International Parliament of Writers, Christian Salmon; Portuguese novelist José Saramago; Nigerian poet and dramatist Wole Soyinka; and myself. At 6 p.m. the previous day, we had held a press conference at the France Television booth in the main hall of the Paris Book Show, where we presented the document "Call for Peace in Palestine," which had been signed by over five hundred writers from more than thirty countries, including several Israeli writers.

On our trip, there were also ten or so reporters, and at the airport gate we all got into a bus that the French consulate sent to pick us up. The highway from the airport stretched into the interior, the landscape becoming more and more desolate. This was a wasteland, hills and mountains of sand and stone forming a bleak panorama, with shrubs and wild grass scattered here and there, that reminded me of the Gobi desert.

In the spring of 1990, the Chinese poet Duo Duo and I took part in the International Poet's Festival in Jerusalem. At that time, we were also ferried around in buses. The trip had been an enormous shift in orientation for us—in language as well as in time and space. I just remember Duo Duo swimming in the Dead Sea, and then regretting it as he crawled back out of the water.

Israel is a paramilitary state, and it is extremely common to see young men holding a gun in one hand while embracing a girlfriend in the other, strolling down the street as though this were the most natural thing in the world. When one brings up the Middle East crisis with Israeli writers, they often say they are dissatisfied with their right-wing politicians but also powerless to do anything. When it comes to the future, most of them simply shift their gaze, their faces full of gloom. We headed for the border between Israel and Syria, where the kibbutzim reminded me of the Chinese military units set up along the Sino-Soviet border in the 1960s and 1970s.

Twelve years had gone by in a flash, from one year of the horse to the next. But this time I was headed for the other side of the border.

Heading into the 1990s, there were real prospects for peace. On September 13, 1993, Rabin and Yasir Arafat shook hands for the first time and signed the first Autonomy Agreement. On September 28, 1995, they signed the second Autonomy Agreement, and, soon after, Israel withdrew its army from the West Bank. That same year, these two men shared the Nobel Peace Prize. Arafat ended twenty-seven years of exile and returned to his homeland. But on November 4, 1995, Rabin's assassination by a right-wing extremist student cast a shadow over the peace process. History is often determined by chance events. If the assassin had not succeeded, the subsequent chain of events might have gone in a different direction. It was just such a stroke of chance that picked out Bush and Sharon from the mass of humanity, setting them on the political stage to bring changes to the whole world.

The incandescent sun, hanging in the sky, stuck to the backs of our heads like the muzzle of a gun. An eagle wheeled above, as though intending to spread its shadow over the earth. A sentry post appeared ahead, and a soldier with a rifle inspected our vehicle's license plate and our border pass. Machine guns stood on tripods on sandbags in the nearby embankment. The road in the opposite direction was jammed with vehicles. Our guide told me that Palestinian vehicles were absolutely forbidden to drive on this road. Our side of the road was not jammed for the simple reason that it headed toward Ramallah, the besieged town from which Arafat ran his operations.

Gradually the sky grew dark, and the scenery changed. First we came to a sentry box next to a dark and gloomy military camp, with tanks parked alongside it. Ahead was a blockhouse; its embrasures looked like empty eye sockets. The door of our bus opened with a grating sound, and the representative from the French consulate, holding a special permit from the Israeli Ministry of Defense, negotiated with the soldier. A cameraman followed him, the light from his flash glaring. Then the soldier called over his superior, most likely the platoon leader. Over a walkie-talkie, the platoon

leader asked *his* superior for instructions. He then asked for our passports
and climbed into our bus to check them one by one. He was very young and
had tired, cold eyes. His face showed a lack of expression that seemed to
say, "You guys are just asking for trouble—have you come here to die?" He
contacted his superior again on the walkie-talkie, waited a good long while,
and finally waved us on. The bus had not gone very far before we came to
another sentry box, but this one did not hold us up for long. Continuing on,
we came to a Palestinian police officer in blue camouflage. He gestured to a
police car that was stopped on the side of the road; it pulled out and led the
way for us, its blue lights flashing. At last, we entered Ramallah.

The Arabic word *ramallah* means "God's high place," although the town is
not even nine hundred meters above sea level. It is situated on the west bank
of the Jordan River, sixteen kilometers north of Jerusalem, and looks down
on the surrounding area. The surrounding hills have numerous springs and
are a well-known summer retreat. Ramallah now refers to the two towns
of Ramallah and Al-Bireh. Ramallah was founded in the twelfth century,
during the occupation of the Crusader armies, but the history of Al-Bireh can
be traced back to the Canaanite period of 3500 BC. Al-Bireh is mentioned in
the Bible seventy-six times, and it is said that the Virgin Mary often stayed
there. The inhabitants of Ramallah used to be mostly Catholics, but after the
war of 1948, there was a large influx of Palestinian refugees. In the 1950s,
Ramallah belonged to Jordan, but in the Six-Day War of 1967 it fell into the
hands of Israel. In 1988, Jordan returned sovereignty over the West Bank to
the Palestinians, but it was in reality still governed by Israel. Only in 1996,
when Israel withdrew its troops, did Ramallah become the capital of the
Palestinian West Bank.

At night, Ramallah looks like a ghost town. No people are on the streets,
there are few cars, and most of the buildings are black and unlit. It was
quarter to seven when we arrived at the Grand Park Hotel. Our hosts were
awaiting us at the door. At their head was Mahmoud Darwish, the most
outstanding Palestinian poet of the present generation, at whose invitation
we had come. When a reporter asked about the purpose of our trip to
Palestine, Soyinka answered the question well:

> It is very simple, we have accepted the invitation of our besieged colleague,
> the Palestinian poet Darwish. On two earlier occasions, we had looked

forward to him visiting the United States to accept an important award from an American university and to interact with other writers. This gathering was delayed due to the events of 1992, and then canceled. As I see it, it is a great pity that he lost this chance to cross borders and travel abroad. Since Darwish was unable to come to us, it was up to us to go to him; it is as simple as that.

The Grand Park Hotel, where we stayed, was quite luxurious, its marble so polished that it reflected your image, and the staff was faultlessly courteous. In besieged Ramallah, this gave the place a certain surreal quality. Darwish was clad in a piece of white silk; his age was difficult to judge. Hardship generally hastens aging, but sometimes it can also erase the marks of time. Darwish had an optimistic face, which seemed to be perpetually grinning. It turned out that he had been born in 1941, and when he was seven years old, his village was attacked by Zionists. When Darwish fled to Lebanon he was separated from his family, and he became an orphan. A year later, he returned to his hometown to find it reduced to ruins and an Israeli settlement built up in its place. He began to write poetry in elementary school, but because he failed his "political review," he could not go on to middle school. He had spent time in prison and had been under house arrest numerous times.

We rested for a while and then walked together to a banquet hosted by the Palestinian Ministry of Culture. Outside, it was a bit chilly, and the moon had risen; everything was covered in its pure light. In the distance, the lights of Jerusalem shone brightly—that holy city of three religions that has been the cause of so many disasters throughout history, all in the name of God. As an activity of the imagination, religion most likely arises from a fear of death and the unknown world. Unlike poetry, it arises from the collective imagination and of necessity forms a relationship with power, and thus it is transformed into an authority, systematized and even militarized. When it encounters another collective imagination, it invariably ends in the clashing of swords and the flowing of blood. The fact that throughout its history China has almost never had religious warfare is probably because Buddhism and Daoism value individual experience. One should not mix with those who travel different paths; if that fails, then one can simply attain Buddhahood on the spot, as the Chinese *Chan* masters say. Furthermore, imagination requires space, and in the Middle East, especially in the holy city, space is extremely limited. The dissemination and feedback of imagination always renders the situation more complex. Take, for example, the farcical first of the eight Crusades to the East. The image of that crusade was initially hooked to the Roman Pope's ambition to unite the Catholic and Eastern Orthodox churches, which, in turn, aroused a hermit slumbering in a French monastery. By fanning the flames underground, kindling fires at the grassroots level, he gathered together eighty thousand poor peasants at the banks of the Rhine and set out for the East. Blind hatred and the promise of heaven were their motives, yet they did not even know for sure where the holy city was, nor had they any supplies; they made their way, robbing and looting, and in the end were cruelly defeated by the Turks, not three thousand of them surviving.

The banquet was a buffet. What surprised me the most was that the excellent wine was a local product. Holding a glass of it, I looked out through the French doors at the night view of Ramallah. An elegant middle-aged woman walked up to me. Her name was Tania. She said she was a soprano, an amateur; I said I was a poet, also an amateur. She laughed. She talked about her mother; she talked about daily life under siege. She pointed out the buildings surrounded by a wall on the mountain and told me that they were an Israeli settlement, that the settlement was continually expanding, and that they often shot in this direction for no particular reason, which had resulted in the killing of numerous children. Just a week earlier, the streets here were full of tanks. Darwish interrupted to say that there had been a total of 140 tanks. Tania practicing in the roar of tanks is an image that has haunted me ever since.

When I woke up the next morning, I did not know where I was. A ray of sunlight slipped in from behind the curtain. I remembered that when I went to the Israeli consulate in San Francisco to get my visa, a young Jewish man at the entrance questioned me. I said I was going to Palestine. He said there was no Palestine. His tone of voice was calm, natural, and brooked no doubt. With one look, you could tell that he had had a good upbringing, was good at heart, but had absolutely no awareness of the tragedy he was denying.

At breakfast, I ran into Juan, Vincenzo, and a Palestinian professor. Juan asked if I wanted to go downtown with them. Juan lives in Morocco and can speak a little Arabic. He writes experimental novels and is a social activist, which makes him a typical public intellectual. This role, quite common in Europe, is almost extinct in the United States. Juan travels all over the world and publishes articles in large Spanish-language newspapers attacking the ills of the time, influencing the direction of public opinion. He had previously taken a television production team to Palestine, and this professor had been their guide.

We took a taxi to the center of Ramallah There was little to distinguish it from a remote town in China's Xinjiang Province or in South Africa—it was poverty stricken but bustling with life. Signs advertising Coca-Cola and Motorola stood at a crossroads. At an open-air market where fresh fruits and vegetables were spread out, vendors cried out calling attention to their wares. The professor greeted everyone on the street, pinched the fruit, tasted the medicinal herbs, asked prices, and chatted about the weather. Juan bought a copy of the English-language *International Herald Tribune* at a newsstand. To my surprise, this newsstand was stocked with all kinds of popular American magazines, like *Life*, *Penthouse*, and *Seventeen*.

The professor showed us the shops and houses destroyed by Israeli fire, most of which had been repaired, though one could still make out the fresh color of recently repaired spots. On the walls, group after group of photographs were pasted, like the rosters of model workers we used to have back home; among the multitude of young men, there was a beautiful girl. They were photographs of the martyrs who had blown themselves up. The professor told me that the girl had died only a month earlier, twenty-eight years old, the first female martyr.

We walked to the cultural center, which was named for the Palestinian poet, educator, and social activist Khalil Sakakini. (His entire life was the stuff of legend. During World War I, he went to jail for sheltering Polish Jews.) The center was a typical example of traditional Palestinian architecture; built in 1927, it used to be the residence of the mayor of Ramallah. After passing through the meticulously ordered garden, we went through an arched entryway. There was an exhibition of paintings on the first floor; the second story was divided into offices, including those of the editorial section of the literary publication where Darwish was the editor-in-chief. The stairs led us to the third-floor conference room.

We sat facing the Palestinian writers, and we delegation members were introduced by Leila Shahid, the official Palestinian representative to France. She was a fat woman who liked to make jokes. Introducing the Italian novelist Vincenzo Consolo, she said his name first with the accent at the beginning, "*con*sole," like a television, a rather material rendition; then she shifted the accent back, making it a verb, "con*sole*," which had a more spiritual quality. That was good—Mr. Consolation.

Darwish was the first to speak, and he mentioned "this bloody spring." He told us, "Your courageous visit is, in a way, breaking the siege. You make us feel that we are no longer alone. We are aware that there has been too long a history, and too many prophets; we understand that this space held in multiple embraces is not a prison and that no one has a monopoly on a land, a god, or a memory. We also know that history is neither fair nor elegant. But our mission is to be human—we are both the sacrificial victims of history and its creation." At the end, he said, "and the incurable disease we suffer from is hope . . . hope will make this place regain its original meaning: a land of love and peace. Thank you for bearing the burden of hope with us."

Hope is a burden indeed. Three days later the Israeli army again occupied Ramallah and the greater part of the West Bank. Nor was the cultural center spared, the works of art and the offices were completely demolished, and even the computer hard drives were removed.

Later there was a press conference held by the Palestine Media Center. Saramago became the focus of attention because before leaving Paris, he had shocked everyone by comparing the Israeli authorities to the Nazis and using words like *Auschwitz* and *Holocaust*. Most of the members of the delegation were uneasy, fearing that his provocative language would affect the goal of our trip. I didn't feel Saramago had done anything wrong. After all, we are not politicians and have no need to use diplomatic language. A writer has the right to use metaphor, and if he can shock society into awareness by using it, this merely shows the efficacy of language. Furthermore, his words were prophetic, as proven by the massacres to follow at Jinin and other places. Israel does not possess exclusive ownership rights to the words *Auschwitz* and *Holocaust*. Those who were victims in the past can become today's tyrants. This is the darkness of human nature, the darkness of the cycle of vengeance, the darkness of hatred that makes people sink into it. The writer is the traveler who passes through this darkness.

During the press conference, I mentioned that in addition to all the other types of siege, there is yet another, the siege of the language of hate. As the conference was ending, Juan, who had been sitting to my left, said he agreed completely; perhaps because Spain and China have similar revolutionary backgrounds, to us problems of language have become even more important.

We had accepted an invitation from the president of Berzeit University to have lunch with the professors there. Berzeit University is in a northern suburb of Ramallah. The bus we were riding in suddenly came to a halt in front of a cement roadblock. We had to walk about five hundred meters and get into cars at the other end. I asked Tania, who was accompanying us on this visit to the institution of which her husband was president, why. She shrugged her shoulders and said, "They are just making life difficult for us." She told me the sentry posts had originally been by the side of the road but were later moved up to the hillside. She pointed to a blockhouse on the hillside; those Israeli marksmen can shoot anybody they don't like the look of. I shivered; this menace frightened me even more.

The far end of the road was crowded with people and taxis. The university and some thirty villages were cut off from Ramallah, which was very inconvenient, but at least it brought the taxi drivers and street vendors some business. Dust flew in the air, people were shouting, and tempers were short. There was a vendor carrying on his back a brass samovar taller than a person, whose spout was elaborately curved, making it look like some unfathomable musical instrument. Suddenly, with a heave of his shoulder and a twist of his waist, liquid trickled out of it like music. He gave our leader, Russell, a free glass, and we all had a sip. It tasted like cold sour-plum juice, and drinking it made me feel much calmer.

We got out of the taxi and walked across the campus. It seemed no different from any other university in the world. Students talked together in small groups, enjoying the afternoon sunshine. The female students seemed quite open, and none was wearing a burka. Berzeit University was Palestine's first institution of higher education. When it was established in 1924, it was only a primary school, but it was gradually upgraded and became a full-fledged university in the 1970s. Over the past few years, fifteen students have been killed in demonstrations. The Israeli authorities routinely force the university to close down, and from 1979 to 1982 it was closed 61 percent of the time. The last time it was shut down was in January 1988, when it stayed closed for fifteen months. During this time, it secretly organized temporary study groups outside the school. Even so, it has taken many students ten years to finish the four-year program.

Unfortunately, no student representatives had been invited to join us, and the luncheon was somewhat flat. The president gave an introductory speech of welcome, and Russell talked about the possibility of Berzeit University's cooperating with another university, perhaps with Princeton, where he taught. One teacher told us that because of the siege, many students slept in the classrooms at night.

I slipped out to wander around the building. Student sculptures were on display in the main hall. One of them astounded me: a bird's egg set in a nest made of iron nails. Such an imagination was heartbreaking; it could only have come from youth wounded by war.

We took a bus from the university to a refugee camp. These "refugee camps" are actually temporary dwellings built for people who have been expelled from their own homes, but they have been "temporary" for generations. We first went to the refugee camp's recreation center. Its door, battered down by a tank, was the first sight that greeted our eyes; the floor was strewn with bits of paper and broken glass. Computers, musical instruments, and bodybuilding equipment—nothing had been spared. The person in charge of the center apologized and said that there was not a single good chair left for us to sit on. He spread open his hands and asked, "What do you think, is this a terrorist base?"

There were great holes in almost every wall in all the houses. This was the result of an explosive weapon newly invented by the Israelis, who were tired of the inconvenience of breaking down doors to get in; now they can simply pass through walls. It seems that this new technology brings with it a new way of calling on people and is changing the traditions of human etiquette. We came to a refugee family's house down a small alley in the refugee camp. When the "guests" came to call, they not only destroyed the television set but also wounded their host. I don't understand Arabic, but the despair and hate in the family members' gestures and expressions were clear at a glance.

At six that evening Arafat wanted to see us. This had not been written on the schedule, but everybody seemed well aware that it would happen. Leila, who also went with us, said that he could see us for only half an hour, after which he was calling a meeting of the cabinet. A police car led the way for us. It was just getting dark when we arrived at Arafat's official residence. The bus went through the main gate, drove through an empty area, and stopped at the entryway of an ordinary-looking house where guards, guns loaded and ready to fire, stood watch. We were brought to a lounge area, where we all talked and joked quite casually, unaccustomed to the pressure of such a formal occasion. After about ten minutes, we were taken to a room across the hall; Arafat was standing at the door, and after Leila's introductions, he shook hands with each member of the delegation. He was flashing his famous smile; he looked just like his photographs, except that he was shorter than I had imagined. Short people have their own way of dealing with the world: in general, they are more confident and stubborn, more pragmatic, and more full of a combative spirit. The strategists and psychological experts in Israel had probably not reckoned with this point.

This was clearly both Arafat's office and his reception room. At one end was a desk, and beside it stood a Palestinian flag. At the other end was a sofa, and on a tea table sat a delicate water lily. Arafat and our leader, Russell, sat in the middle of the sofa. According to prior arrangements, this was not to be an open meeting, so all the reporters were chased out. Russell first said a few words on behalf of the International Parliament of Writers and expressed support for Palestine's independence and freedom. He emphasized that we had come especially to see Darwish. Arafat pointed at Darwish and joked, "He's our boss." Each delegate said a few words, which Leila translated, and Arafat often answered in English. Soyinka said he hoped that they would not write hatred and conflict into their textbooks. Arafat made a decisive gesture and said, "Absolutely not. We are doing quite the opposite, not paying nearly enough attention to historical description." At the mention of hatred, he sighed and said that when he was a child, his home was near the Wailing Wall, and he used to play with Jewish children all day. Now that is almost impossible. I was the last to speak. I said that he had been a hero of mine ever since I was a child, and I wondered if he still held on to his early ideals after so many years and difficulties.

Arafat jumped up excitedly and pointed to the large photograph of the Temple Mount behind him—particularly the striking gold leaf Dome of the Rock and the Jewish temple beside it. The Temple Mount is a holy place not just of Islam, but also of Catholicism and Judaism. Jesus preached there, and it also contained the first altar of the Hebrew patriarch, Abraham. Arafat drew a large circle with his finger, indicating that living together in peace was his ideal. He was also able to use metaphor to observe and explain the world in different ways, from different angles. It was difficult to imagine his opponent Sharon using metaphor. Sharon's language was as blunt as a tank. And three days later, Sharon's tanks would burst into Arafat's official residence.

The visit lasted about an hour, running over the allotted time, and the cabinet meeting had to be postponed. Arafat posed for pictures with each of us. He also ran back and forth, fetching illustrated brochures of a Palestinian Bethlehem development plan for the year 2000, along with souvenir badges that he gave to each of us. Breyten asked him to autograph his brochure. As we were about to leave, the mischievous Breyten drew close to Arafat's desk. The head of the guards tried to stop him, but he managed to slip by and steal a piece of chocolate from Arafat's desk and put it into his mouth.

At eight that evening, at Ramallah's Al-Kasaba Theater, we held a reading with a group of Palestinian poets. The house was packed. Someone told me that on account of the siege, there hadn't been this kind of cultural event for a long time. Darwish read first. From the sound of the appreciative sighs in the audience, one could sense that he was the pride of Palestine. His poetry made me think of the late Israeli poet Yehuda Amichai, whom I had met twelve years earlier at the Jerusalem International Poet's Festival. There was, to my surprise, a certain similarity of tone in their poetry: the lonely quality of their words, their impotent resignation and alienation regarding the state of things, their fear of the clamorous crowd, their attempt to protect the last bit of dignity by self-mockery. I don't know if they ever met, and maybe that is not important. What is of importance is that it would be enough if the two peoples were able to really listen to their poets. As Paz said, poetry is a third voice, apart from religion and revolution. This voice cannot truly eliminate hatred, but perhaps can, to a degree, serve to alleviate it.

This was the night that poetry broke the siege of the language of hate.

Early the next morning, we were to leave Ramallah and go to the Gaza Strip. I woke up early and turned on the television. The first item on the CNN six o'clock news was a shot of Arafat meeting with us, and following this, a Palestinian spokesman announcing that Arafat had decided not to attend the Arab summit meeting being held in Beirut. I did not see the connection between the two stories, but the decision had obviously been made at the cabinet meeting. The superimposition of the two images gave one a feeling of having overstepped one's station. Was it the support of the international writers that made him strengthen his determination to struggle to the end?

Beginning the previous evening, two or three armed police had been stationed at each floor of the hotel, standing watch with guns in hand. I heard it was because of Saramago's provocative remarks, which had prompted the president of Portugal to personally call Arafat, in the hope that Arafat could guarantee Saramago's safety.

Darwish and the rest came to the hotel to see us off. Tania gave me a tape of a concert she had performed in Paris and a book she had written. The last thing she said was, "Compared with Gaza, this place is paradise."

The road from Ramallah to Gaza is not long, but it took us almost three hours of inching along in traffic. At the border inspection station before entering Gaza, we switched to a U.N. vehicle; we were accompanied by the U.N. representative in charge of the central aid office in Gaza. Our luggage was specially searched, separately from us, and we had to go through customs in a different car. Our passports were taken, and we waited for more than an hour before an Israeli official finally came out and confirmed our identities. Leila told me that we were lucky, because without the United Nation's help, it would have been extremely difficult to get into Gaza. And unless they have special approval, Palestinians can never leave.

We entered Gaza two hours later than scheduled. As soon as we passed the border, our car was surrounded by local journalists who had been impatiently waiting for us. But as time was pressing, we decided not to give any interviews for the moment.

Leila opened the car door and began explaining this calmly, but quickly lost her temper, and the reporters had no choice but to stalk off. With her hands on her hips, she told us, "They used to behave better and keep their promises, but now all they care about is American dollars, and they'll beat their brains out to get one. Ugh!"

Then a middle-aged man came up to us. His name was Raji, and he was the director of the Palestinian Centre for Human Rights. Beads of sweat seeped out onto his balding head. His English was fluent, but it had an obvious restlessness, his words bouncing around like spent shells. He was a lawyer and was active in human rights for many years, and he had been imprisoned by the Israelis. As the bus moved forward, he stood at the door and told us about the situation in Gaza.

The Gaza Strip is a narrow belt of land that runs along the Mediterranean Sea, forty-six kilometers long and six to ten kilometers wide, about 360 square kilometers in area. In Gaza, one of the most densely populated areas on earth, twelve hundred thousand Palestinians occupy 60 percent of the land. Israel controls 40 percent of the land, including the settlements, the military base, and the buffer zone, yet there are only six thousand Israeli immigrants, making up about 5 percent of the total population. Three-fourths of the people of Gaza are refugees who were driven from their homes by Israel in 1948 and their descendants.

The only large highway crossing Gaza is controlled by Israel and is reserved for the use of the Israeli military and settlers. Palestinians can only crowd onto a single unpaved road, and even this road is divided by two guard posts and is closed to traffic after 5 p.m. Rush hour is simply a disaster, with a line of cars stretching into the distance in front of the guard posts. The road is narrow, and accidents are frequent. Just in front of us, a truck had overturned by the side of the road. Karen, the U.N. assistant representative in Gaza, was sitting next to me. She told me Israel was afraid of suicide car bombings and made it a rule that every car had to have at least two people in it or it would not be allowed on the road. She said that even when she was driving a car with the U.N. logo, she tried to have her son sitting with her as often as possible, just in case.

The car made a turn and went down a road along the seacoast. Blue sky, white waves, green trees—it was enough to take one's breath away. Raji told us that not long ago a delegation from Spain had visited and that they were shocked by the poverty of their Mediterranean neighbors. Israel holds maritime power, and Palestinian fishermen can fish only within six kilometers of the coast. Passing by a field of strawberries, Raji said many of the strawberries that Europeans eat are from Gaza, but that they have no idea that's where they come from because Gaza strawberries must first be shipped to Israel, where they are packaged and given an Israeli label before they are exported. Worse yet, even Gaza's groundwater is siphoned off by the Israelis, then sent back through pipelines and sold to the Palestinians in Gaza. Such bald exploitation, with no need for concealment or obscurity, should be enough to make all the capitalists of the world sick with envy.

We came into the neighborhood of an Israeli settlement on the beach. There seemed to have just been a battle here. The road was pitted, and the surrounding buildings had all been demolished; the ruins were covered with the scars of gunfire. The settlement, circled by a high wall, had a blockhouse standing guard. This was one of the nineteen settlements in Gaza. Raji told us that at this intersection alone, more than eighty people at a demonstration had died beneath these guns, most of them young people.

Unlike the West Bank, Gaza is surrounded on all sides by Israel's barbed wire barricade. As I see it, aside from economic extortion, the Israelis are content to let the Palestinians live or die as they will. The Palestinians not only lack the freedom to come and go from Gaza but are also under severe restrictions for traveling within their own land. If Gaza is a large prison, then these settlements are small prisons, prisons within a prison, besieged on all sides by hatred. It is simply impossible for the Jewish settlers to have any contact with the locals; in their comings and goings they always have military escorts. Just what kind of person would be willing to move here? Karen pointed to her skull. Why? Is it a mental problem? Karen laughed and replied, "No, they are just duped by advertisements—the beautiful landscape, low-priced houses. Many of them are old Jewish people from the States."

I asked Breyten if the situation here was in any way comparable to the old apartheid system in South Africa. He sighed and said he didn't think anybody could top the efficiency of Israeli officials. It's as though everything has been carefully planned with computers: how to squeeze out the maximum, how to impose the greatest difficulty on their lives.

We continued on to the province of Rafah, which neighbors Egypt, at the end of Gaza. Before getting out of the bus, Leila warned us that this is an extremely dangerous area, that Israeli soldiers may shoot at any time, and that everybody should stay together as much as possible and shouldn't wander off. With a group of children pressed around us, we followed a wretched street, at the end of which was a great tract of ruins with heaps of rubble, brick and tile, and shards of glass. The border wall was just fifty meters away; Israel's blockhouses and tanks stared menacingly.

Raji told us that in order to establish a buffer zone at the border, Israeli troops had destroyed almost four hundred refugee homes in this area. On January 10, 2002, alone, fifty-nine houses were torn down, and two days later forty more were demolished. At a result, seventeen hundred refugees had no homes to return to. At best, they were allowed forty minutes to gather some of their things; at worst, they were given no notice at all. As we stood there, a path opened in the crowd and a middle-aged woman (who looked much older) came toward us. With Leila translating, the woman related the terrible events of January 10. At two in the morning, with no warning, Israeli bulldozers roared in; adults were shouting and children were wailing. Scrambling and crawling, she managed to save her thirteen children, but all of their belongings were buried in the rubble. Next came the complaint of an old man. He had heard that Russell was an American, and shouted hoarsely, "Why do you Americans give airplanes and tanks to Israel? Who is the terrorist? Sharon is the real terrorist!"

My rage left me utterly spent, and I wandered around on my own. On the street, I ran into Soyinka and Juan, and we walked together in silence. Not far ahead, a high-pitched loudspeaker broadcast music and slogans. On a banner at the mouth of an alley was someone's photo. We guessed it must be that of a new martyr. Shadows swayed in a house where a feast was taking place; several elderly people were seated along the wall, smoking. It was full of cheer—like a funeral in our northern villages in China. A young man stopped us and invited us in. When he saw that we understood no Arabic, he called someone over who said "welcome" to us in English. Soyinka pointed at his watch: "Thank you very much, but we have to leave right away." They were a little disappointed.

When we got back to the coach, Leila shouted, "I have been looking everywhere for you. We have to make it to the guard post before four-thirty, otherwise we won't be able to get through." A child of six or seven pulled on my hand, wanting me to take his photo; he squatted beside the coach, making a V with two fingers.

Our road led us past the Rafah provincial highway police station, where we stopped briefly. This place was quite close to the U.N. offices and not long before had been hit by a missile from an Israeli helicopter, which had blown off the roof and burst out the doors and windows. Hearing of our presence, the provincial governor rushed over. But because we were pressed for time, we could only hurriedly shake hands and say our good-byes.

We raced to the guard post, and even though U.N. vehicles go through a special lane, there was still a line. The other lane was so packed with cars that you could not see the end. Raji wiped sweat from his forehead and said, "I have lived forty-eight years and have never felt such despair. It is not poverty that people fear, but humiliation. Think about it; passing through a checkpoint every day is a form of humiliation."

Breyten pointed out the window to a young man who worked for Raji. His name was Li Zhiyi. He was an American-born Chinese whose parents had come from Taiwan, but he couldn't speak much Chinese. He was a tall young man, handsome and intelligent. While he was studying sociology at Harvard, he did volunteer work in India, and last year, after graduation, he came here to do an internship. He had planned to stay only three months but had extended his stay once, and then once again, and now planned to spend the summer here before returning to Harvard to work on his Master's degree. He said his parents were both in hi-tech fields and didn't really understand him, and that they were worried about him. I agreed to give his parents a call when I got back to the States to put their minds at ease. While he spoke with me, he also chatted and joked with some young Palestinians. His Arabic seemed fluent. I was proud of him; not many overseas Chinese kids can separate themselves from mainstream culture and get beyond the boundaries of material life.

When the topic of suicide bombings was mentioned, he said that more than fifty incidents were entirely the work of people living on the West Bank, because people in Gaza have no way to get out. Here in Gaza, it is also very difficult to get close to the settlements. Of course, there were those who risked their lives trying. He had known a young Palestinian who ended his life this way shortly after getting married.

We came to a hotel by the sea. Breyten and I were leaving on a plane the next day, so we still had to hurry back to Tel Aviv. Leila agreed to have someone drive us at 10:30. The other members of the delegation were going to stay two more days in Israel to meet with local poets and antiwar groups.

Breyten and I were both tired and agreed to meet at the bar downstairs for a drink. The bar was deserted. We asked a waiter, and he said that they were not selling any liquor because of the intifada. I did not understand. Breyten told me this word referred specifically to the Palestinian resistance movement. Stymied, we went and knocked on Russell's door. He still had half a bottle of scotch. The window of his room faced the Mediterranean Sea. The sky was gray and cloudy, and the water looked black and gray, with layer after layer of white waves cresting up.

Twenty minutes later, we all gathered downstairs and walked to the offices of the Palestinian Centre for Human Rights to hold a press conference. Saramago again was the focus of attention. In French, he said that some people dislike it when he uses this or that kind of word, but regardless, we must admit that this is a crime against humanity.

A conference with Palestinian writers in Gaza followed. Probably as a result of the scotch he had drunk, Russell was not his usual thoughtful and cautious self and said, with some emotion, "I have spent most of my life being in the wrong place at the wrong time, but this time I have chosen the right place and the right time."

The Palestinian writers spoke marvelously. A young local writer said he had just gotten one of Saramago's novels from a friend and was reading it. He lived far away and would not be able to return home this evening as the roads would be closed. He gave this Arabic version of the book to Saramago.

At eight that evening a reception was held in an elegant, old-style Arab hotel. The vaulted main hall was encircled by a corridor, and candlelight flickered everywhere. I was weaving in and out of the pillars and ran into Madeleine Mukamabano from the France Culture radio station. Her entire family had died in the ethnic strife in Rwanda. When the International Parliament of Writers met in Lisbon in 1994, she, as an eyewitness, described the terrifying slaughter. When she talked about her impressions of Gaza, she said she felt it was more awful than what had happened in Rwanda.

Compared with the mass slaughters, this was a daily torment of both the body and spirit, more dispiriting and more painful.

The time for our departure came quickly, and we looked everywhere for Breyten. Someone said they had seen him upstairs. I looked everywhere, but there was no trace of him. I returned to the hotel to get my bags. A U.N. jeep was parked at the gate of the hotel. I asked the young Finn driving the jeep to wait, and I returned again to look for Breyten. He finally appeared at the gate, a little unsteady of gait. I asked him if he had been drinking. He held his index finger to his lips: "Shh. Intifada."

There was an Israeli inspection station just as we left Gaza. On the soldiers' instructions, the driver parked the car in a cement stall for vehicle inspection. A young woman soldier flirted with the two male soldiers. We dragged our luggage into a room where a man in glasses was friendly but didn't let that get in the way of his carrying out his duties, as he searched us from top to bottom.

The moon was bright and few stars were visible. There were almost no cars on the highway. I slept the whole way, and when we got to the hotel in Tel Aviv it was already 12:30. Yael Lotan was waiting for us at the desk. She was Jewish, about forty; she ran a small publishing house and had volunteered to arrange some activities on this side of the border for the International Parliament of Writers. Breyten and I had to get up at 5:30 the next morning, and Yael insisted on going with us to the airport. I invited both of them to have a drink. First we went to the hotel bar, but the jazz band performing there was too loud, so we went to my room and ordered a bottle of red wine. Yael told us that Saramago's speech had made some big waves. He is very popular in Israel, where one of his novels has sold sixty thousand copies, making it a bestseller there.

I asked Yael what she thought about the suicide bombings. She shrugged her shoulders, and the lenses of her glasses flashed in the lamplight. "I like red wine. I like books." She paused and said, "If I get blown up one day, I will have deserved it." She was willing to pay the consequences of the choices of her people.

I only got a couple hours of sleep, crawled out of bed, and met Breyten in the lobby. Yael sauntered in late, which drove Breyten into a frenzy of impatience. It was fortunate that Yael was with us; when she greeted the airport security staff in Hebrew, they were considerably more polite to us. A girl questioned me. Because my passport had been stamped, I could not deny that I had been to Ramallah and Gaza. Whether blunt or oblique, her questions, though complex, came down to simple matters: Who are you? Where are you coming from? Where are you going? It made me feel foolish, since these are the very questions that I myself have trouble figuring out. Afterward, Breyten and I compared notes. Fortunately, he had not said anything about Arafat; otherwise we really would have been in trouble.

The earth moved under our feet. We were on a British Airways flight to London. I opened the local English newspaper, the *Jerusalem Post*, where there was a report on Arafat's meeting with us and the open letter that the former Israeli ambassador to Portugal sent to Saramago. In it, he said, "You chose to use a metaphor that we cannot accept; and what is even more difficult for us to accept is a person who knows the power of words."

Twenty-four hours later, Israeli forces mounted a large-scale attack on the West Bank and surrounded Arafat's official residence.

Translated by Matthew Fryslie

# Imperial Crisis and Domestic Dissent

Carolyn Eisenberg

Among leftist historians and writers on American foreign policy, one can observe a certain paradox in discussions about the current Bush administration. On the one hand, there is a powerful sense that we are in an exceptionally dangerous moment in international history and that the White House is taking our country on a new and alarming route. On the other hand, there is an acute awareness that American imperialism and a propensity for war are longstanding features of our national development. How can these attitudes be reconciled? What are the dynamics of contemporary policy formation, and how does current decision making relate to previous patterns? Finally, what role can historians play in educating the public and contributing to the growth of a resistance movement here in the United States?

*positions* 13:1 © 2005 by Duke University Press

**What Is New About a Strategy of Preemption?**

In the months following the attacks on September 11, 2001, the president and his top officials sent strong signals that national security policy would be dramatically changed. Having identified specific countries—Iraq, Iran, and North Korea—as an axis of evil that could not be tolerated in a terrorist era, they began building a case for a military response. Their views were publicly codified in the September 2002 National Security Strategy of the United States of America. Although the thirty-one-page document was heavy on platitudes and familiar prescriptions, it contained a fresh warning:

> Traditional concepts of deterrence will not work against a terrorist enemy whose avowed tactics are wanton destruction and the targeting of the innocents. . . . The overlap between states that sponsor terrorism and those that pursue WMD compels us to action. . . . The United States has long maintained the option of preemptive actions to counter a sufficient threat to our national security. *The greater the threat, the greater is the risk of inaction—and the more compelling the case for taking anticipatory action to defend ourselves, even if uncertainty remains as to the time and place of the enemy's attack. To forestall or prevent such hostile acts by our adversaries, the United States will, if necessary, act preemptively.*[1] (emphasis added)

At the time this document was issued, there was little doubt that Iraq had been selected as the first target. The only ambiguity was whether the U.N. Security Council could be persuaded to endorse this project. In either case, the Bush administration seemed determined to invade Iraq, and if this proved successful, to attack other nations accused of harboring or abetting terrorists.

Since the promulgation of the 2002 National Security Strategy, many mainstream foreign policy pundits have lamented the president's departure from previous norms. According to their narrative, U.S. policy during the Cold War was characterized by concepts of deterrence and containment. They suggest that in the good old days, the United States relied on diplomacy, cooperated with allies, respected the sovereignty of other states, abided by international law, and deferred to international institutions. Over decades, this approach yielded high prestige and practical results. By behaving in a prudent, principled, and pragmatic fashion, the United States had managed to peacefully vanquish the Soviet empire.

Of course, revisionist historians have long challenged this description. They have produced a formidable literature to demonstrate that the terms *containment* and *deterrence* are ideological constructs that have neatly masked an aggressive foreign policy in the language of national defense. In actuality, American interventions around the globe—whether in the form of rigged elections, military training and assistance programs, covert operations against undesirable governments, or the deployment of half a million troops to Southeast Asia—grew out of a bold, expansive agenda for organizing the world along principles favorable to the United States. In the service of that agenda, American leaders had frequently engaged in high-risk policies that antagonized others and exposed the nation to violent retaliation.

To understand why mainstream commentators see the Bush policy as something new, it is worth noting that the administration is going far beyond the ordinary usage of the term *preemptive war*. In popular understanding and international law, this refers to a very clear situation in which one country is faced with an imminent attack from another. Under such conditions, there is a recognized right to strike first, a right that American leaders have always claimed.

That norm was manifest in the nuclear field, when during the 1970s and 1980s, the U.S. government invested heavily in an arsenal of "first-strike" weapons, which were partly justified by the need to head off an impending Soviet missile attack. Despite domestic and international efforts to gain American adherence to a principle of "no first use," this was one major reason why a succession of presidents refused to do so.

It is noteworthy that the Bush administration has taken a more extreme position. In typical Orwellian fashion, it is advancing an agenda of preventive war in the language of "preemption." Its officials are claiming the right to attack another country, even if it poses no demonstrable imminent threat, but merely the possibility that at some unspecified time in the future it might become dangerous.

This is not entirely new either. Since the inception of the Cold War and even before, the U.S. government has used military force against other countries when there was no indication that those countries were preparing an assault on our national territory. Yet in most cases—notably Korea and Vietnam—the American initiative was described, whether accurately or not, as a response to some act of aggression by the other side. What is re-markable about the 2002 National Security Strategy is that now even this fig leaf has become superfluous.

The Bush administration's decision to publicly assert the American right to invade other countries, without any of the usual justifications, reflects the priority it places on military activity. This is an administration that views war making as a policy of choice. Throughout the Cold War, American leaders relied on military superiority in order to coerce other countries, and when small states proved pesky, they were quick to send in the marines. However, U.S. presidents were quite reluctant to go to war when opponents were well armed and there was likelihood of serious resistance.

The war in Vietnam is, from this standpoint, the exception that suggests the rule. There never was a clear decision to go to war. U.S. military in-volvement occurred in an incremental way, which ultimately narrowed the options. It was because President Kennedy had the illusion that the United States could remain in an advisory capacity to the army of South Vietnam that he dispatched the first large increment of troops.

By contrast, the neoconservatives in the Bush administration came into office itching for a fight, believing that American international goals could best be served through wars against major adversaries. From that standpoint, the significance of the 2002 National Security Strategy was its public nature. In the eighteen months that followed the attacks on September 11, White House officials were conditioning the American people to the idea of a full-scale invasion, first of Iraq and later other countries.

They were also preparing the public for the possibility that the United States might go to war without the support of allies or the international community. Unlike previous administrations, which had generally stressed the need for international legitimacy and cooperation, the Bush team viewed these items as desirable but unnecessary.

**Why War?**

These shifts leave us with further questions. What explains this special enthusiasm for military confrontation? In exploring the matter, I would like to suggest some general propositions about the way American policy evolved during the Cold War.

Among many revisionist historians, it is a truism that during the Cold War the United States behaved in an imperialistic fashion and that this was rooted in the domestic political economy of the United States. Put simply, American capitalism generated a need for constant interventions around the world. Hence, the growth of our outsized military was the inevitable accompaniment of an ambitious international agenda.

As for the competition with the Soviet Union, this was often described as a mask for other objectives or as the unfortunate by-product of America's need to control the global economy. In other words, officials were manipulating fears of Soviet aggression in order to justify actions that were taken for other reasons. When put in this frame, American militarism appears as less cause than effect. It is the means by which the U.S. government protects corporate interests abroad.

This interpretation yielded a certain weird optimism about the future. For if the goal of American military might is to protect profit, then there is a kind of rational hidden hand at work, and nothing too dangerous can happen, at least not to Americans. This outlook explains the complacency among many leftist writers during the early Reagan years, when the administration seemed to reject arms control and embarked on a massive nuclear buildup. It was not until British historian Edward Thompson issued his doomsday warnings about where the nuclear competition was heading and a powerful European peace movement began to challenge American policy that revisionist scholars in the United States took a fresh look. If Edward Thomson and others were correct in saying that the very logic of nuclear competition was to make an apocalyptic war more probable, why would corporate-minded officials pursue this course?

One answer is that American foreign policy during the Cold War era was not simply about expanding profits and that American militarism in its post-1945 incarnation had a wider purpose. It grew out of the specific circumstances existing at the end of World War II and was the means by which American officials could best enhance the power of the nation-state while establishing a global economic framework that would facilitate the international interests of capital.

This might seem like a theoretical nitpick. However, by taking seriously the nationalist foundation of American policy, we can more easily recognize that over the course of a half century, American militarism has become an important phenomenon in its own right. It is not simply a consequence of economic interests, but actually shapes the way in which the U.S. government makes decisions in the international field.

In this regard, it is useful to consider some quite familiar features of Cold War America that have persisted into the present era. The purpose in itemizing them is not simply to notice their existence, but to suggest that they exercised then, and exercise now, a substantial influence on policy.

1  The first is the tremendous centralization of power in the executive. American presidents and their small circle of advisers have an enormous, at times unbridled, ability to make decisions. Obviously there are many filters that operate to produce politically reliable people at the top. However, once in power, the predilections of these individuals, even when they are incompetent or irrational, can be determinative.

2  The second is the importance of the national security managers, a layer of people who are not clearly linked to one political party but who exert leadership roles within the relevant bureaucracies. Frequently, these experts will cycle between government service and the private sector, with strong links to the corporate world. Yet even when these links are present—with, for instance, Averill Harriman, the Dulles brothers, Robert McNamara, and even Dick Cheney—these figures are not simply thinking in the fashion of businessmen. For these people are nationalists as well as capitalists. Their prescriptions reflect a concern for the power of the nation-state, along with the prerogatives of capital. Moreover, they are immersed in a culture in which the instruments of war, the threat of war, the conduct of war, and, indeed, the prospect of nuclear engagement are regular fare.

3  A related phenomenon is the military-industrial complex, described by President Eisenhower decades ago. It is much bigger now. There is a vast network of private companies and governmental bureaucracy, employing millions of Americans, whose main activity is preparation for war. One obvious result is that these entities have a continuing stake in a threatening military posture by the United

States. That very disposition increases the probability that in times of heightened conflict, the country will resort to war.

4  Although less concrete, perhaps the most crucial feature is that: when a major power such as the United States relies so heavily on military strength, it makes the world a more dangerous place. The very emphasis on violent methods and coercion deepens antagonism, stimulating both fear and anger on the part of opponents and prompting a quest for weapons and redress. In the competition with the Soviet Union, there was a self-defeating dynamic in which each side's accretion of military might was a stimulus to the other's. Insofar as the rivalry swept up many nations and groups, left in its wake were a variety of armed and aggrieved people whose discontents did not evaporate when one side left the field.

All of these factors help to explain why the collapse of the Soviet Union did not lead the United States to disarm. The tragic legacy of the Cold War was an ideology, a set of leaders, a network of bureaucratic and economic interests, a cluster of habits, and an array of international foes, whether real or imagined, that perpetuated the drive for military power.

Indeed, for many American officials, the great danger of Gorbachev's surrender was that it might jeopardize public support for a large defense establishment. A telling moment came in 1989, when the Germans tore down the Berlin wall. To the surprise of American reporters, the first President Bush seemed inordinately grim. He later explained this perceived grimness as the manifestation of a desire to avoid gloating over a Soviet defeat. A more practical consideration was his apprehension that the removal of the wall and the possible reunification of Germany might eliminate the rationale for NATO. Such alarm was premature. In the ensuing months, the American negotiating team (which included Condoleezza Rice) prevailed on the Soviets to allow a united Germany to enter the alliance, making the organization even stronger than before.

A similar concern inspired Bush Sr. to go hurtling into the Gulf War. In light of American concerns about oil, the Iraqi invasion of Kuwait would have been unacceptable under any circumstances. What was so striking in this instance was the president's eagerness to remove the Iraqi forces through military means. Although promising diplomatic efforts were in progress, Bush upended them by sending in the troops.

Thus, paradoxically, the disappearance of the Soviet rival increased the American propensity for war. This was partly for domestic reasons, namely the need to convince a more skeptical public that a vast military apparatus was still useful. At the same time, since there was no longer a Soviet counterweight, many officials were convinced that going to war had become a less costly and more efficient way to solve a range of international challenges.

## Why Iraq?

It is against this background that we can most fruitfully consider what at first glance seems an utterly irrational response to the attacks of 9/11: the decision to invade and then to occupy Iraq, a country that had nothing to do with the actions of Osama bin Laden.

When confronted with this absurdity, the reflexive response of leftists everywhere is to say "it's all about oil." What else could account for such a ludicrous diversion of resources? It is certainly true that the Bush officials are concerned about oil: they are interested in controlling the supply inside Iraq and, by establishing new bases there, hope to widen U.S. control over the oil supply in the entire Gulf region.

However, until 9/11, neither of these priorities was of sufficient weight to motivate an invasion. Indeed, the first President Bush had deliberately refrained from attacking Baghdad because he was "concerned about the long-term balance of power at the head of the Gulf. Breaking up the Iraqi state would pose its own destabilizing problems."[2] For similar reasons, in the late 1990s, a Council of Foreign Relations study group rejected the idea of military action, despite its recognition that economic sanctions were beginning to crumble. While President Clinton was tempted by the military option, the costs of combat and the potential shock waves throughout the region induced considerable caution.

Of course, the neoconservatives who came to power during the presidency of Bush Jr. were a different breed. As has been widely discussed, many of them—including Vice President Cheney, Secretary of Defense Donald Rumsfeld, Deputy Secretary of Defense Paul Wolfowitz, and a bevy of subordinates—were calling for the overthrow of Saddam Hussein years before the planes hit the World Trade Center and the Pentagon. This obviously undermines the administration's claim that its actions were inspired by a worry that Iraqi weapons of mass destruction would be handed over to terrorists.

While such skepticism is warranted, this does not translate into the quick conclusion that the Iraqi war is all about oil. In understanding the thinking of the neocons, it is important to recognize that their oil strategy is encompassed in a wider view, as is their commitment to Ariel Sharon's party in Israel. For these are ideological extremists who hold a vision of a world order, which they articulated with disturbing clarity in the reports of the Project for a New American Century.[3]

It is a vision of a world in which the United States, as the one remaining superpower, has the opportunity to use its military supremacy in new ways and to create an international order in which the U.S. government will be permanently dominant and in which its version of free-market capitalism can be extended. As the neoconservatives dreamed of the future, the seizure of Iraq was not an end itself but the first step in a larger military plan.

Furthermore, in understanding the decision to invade Iraq, it is not sufficient to focus on the specific objectives of the Cheney-Rumsfeld group. Although this faction occupied a strategic position within the Bush administration, until 9/11 there was only a slight prospect that their wishes concerning Iraq would be heeded. Under Colin Powell's leadership, U.S. policy was moving in the opposite direction, toward the liberalization and more precise targeting of economic sanctions.

In actuality, the terrorist attacks did change a number of things. They made a convert of the commander in chief, who might have wished to drive out Hussein from the beginning but was too timid to do so. They turned some centrist and even liberal members of the foreign policy elite into enthusiasts for what had previously appeared a needless, high-risk adventure. They rendered the normally malleable members of Congress even more pliant than usual, reduced a conformist media into servility, and made a terrified American public an easy mark for outlandish propaganda.

In short, there are many reasons for this foolhardy decision, but a crucial one is this: as of September 10, 2001, the United States was a country wired for war. This had been the case for decades. However, there had not been an attack on our shores since Pearl Harbor. Given the long-standing American propensity to use, or to threaten to use, military power in a wide range of difficult situations and the careless assumption that America's military advantage would prevent any attack on our vital interests, it was a foregone conclusion that the response to something as devastating as 9/11 could only be war. How long such a war would continue would reflect the strategic preferences and talents of those in the White House and the fortitude of enemies. In these respects, we have not been lucky.

We are, unfortunately, not at the tail end of the Iraq campaign, as many would like to think, but at the beginning of a whole new era of military confrontation. If the Bush administration has its way, we will be expanding our armed forces during the second term, whether through the draft or some other means. And the dangers we face internationally will surely grow. The policies the U.S. government is now pursuing in Afghanistan, Israel, and Iraq have already fueled a fresh cycle of violence that will be difficult to stop, even with a more prudent president, who is eager to apply the brakes.

## What Role Can Historians Play?

Historians need to resist. For most of our lifetime, American foreign policy has exacted a fearful price from people around the world, and it has long been dangerous to our own populace. It is now more menacing than ever.

Some administrations are more reckless and irresponsible than others, and some presidents are dumber than others. At present, we are in the hands of reckless ideologues who are truly ignorant about the rest of the world and are subject to grandiose delusions about what military force can really achieve.

Even if we historians have no ability to educate our present leadership, we can surely educate the American public. In dealing with students, we need to put forward alternative ideas about the roles of militarism and capitalism in shaping the present world. I am not advocating the kind of one-sided presentations that many of us experienced when we sat in classrooms. However, as teachers and writers, we can offer the missing perspectives and the information that young people need to consider. And we can create an educational atmosphere in which divergent ideas are truly engaged.

Ironically, my generation was galvanized by the Vietnam War, and that experience created a hope that scholarship and teaching could nurture a critical sensibility that would reverberate throughout our society. Yet while many constructive changes have taken place within our discipline, it is on this very topic—the American role in the world—that we have been least communicative and least effective. This failure is perhaps one unfortunate by-product of the emphasis on social history and the rejection of projects that focus on the predilections and practices of powerful white men.

Whatever the exact reason, the educational task of nurturing a critical sensibility about American foreign policy remains unaccomplished. It is now an urgent responsibility, which I hope we can meet.

## Notes

This essay is a revised version of a talk presented in January 2003 at the Historians against the War Roundtable, American Historical Association Convention, Washington, DC.

1  White House, National Security Strategy of the United States 2002, September 17, 2002, www.whitehouse.gov/nsc/nssall.html.

2  George Bush and Brent Scowcroft, *A World Transformed* (New York: Random House, 1998), 487.

3  See, for example, Project for the New American Century, "Rebuilding America's Defenses," September 2000, www.newamericancentury.org/RebuildingAmericasDefenses.pdf. A complete set of all reports from the Project for a New American Century can be found on the organization's home page, www.newamericancentury.org.

## Good-bye Kitty, Hello War:
## The Tactics of Spectacle and New Youth Movements in Urban Japan

Sharon Hayashi and Anne McKnight

Tokyo's Miyashita Park is usually an oasis of scrubbiness in the semiotically saturated landscape of Shibuya, the capital of Japan's retail consumer culture. Located off the crowded and information-filled main shopping streets that branch out from the busy train station, Miyashita Park is a weedy and unkempt space that has recently become home to a tent city of homeless residents. The uncared-for, grassless (and, more strikingly, signless) neglect of this pocket park contrasts vividly with the branding, advertising, and signage that mark other nearby spaces. On October 5, 2003, the park hosted an event that was even more incongruous with the Shibuya streetscape: the fourth set of political rave demonstrations focused on the occasion of George W. Bush's October 17–18 visit to Japan and his more desultory visits to other Asian countries to garner support for the continued war in Iraq. Another rave demo took place in Kyoto on October 19 and followed a similar route, through Kyoto's Shijô, a main drag of consumer culture.[1]

*positions* 13:1 © 2005 by Duke University Press

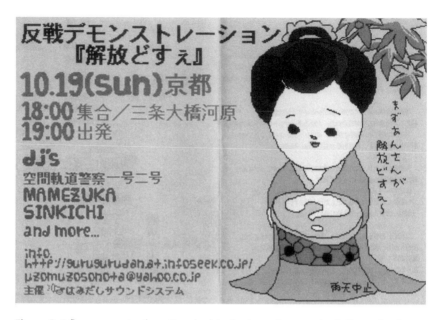

**Figure 1** A flyer announcing the antiwar/reclaim the streets demonstration in Kyoto, October 19, 2003. The character pictured is modeled on Otabe-chan, a character from a well-known Kyoto sweetshop and an apprentice geisha (*maiko*) who advertises a famous local sweet. Her come-hither glance at tourists is transposed here into an invitation to move from store to street to join the protest.

These rave demo protests, which have been going on since early 2003, have used different strategies to reclaim in each city a space thoroughly saturated by consumer culture and populated by youth. The strategies for these protests differ from strategies for other antiwar and antiglobalization protests whose internationalism is signaled by the presence and pressure of transnational NGOs and by communication in English in parallel with communication in Japanese. While using media tactically, rave demos experiment with new forms of music (anarchic noise and techno beats) and media (3–D videos projected onto the sides of buildings through the course of a rave demo). Organizers have attempted to mix art and activism in public spaces of Tokyo and Kyoto to convince their own demographic of youth culture of two things, in a manner that treats ideology differently than citizens' movements or political parties do. First, the organizers try to show that youth subculture

**Figure 2** In a tactical use of local iconography, the flag in the background reframes the name of the local baseball team, the Hanshin Tigers, to read "Hansen Tigers," or "Antiwar Tigers."

is already written into the world, despite its feelings of alienation. Second, they try to mobilize the political potential of the crowds by reintroducing elements of the pleasure principle of mass culture into ideologized political protest, particularly by using mediated musical forms such as techno and DJ sound trucks, with dance, identity-camouflaging cos-play costuming (a subculture that consists of playing with the costumes and roles of familiar manga and anime characters), and neo-folk elements like *chindon* bands. Most recent is the occupation of Miyashita Park to stage a symposium and simultaneous musical events. In this case, the term *occupation* refers not only to opposition to sending troops and funds to Iraq but also to the local policy of requiring permission to conduct political gatherings, the "occupation" of public spaces like Miyashita Park by the increasing ranks of homeless people, and the global issue of the occupation of Palestine.

Our article presents the recent political demonstrations put on by members of a loosely organized youth culture in urban Japan, broadly conceived from a demographic of people ranging in age from their late teens to late thirties. This new social formation of economically oriented antiwar protesters has combined with a new cultural formation of tactical media to respond to three ways in which local experience is written into global issues: the decision to send money and troops to Iraq as "peacekeepers," narrowly staying within the bounds of Article 9 of the constitution, which forbids Japan's rearmament and outsources the use of military force to the United States and its allies; the neoliberal economic policies of Japanese Prime Minister Jun'ichirô Koizumi and Tokyo Governor Shintarô Ishihara that are widely seen as hastening the shift to a flexible labor market of *furiitaa*, or freelance workers; and the desire to reclaim a space for public demonstration in which the public is not always understood as being the same as the nation, and is often experienced through the cosmopolitan media flows and artifacts of popular culture. While there are obvious parallels to antiglobalization protests and new social movements elsewhere in the world, we see these protests as significant because of the way they situate international relations as something immanent to protesters' and spectators' own lives—that is to say, the international or global is felt, invested, and represented within what are technically state boundaries and within what is often topologized as the local neighborhood culture of Shibuya. We use the term tactical media here as it has been used by media activist organizations drawing on Michel de Certeau's idea of a tactic in his book *The Practice of Everyday Life*. Here a tactic makes explicit an operating logic of everyday life to effect a redeployment or transformation of that logic on the part of users. In the rave demos, tactical use of media departs from the realist use of media to convey information and instead emphasizes how consumers use the representations (images, texts, artifacts) around them.[2]

Parading through Shibuya on October 5, four–ton trucks on which huge speakers playing techno music with thumping bass were strapped shook youthful shoppers and clerks out of shops to look for the sound source. Called rave demos, or sometimes sound demos, in deference to the presence of large sound systems, the protests use the nomadic reclamation of space, dancing, DJ-ing, and music characteristic of global rave culture to push an

**Figure 3** Speakers are loaded onto trucks in preparation for the October 19 rave demo in Kyoto.

antiwar, anti-Koizumi and anti-Ishihara message. About 700 people—and 500 riot police—took part in the rave demo, attempting to use the power of the spectacle to get people to join in the protest.[3] The goal was to use sound to appeal to their curiosity and dance music to draw them into a mass phenomenon whose source they might not even have been able to see. Along the course of the rave demo, some people become piqued by the sounds, while others become curious. This method of constituting communities through gossip about the effects of remote events, in fact, recalled the virtual nature of their relation to the war itself as mediated by discursive networks of print and image.

The October 5, 2003, occupation of Miyashita Park included a performance of ECD's rap song "Us Guys Don't Just Do as We're Told" (figs. 4–5), which offers a site-specific account of the landscape of the demonstrations.[4]

ECD
言うこと聞くよな奴らじゃないぞ


オタマジャクシで街を埋めつくし
小田マサノリで道をハメはずし
通りは踊り場　用事は放り出し
ポリは怒り出す　総理は言いつけろ
ありえない景色　かつてないクライシス
渋谷どーなる　知るかグローバル
ひびけ　斗缶　たたく3時間
反戦　反弾圧　反石原


言うこと聞くよな奴らじゃないぞ（X4）


世界残酷AIN'T NO JOKE
SHOCK連続それをふりほどく
ひっぱりあげる倒された仲間
やっぱりポリスFUCKだ人殺し
実力行使　直行鉄格子
わかっちゃいるけど第一解放区
毎度の態度悪い暴れん坊
FightのRight種類ただ連呼　殺すな


言うこと聞くよな奴らじゃないぞ（X4）


はね返しはね返しはね返しふくらむ
前進こばむ行進　新提案
理解しがたいと固い頭には
心配　何が起きるかわかんない
年代　超えて無関係つながり
何枚写真撮っても　手がかり
あるわけないバックも目的も
鳴り物　準備集合罪　WACK


言うこと聞くよな奴らじゃないぞ（X4）

**Figure 4**   The lyrics of ECD's song "Us Guys Don't Just Do as We're Told" place what it calls the "unruly rally" of the rave demos in the context of Shibuya during neoliberal economic changes.

Us guys don't just do as we're told

ECD

Fill the town with musical notes
Going crazy with Oda Masanori
Street's a disco, closed for business
Cops fly into a rage, tell it to the PM
Impossible scene, crisis never before seen
What's gonna happen to Shibuya? Ever heard about globalization?
Ring out! Beating on an oil drum for three hours
Anti-war, anti-oppression, anti-Ishihara

Us guys don't just do as we're told (4X)

Cruel world ain't no joke
Waking up from serial shock
Helping up fallen mates
Fucking police murderers
Use of force, straight to jail
We get it but it's still free zone number one
Those bad boys
Fight for your right types just calling out, do not kill

Us guys don't just do as we're told (4X)

Fighting back, fighting back, fighting back, swelling
Unruly rally, a new strategy
When it's hard to understand the hard-headed
Worry, don't know what's gonna happen next
Crossing generations, connecting the unconnected
No matter how many photos you cops take
Doesn't tell you a thing about the groups or their goals
Making noise, the crime of premeditated gathering WACK

Us guys don't just do as we're told (4X)

**Figure 5** Translation of ECD's song "Us Guys Don't Just Do as We're Told," a variant of which was performed at the October 5, 2003, rave demo.

ECD, a first-generation Japanese producer/musician with hip-hop roots who released his first record in 1990, is known for turning to local references. Here his lyrics create and make an invitation to a rhetorical community ("us guys") that calls out an anti-Ishihara/anti-Koizumi platform and becomes an activist community working to reclaim public space and its terms of occupation. ECD also puts some distance between this movement and old-style peace demonstrations.

The occupation of separate areas of Miyashita Park by different musical constituencies just prior to the rave demo formalized the way that different groups with different agendas and investments in politics have responded to the rave demos. On the day of the demo, completely incompatible musical performances by free improv musicians and techno DJs flanked a symposium that resembled a teach-in, where spectators sat cross-legged on the ground. Passersby carrying shopping bags drifted in and out, using cell phones to alert their friends to the goings-on in the park. Lacking demographic or ideological unity, or even the unity of identity known as taste, the very baggy composition of the crowd was one of its primary characteristics. "Baggy" had in the 1970s been the quality that Marxist labor organizer and historian Takaaki Yoshimoto cited to describe the way in which the "national" contained everything within its parameters.[5] We think that the composition of the crowd is more than a sampling of musical taste markets, since social commentators on youth culture often dismiss such gatherings. Moreover, the fragmentation of the crowd was markedly different from the sectarian protests against the U.S.-Japan Security Treaty (AMPO) ratified in 1960 and 1970, protests whose splitting is often cited as a symptom of or conduit for the demise of the Japanese left. Without imposing a unified ideological stance, the rave demos have indicated both a disenchantment with official politics and discontent with the neoliberal measures proposed and enacted by Prime Minister Koizumi and Tokyo Governor Ishihara. The baggy composition of rave demo and symposium participants shows how new arrangements of experience ally vastly different groups of people, all of whom are affected by shifts in the flexible, globalized labor market—twentyish *furiitaa*, students on the verge of getting a job, and downsized office ladies (OLs) and salarymen. The multiple agendas of protesters signal the emergence of new alliances based on new arrangements of war, security, economic growth, and work and working time and forges connections to economic and cultural movements beyond the national.[6]

## Background: 9/11 and 9/17

President Bush's October 17, 2003, visit to Japan linked two clusters of security issues—the 9/11 World Trade Center destruction and the September 17, 2002, meeting between Prime Minister Koizumi and North Korean leader Kim Jong-Il. At this meeting, Kim admitted to the kidnapping of roughly a dozen Japanese citizens by North Koreans during the 1970s and 1980s. Featured since then on late-morning television talk shows, manga, and daily newspapers, the presumed North Korean security threat to everyman was what led to the "state of emergency" measures that passed both houses of Japan's National Diet and were ratified in June 2003.

The paralleling of security threats extends the Japanese government support for U.S. antiterror efforts beginning in October 2001, when Japan started giving naval logistical support to U.S. troops in Afghanistan by refueling ships. These reactions echo the passing of the wiretapping law (1999), regarded as a security measure against violence by AUM-like sects, and the nationally accessible JUKI-NET, an online resident registry system launched in 2002. Alongside such state-motivated efforts to promote nationalism, popular nationalism has increased following the Taepodong missile launches by North Korea, beginning in 1998. This sharp rise in nationalist sentiment and its management have changed popular conceptions of the body politic, resulting in increasing attention to systems that enable the criminalization of noncitizen Korean residents of Japan and broader categories of foreigners. In an array of recent protests that have taken place since the May 2003 institution of the state of emergency measures (*yûji hôsei*), writers and academics as well as fringe intellectuals have evoked the 1960 and 1970 AMPO (U.S.-Japan Security Treaty) protests, expressing their exasperation at a seeming reaffirmation of deference to U.S. security wishes and the world order in which Japan becomes implicated politically and economically.

As different modes of production come into being with downsizing, outsourcing, and an increasing dependence on *furiitaa*, a different type of disenchantment demands a different type of political movement. In Japan, this is demonstrated in the largely nonsectarian movement of different youth cultures with a common investment in using sound, dance, and items of the surveillance-industrial complex, such as cell-phone cameras, to occupy the streets. Flexible labor and virtual war encourage flexible protest and virtual protest. While they do not identify themselves as *otaku*, it has been the highly fragmented and largely nonsectarian groups of freelance workers— music writers, graphic artists, computer geeks—who have organized and launched these protests, acknowledging that they are currently living in a "state of emergency." The term *furiitaa* was initially popularized during the 1980s bubble era. A *furiitaa* (from the English *free* and the German *arbeit*) was a freelance worker who valued the open-ended nature of free time over money. In the bubble context, it was possible for flexible labor to retain a countercultural stance of being time-rich, if cash-poor. Government and think-tank statistics typically started to register *furiitaa* beginning in 1990, when they comprised 1.82 million people or 10.4 percent of the workforce (even apart from the more traditional flexible labor pools of students and housewives). In 2001, the figure rose to 4.17 million or 21.2 percent of the workforce as, in the deregulating economy, the force behind the *free* of *furiitaa* has come from the employer rather than the employee side: *furitaa* has come to signify the increasing demographic of freelance workers, a pool from which employers are free to pick workers for jobs that are increasingly contract based and without the benefits of full-time employment (and also, probably not coincidental to the galvanization of movement, increasingly male in composition, though still predominantly female).[7]

## The Olympics, Expo 1970, and the Roots of Virtual Protest

New social arrangements of labor and information culture as inspirations for new types of political movements are found in the ways that many youth subcultures locate the pleasure principle in two arenas: music and dance in club and mobile rave cultures, and surveillance as a pastime—taking and swapping pictures, feeling secure and protected by the vigilant security cameras that are found throughout the cities. The idea of the rave demo harnesses these elements of mobility and exhibitionism: the desire to be seen, the desire for community, and the desire to make something positive rather than enslaving from elements of mass or technical culture.[8]

The relationship between spectacle and exhibitionism, and the personal relationship to technological development, are usually traced back to two events: the 1964 Tokyo Olympics and the 1970 Osaka Exposition. The year 1964 is seen as significant because of the reconstruction of Tokyo for display to the international gaze.[9] In turn, 1970 is seen as a turning point for leftist activism because of the way in which it presented technology as a spectacle whose displays and fetishistic explications of futuristic technologies distracted the masses from participating in public discourse. In the cultural sphere, the 1970 expo is commonly noted by electronic musicians and music writers and celebrated by electronics manufacturers as a turning point, as the locus classicus of Japanese media society. The expo was seen as a giant bait-and-switch maneuver to opt out of a national participatory democracy based on popular governance in favor of techno-culture's promise of another globalized utopia realized through markets and technology. Writer and art activist Masanori Oda points out that on June 23, 1970, the day that AMPO was ratified, there were 222,000 visitors to the expo; eventually, more than 60 percent of the population of Japan would attend.[10] Another prescient dimension of the expo was the forced mobility of its spectators. As the rave demos were paced by a police van crowded with videographers, visitors to the expo commonly complained that they were watched and were forced to be constantly mobile by announcements and guards on the exhibition grounds.

In general, a recognition of the commodification and alienation of society informs a movement. The acceptance of the materials of consumer culture and the adoption of promotional strategies antagonizes some veteran leftists, such as Tomoya Takaishi, who uphold the activities of the Shinjuku Folk Guerrillas involved in the AMPO protests as a model of protest. In 1970, radical students simultaneously denounced as apolitical both the university and U.S. imperialism in Vietnam, and brought debate and antiwar songs into the public arena of the Shinjuku Station west exit plaza. The Folk Guerillas performed in the underground space at Shinjuku Station, which was then occupied by ten thousand people, until scuttled by the riot police. Takaishi criticizes the current protests for the emotive coercion of their message and implies that the subjectivity of today's protester is different:

There's no thinking in it. You could brush this off by saying that these are different times, but actually our way of forming connections between people was very different. The Folk Guerillas didn't go around mobilizing people, the circle around us grew and spread larger on its own. It wasn't just for the sake of revving people up; each person went through the work of thinking things through, and they were prepared to be arrested when they went into the plaza. The huge reverb sound of the sound demo, that in itself has so much power that it's its own kind of violence.[11]

While the use of music and the desire to establish a position within a spectacle to mobilize crowds haunts the history of Futurist techno-gone-fascist and right-wing marches both past and present, we probably cannot draw a clear distinction between left- and right-wing rallies, especially given the general directionlessness of the pleasure principle of popular culture. Could the fear of returning or replicating the pleasures of fascism be one of the reasons (aside from a polemical refusal to appropriate elements of consumer culture) that so-called serious leftists have steered clear of pop culture, pop music, and manga, leaving the terrain wide open for the popularity of "true story" manga?[12]

This is not so for the rave demos. Carefully negotiating its time slot to accommodate retail operating hours, the parade route of the Tokyo rave-demo unfolded on a Sunday night, through a route that linked all the major department stores in Shibuya and passed by the NHK's studio headquarters, itself a legacy of the Olympics. Shibuya's importance as a base derives from its place in the economic development of virtuality. Now known for its scrambled crossing, its crowds of cram-school commuter teenagers, and a number of record stores per capita second to none, Shibuya is the product of the Olympic construction boom during which Tokyo was reconstructed as an international showpiece. In 1964, Shibuya was redeveloped from a neighborhood of public buildings to the flagship of Japan's retail industries. Streets were renamed from the democratically bland Town Hall Street (Kuyaku-sho dôri) to the upscale pastoral Park Avenue (Kôen dôri), forming a boulevard along which the two major department-store groups, Seibu/Parco and Tôkyû, clustered buildings. Continually under renewal, the stores fostered a retail culture beginning in the early 1970s that revolved around introducing young local designers, leasing space to in-store boutiques, and introducing consumer credit to enable purchase over time, to cater to youth, who by the early 1980s sought market differentiation and brand goods rather than a place in mass culture.[13]

Just as Shibuya is different from AMPO-era Shinjuku and its public-sphere based protests, the impersonal strategy of occupying public space through music and dance differs from critiques of the everyday undertaken by the *angura* movement, the 1960s countercultural underground that criticized state policy and violence and that privileged populism and the individual. Street theater and performance-art happenings of the 1960s and 1970s often used neofolkic elements to defamiliarize elements of everyday life, using a one-two resistance punch of theater and graphic design to bring out suppressed ideology. The rave demos, in contrast, addressed a new awareness of the kind of virtuality that is represented by shopping, finance capital, digital sound and video, and a relation to war.[14] Rather than privileging the people as a site of action or authenticity, the rave demos' site, publicity, and objects of critique all draw on these virtualities to emphasize less ideologically certain processes of becoming rather than being. This tactic resonates with other recent examples of art activism that write Japan into the world. Yûtaka Tsuchiya's 2003 DV-film *Peep "TV" Show*, for example, features two protagonists from the Shibuya subcultures who try to understand how, as one of them says, "this is where the plane [of September 11] hit us."

When explaining their choice of tactics, rave demo organizers often refer to prior symbolic uses of material structures to which they are responding. Music writer Maki Mizukoshi distinguishes the rave demo's use of Tokyo as a space of spectacle from ways that Tokyo has been used recently as a backdrop for displays of military preparedness. Referring to Ishihara's series of drills that navigate Self-Defense Forces through Tokyo, as well as his advocacy of Japan's reviving its economy by developing its security and weapons industries, she remarks: "Shintarô Ishihara did his audition for the big-time as Governor here, and used the street as a backdrop for film production, which ends up making the street a function of the city administration." She notes that the post-Ishihara redemption of public space also invoked by pop figures like revisionist manga historiographer Yoshinori Kobayashi reduces and limits all discussions of the economy to those that can be framed in national terms, including the GNP and national defense.[15] For her, the strategic choice of staging an anti-Ishihara sound demonstration in the heart of Shibuya reclaims those streets while exploiting their physical architecture. In contrast to the valleys of cramped Shinjuku streets, which reduce visibility and prevent sound from traveling, the wide boulevards of Shibuya offer an ideal acoustic environment and visual display for the rave demonstrations.[16]

We see the tactical use of post-expo media in three examples below: a graphic from a Web site that gives step-by-step instructions for how to protest; a set list from the October 19 rave demo in Kyoto; and a graphic from an antiwar Web site that draws on earlier traditions of antiwar protest from the Vietnam era.

Our first example, a composite of a plundered graphic, how-to-manual text, and the Web site designer's own fingerprint, shows Elvis affirming the right to remain silent, in a set of Web pages titled "Anti-Police Academy Guideline" (fig. 6). The image inverts the status of everyman conferred on the pop culture Elvis by virtue of his military service. The text spells out the right to noninterpolation into official service by adjudicating or acquitting oneself as a criminal. The highly local nature of the referents used in rave demo graphics appears in the array of how-to-demonstrate guides in globalization protests, such as information on legal rights, and the practical advice on police control follows a similar logic. In many elements of the rave demos' tactical use of media, pop, and animé-based graphics, soft lettering and pastel coloring personalize the situation of protest and take the edge off the hard reality of police control and the possibility of arrest. This image can be seen as being used tactically by its redeployment and inversion of the way the state should not discriminate between a celebrity and everyman. Though the graphics depend on images recruited and transmitted virtually through new media, rhetorically the insistence on rights does not depart far from earlier public-sphere protests, as following these rules reaffirms the juridical power accorded to the state.

The second tactical use of media recycles a protest graphic from 1967 anti-Vietnam war protests sponsored by the Citizens' Federation for Peace in Vietnam (Beheiren) (fig. 7). This calligraphy graphic by Tarô Okamoto stood out strikingly in a full-page ad in the *Washington Post*, and its redeployment

**Figure 6** Thumbs up for knowing your civil rights as a protester. Credit: ASC

in Internet terms differs somewhat from the public-sphere claim on the state seen in our first example. The 1967 style of the black-and-white *korosuna*, or "do not kill," graphic is remarkable because its execution uses line and force to disalign the character that most localizes the impact of *kill*. The strokes are spiky and tilted in perspective, so that the "do not" message appears to be trailing behind. Materializing the imperative "do not kill" in this way works to emphasize the violence of war and, by keeping the sign legible, makes meaning rest in the act of killing. A pro-peace message is not conveyed. In a second use of the graphic and slogan of *korosuna*, a group of artists loosely brought together under the *korosuna* banner has recently staged happenings and performances and taken up this 1967 graphic for a kind of organizational branding. Part of this group's activities are in conjunction with the rave demos, which jolt unsuspecting spectators out of peaceful slumber. Like the rave demos that its members have also participated in, the group emphasizes the importance of the physical space of demonstrations as a temporary meeting point and possible space of transformation. What interests us is how new media in the group's activities work with or discard notions of *public* and *space* that correspond to modernist design and subjectivity. The group's use

**Figure 7** Taro Okamoto's graphic from the *Washington Post*, April 30, 1967. The graphic derives from the characters for *korosuna*, or "do not kill."

of graphic design explicitly invokes earlier anti-Vietnam protests, especially in its focus on the U.S.-Japan bilateral framework within a world system. But here the Web-based message shifts the 1967 graphic's sense of dynamic action into an experience of movement within space.[17] At the level of citation, the new use of the graphic both questions the appropriateness of calling the attacks on Iraq war and summons an awareness of the postwar search for peace and prosperity. As an assemblage, the site's graphics proliferate fluttering red *korosuna* icons, a brash bloody red that extends to totalize and make congruent the typography of the entire site. The site contains images, picture archives, organizational statements, sound samples, bibliography, and announcements of future "shows."

In using the 1967 image, the new *korosuna* graphic seems consistent with the tradition of public sphere criticism, which saw modernist space as a grid with centralized infrastructure overseen by a potentially phantom gaze. But Net-specific tendencies are also here. The graphic seems to indicate a different mode of violence vis-à-vis the public sphere. It sometimes verges on illegibility. Unlike the clear disalignment of the 1967 graphic, the new *korosuna* graphic can seem to blur into other levels of citation, like horror-movie splotches or the gaudy garnish of gratuitous design elements. As a movement, the group mobilized by the *korosuna* graphic could function only through the anonymity of the Internet, from which its ever-changing members are pooled.

Our third example (fig. 8) takes expectations from the world of local pageant and reframes the ritual object in the spectacle of consumer culture. As riot police struggle to contain and hurry along demonstrations, protesters have developed various strategies for stalling and taking up space. Dancing, instead of marching, has been the most effective way of disrupting the strict timetables of enforced mobility set by city officials, and police have kept their distance from heavy and precarious *mikoshi* (palanquins) carried by demonstrators. Again we recall our initial concept of tactic: "I call a 'tactic,' on the other hand, a calculus which cannot count on a 'proper' (a spatial or institutional localization), nor thus on a borderline distinguishing the other as a visible totality. The place of a tactic belongs to the other. A tactic insinuated itself into the other's place, fragmentarily, without taking it over in its entirety, without being able to keep it at a distance."[18]

Last is a set list of the music that provides the skeleton of rave-demo protests (fig. 9). DJ Sinkichillout's nine-song set was the first of four sets in the October 19 Kyoto protest. His selections include the J-rap pioneer Seiko Itô, as well as DJs with Tokyo ties such as Jeff Mills, formerly of Underground Resistance (UR), remixes of punk ballads (from the punk band The Blue Hearts), and a track by KLF (most often read as Kopyright Liberation Front), notorious for their "burning a million pounds" stunt and for the bombastically inclined theater in their ambient house music. DJ Ei'ichi Seino's set list for the May 23 Tokyo rave demo moved between the anthemic music of rock and the beats and textures of club culture, drawing from a many-layered retro archive, ranging from club music designed to power people onto the dance floor (Stefano Greppi), to retro ballads (John Lennon). The songs emphasize movement and pleasure, rather than an analytical relation to space. His set list was chosen by polling a selection of his friends and contacts on the Internet, asking them to name their favorite protest song.

## No Parking: Reclaiming the Streets

As we have seen, Takaishi's experience of the AMPO protests frames the protests' social and cultural organization in terms of critical and organic

**Figure 8**  Artist
Muneteru Ujino's neo-folk
*mikoshi* loads down a
typical festival implement
with elements of
decorated-truck culture.
Photo by Chiaki
Oshima

debate by sovereign subjects deciding to participate in an oppositional movement. But music writer Tsutomu Noda claims that the folkic "outside" has
lost its oppositional edge and bleakly refuses to find any outside standpoint
for the movement. He remarks:

> Just as we know from the fact that street magazines are stand-ins for fash-
> ion catalogs, according to Japanese youth culture, the "street" is nothing
> more or less than the place where you're drunk on capitalism.... [The
> streets] are overflowing with street musicians. Even on March 20th, they
> were all over Shibuya station, and they were more worried about singing

1. HITECK JAZZ / UR
2. ? / KLF
3. ? / SEIKOU ITO & MAGIC UNSUMBLE
4. VIVA BLASIL / BATUKADA
5. rmx / THE BLUE HEARTS
6. RIGHT FOR YOUR RIGHT / BEASTIE BOYS
7. ONE / SUNSCAPE
8. ? / AKFEN
9. MAKOTO KAWAMOTO / EYE rmx

**Figure 9** DJ Sinkichillout's set list from the October 19 rave demo in Kyoto

their songs than the beginning of a war. These guys are pretty much the "front lines" of the major labels, and even the word street has been killed off by capitalism.[19]

Whether advocating rave-demo tactics or suspicious of their reproduction of consumer culture's place of enunciation, for the recent wave of protests, there seems to be general agreement that a significant departure appears in their treatment of the city. AMPO protesters, for instance, saw the city as a forest into which they could disappear. The citizens' network Beheiren could help U.S. soldiers in Vietnam desert from the military; students could throw away their books and get out into the streets, an uncharted space. In contrast, the rave demos tend to see the street as a space of social control and attempt to redefine it from within existing parameters.[20] The image of the pedestrian stepping out of the frame in fig. 10, into the wide-open spaces, is a situationist-inspired *détournement* of the graphic design of a Tokyo municipal traffic safety campaign.

The rejection of organized politics is mirrored in the rejection of formal spatial organization during the demonstrations. Rather than imposing a political program, spaces are opened up for individual participation and ever-changing combinations of participants.[21] The explosive megaphone and drum performance group TCDC (Transitor Connected Drum Collective) is one such unit that has added tension and entertainment to rave and other demonstrations across Tokyo with its unpredictable sound and actions (figs. 11–14). Among the more playful situationist-inspired tactics it has employed has been the fashioning of oil tins into drums to highlight

**Figure 10** Sticker for the October 5, 2003, rave demo. Design by Masanori Oda

the involvement of the oil industry in the invasion of Iraq. A self-identified, latter-day *chindon* band, TCDC exploits the same porousness between street and shop enjoyed by the original *chindon* bands, mobile crews of noisemakers hired to drum up attention for shop openings and special events in the early 1930s.[22]

The anarchic nature of the dancing and *zatsuon* (techno, noise, drums, megaphones, screams) employed by TCDC and other participants in rave demos has introduced contingency and openings into the space of protests that reject the geometry so admired by militarized right-wing organizations.

**Figure 11** Rapper ECD on sax and lead singer of the punk band Guchi (Complaint) at the October 17, 2003, anti-Bush demonstration. Photograph by Emilio A. Templado

**Figure 12** Riot police attempt to hem in the demonstrators but fail to stifle the anarchic sounds produced by TCDC. Photograph by Emilio A. Templado

**Figure 13** TCDC, a self-styled latter-day chindon band, drums up attention for the demonstration. Photograph by Emilio A. Templado

The protests have specifically emphasized their use of sound as distinct from music for several reasons. One is to acknowledge the link to prior uses of sound trucks, largely by right-wing ideologues who bark out diagnoses of social ills from atop their trucks while parked or meandering in public spaces. Another is to differentiate their use of music from the spells cast by lyrics and technology. Still another is to align the different kinds of music and sound—rap, *chindon*, dance, noise, rave, and punk—by their effect of overcoming distance between street and shop and making networks where sound can go that people cannot.

TCDC's tactical use of noise employs maneuvers of randomness, varying intensities, and disruption. This resonates with the tactics of the Tokyo-based Against Street Control (ASC) sound-demo organizers as a whole. While holding out no hope for revolution with a capital R, they are attempting to exploit openings and opportunities nonetheless. De Certeau continues to suggest a definition of tactics:

**Figure 14** Masanori Oda smashing an oil tin drum. Photograph by Emilio A. Templado

It has at its disposal no base where it can capitalize on its advantages, prepare its expansions, and secure independence with respect to circumstances. The "proper" is a victory of space over time. On the contrary, because it does not have a place, a tactic depends on time—it is always on the watch for opportunities that must be seized "on the wing." Whatever it wins, it does not keep. It must constantly manipulate events in order to turn them into "opportunities."[23]

## Notes

1 Information and discussion on the Kyoto demonstration can be found at gurugurudan.at .infoseek.co.jp/. For information about and discussion of the Tokyo demonstrations, see asc.shacknet.nu and dop.is-a-geek.net/.

2 Michel de Certeau, *The Practice of Everyday Life*, trans. Steven Rendall (Berkeley: University of California Press, 1998), xix.

3 Newspaper coverage was slim and probably undercounted the number of participants; these figures are from "Shisô nai kedo rôjô wa shinkûkan: Shibuya de 'hansen' tekuno dai-onkyô"

("No Thought in It, but a New Sense of Space in the Streets: Big 'Antiwar' Techno Vibe in Shibuya"), *Tokyo Shinbun*, October 13, 2003.

4 Lyrics reflect the October 5, 2003, Miyashita Park occupation performance. To listen to an online version of this song go to the sound archive under the menu at asc.shacknet.nu/index_02.html.

5 The remark comes in the context of a discussion in which Yoshimoto explains how he discovered how Japanese political ideology differed from Western political ideology. Takaaki Yoshimoto, *Kyôdô gensô ron* (*On Communal Illusions*) (Tokyo: Kadokawa Shoten, 1982), 8.

6 Protesters were largely freelance workers dealing in symbolic capital. An example was recently made of a bookstore employee arrested for defacing a bathroom in a public park in Suginami Ward by spraying antiwar graffiti on the outside walls. Although his political (anarchist) sensibilities do not extend to the entire group of rave-demo protesters, the writing was clearly legible and said *supekutakuru no shakai* (society of the spectacle) and *hansen* (antiwar). The defendant was indicted under the most serious possible charge, for which prosecutors sought an eighteen-month prison term, rather than a fine or a shorter term for a lesser charge.

7 See Tessa Morris-Suzuki's *Beyond Computopia: Information, Automation, and Democracy in Japan* (London: Kegan Paul, 1988) for an account of government white-paper statements and projections for a late-twentieth-century shift to increasingly flexible labor pools. She too remarks on the gendering of information-society labor: "During the period of rapid industrialization, the corporate sector expanded by drawing the pool of (mostly male) self-employed agricultural workers into the full-time work force. In the phase of 'informatisation,' it has expanded instead by absorbing the pool of (mostly) unpaid houseworkers into part-time, temporary and contract employment" (135). Of course, these houseworkers would also have been practitioners of flexible, unpaid, labor. Japan has long legacies of many kinds of migrant and temporary workers. For another contemporary account of day laborers in Tokyo as flexible labor, see Edward Fowler's *San'ya Blues: Laboring Life in Contemporary Tokyo* (Ithaca, NY: Cornell University Press, 1996).

8 Recent writing on the relationship between urban planning and surveillance stresses the transition from a spatialized, disciplinary society based on direct observation or containment to a society of control based on the manipulation of databases within which elements of people's identities may be encoded and classified. See Stephen Graham and Simon Marvin, *Splintering Urbanism: Networked Infrastructures, Technological Mobilities, and the Urban Condition* (London and New York: Routledge, 2001). *Splintering Urbanism* is a geography of the modern, networked city that argues that as infrastructures and technologies that transport and communicate are unbundled from integrated networks and privatized, urban space fragments and stratifies, creating a new spatialization of the city based on position and access to interconnected networks. One network that makes some spaces hubs and tunnels under others is surveillance networks. Specific modes of surveillance made available by digital technologies' automation and algorithmic profiling are treated by Stephen Graham and David Wood in "Digitizing Surveillance: Categorization, Space, Inequality," *Critical Social Policy* 23 (2003):

227–48. Thanks to Yumna Siddiqi for this reference. This fall, Tokyo's Suginami Ward began drafting regulations on the placement of surveillance cameras in public spaces. In December 2003, Yokohama became the latest city to move to install anticrime surveillance cameras in all schools.

9   See Yoshikuni Igarashi, *Bodies of Memory: Narratives of War in Postwar Japanese Culture, 1945–1970* (Princeton, NJ: Princeton University Press, 2000).

10  Masanori Oda, "Tôkyô fôku gerira nô ritânzu"; Besshô: Shôwa zankyô gôgai-den ("Tokyo Folk Guerilla Does Not Return"; Special Issue: Cruel Reverb of the Shôwa Era), *10 + 1*, no. 31 (2003): 21.

11  The interview appeared in one of the few news reports of the demonstrations, the *Tokyo Shinbun* article mentioned in note 3.

12  Here we are referring to the *Gomanizumu sengen* (Manifesto of Arrogance) series of manga by Yoshinori Kobayashi, which emerged in the mid-1990s. Kobayashi is a best-selling writer with a charismatic TV presence. His manga were widely critiqued for their outright denial of Japanese atrocities during the Pacific War. He is criticized both for the specific content of his charges and for his historiography in the service of revisionist nationalism. His 2001 manga, *Taiwan-ron (On Taiwan)*, sparked protests in Taiwan, as, again, his manga argued that comfort women from Asia were not pressed into service but rather both chose and profited from their stints in military prostitution. While Kobayashi maintains his status as a charismatic auteur, his interests collaborate with more scholarly approaches to history in both popular journalism and the academy. For a map of popular and academic nationalism in the mid-1990s, see J. Victor Koschmann, "National Subjectivity and the Uses of Atonement in the Age of Recession," *South Atlantic Quarterly* 99 (2000): 741–61; and Tessa Morris-Suzuki, "Unquiet Graves: Katô Norihiro and the Politics of Mourning," *Japanese Studies* 18 (1998): 21–30. Also selling briskly in fall 2003 was a "true-story" manga based on the supposed life of Kim Jong-Il, by the same group that has organized the popular academic nationalist movement to revise textbooks to deny Japanese atrocities in the Pacific War.

13  The most comprehensive history of Shibuya retail development published in English is Tom Havens's *Architects of Affluence: The Tsutsumi Family and the Seibu-Saison Enterprises in Twentieth Century Japan* (Cambridge: Council on East Asian Studies, Harvard University, 1994). The Japanese literature places Shibuya in economic history and urban studies. See Shunya Yoshimi's *Toshi toshite no doramatorugii: Tôkyô sakariba no shakaishi (The City as Dramaturgy: The Social History of Tokyo's Mass-Culture Quarters)* (Tokyo: Hirobuntô, 1988) for a media sociology. For a popular economic history of Shibuya's retail development since the 1960s, see Akira Nishitani and Mamiko Hatta, *Shibuya-kei keizaigaku: kono machi kara benchâ bijinesu ga umareru riyû (Shibuya-kei Economics: Why Venture Business Was Born in this Neighborhood)* (Tokyo: PHP Kenkyûjo, 1999).

14  For a vividly illustrated account of the avant-garde theater's use of graphic design, see David G. Goodman, *Angura: Posters of the Japanese Avant-Garde* (Princeton, NJ: Princeton Architectural Press, 1999). For an example of a "situation" in motion, see the improvisational

performances of dramatist Jurô Kara and graphic designer Tadanori Yokô in Nagisa Oshima's 1969 political modernist film *Diary of a Shinjuku Thief* (*Shinjuku dorobô nikki*).

15   Maki Mizukoshi, in Tsutomu Noda, Itaru Mita, and Maki Mizukoshi, "Dansu tû demon-
sutoreishon" ("A Demonstration to Dance To"), *Gendai shisô* (*Modern Thought*) 31 (2003):
99.

16   In *Audio-Vision: Sound on Screen* (New York: Columbia University Press, 1994), film the-
orist/historian Michel Chion develops the concept of the acousmatic, which is defined as
"sounds one hears without seeing their originating source" (71). Like the perception of sound
and vibration at the rave demos, the off-screen nature of filmic sound is significant because it
is not (at least initially) spatially magnetized by the image. Where the image is unexplicated
by tracing it to a sound source, the image becomes open-endedly meaningful through the
sound's nature, properties, and powers—the material qualities of the sound, in other words,
and not the agent of its production. Due to the sound's disembodied status and pending sense
of mystery, in conventional cinemathe sense of agency is potentially complicated until the
sound becomes bound in space or character. As Chion writes, musique concrète theorist-
practitioner "[Pierre] Schaeffer emphasized how acousmatic listening, which we shall define
further on as a situation wherein one hears the sound without hearing its cause, can modify
our listening. Acousmatic sound draws our attention to sound traits normally hidden from us
by the simultaneous sight of the causes—hidden because this sight reinforces the perception
of certain elements of the sound and obscures others. The acousmatic truly allows sound
to reveal itself in all dimensions" (32). This slightly idealistic account finds itself closer to
phenomenology than does Jean Baudrillard's use of the spectacle in *The Gulf War Did Not
Take Place* (Bloomington: Indiana University Press, 1995). Nonetheless, the two notions of
acousmatic and hyperreal share an emphasis on the effects and affects of experiences from
combined indexical (hi-fi, analog photographic) and virtual (digital) modes of representation
on faraway listeners and viewers.

17   A sketch, in Japanese, of the decisions made and the players who participated in composing
the 1967 ad, drawing graphically on the original image, can be found at www.tententen.net/
korosuna/001/newshit.html. The text notes that permission was obtained from both the Tarô
Okamoto Memorial Hall and a former Beheiren leader.

18   de Certeau, *The Practice of Everyday Life*, xix.

19   Tsutomu Noda, in Tsutomu Noda, Itaru Mita, and Maki Mizukoshi, "Dansu tû demon-
sutoreishon" ("A Demonstration to Dance To"), 99.

20   Various flyers and statements handed out at the October 5 demonstration explicitly invoked
the global Reclaim the Streets (RTS) movement. Insofar as it has a central rallying point,
the RTS movement began in 1991 in London as an anticar protest and extended to include many protests against various privatization measures in London and elsewhere. See
www.reclaimthestreets.net/ for a set of sites linked in rhetoric but diverging in issues (vis-à-vis
capitalism, the status of globalization, the definition of *public* and *public space*, and specific
local issues deriving from or relating to privatization and commodification of daily life).

21  Although it is tempting to interpret the current concern with appearing to be intelligible in public space as having to do with the post–9/11 security frenzy, the rave demos were not the first intervention of sound over borders for the purpose of forming communities that people could not cross. On May 18, 1952, Paul Robeson was refused entry by the United States into Canada, where he had been invited to give a concert in Vancouver by the International Union of Mine, Mill, and Smelter Workers. Standing on a flatbed truck just over the border in the state of Washington, Robeson sang to an estimated forty thousand people. The concert, known as the Peace Arch Concert, was recorded and released by the union. A reissue is available from Folk Era Records. For an analysis of Robeson's sound demo in the context of Cold War cultural policy, see Mark Kristmanson, *Plateaus of Freedom: Nationality, Culture, and State Security in Canada, 1920–1960* (Oxford: Oxford University Press, 2003). Thanks to Graham Carr for this reference.

22  *Chindon* has recently enjoyed a revival as a musical form in its own right. For a broad compilation of studio and street recordings of working *chindon* musicians, see Masami Shinoda, ed., *Tokyo Chindon, vol. 1*, (Tokyo: Puff Up, 1992). The CD packet includes essays by musicologist Shûhei Hosokawa and *chindon* musician Wataru Ohkuma. An example of the pop appropriation of *chindon* is found with an array of early-twentieth-century protest songs from Ainu, American, and Korean forms on Soul Flower Mononoke Summit's 1997 CD *Levelers Ching-dong* (*Respect*).

23  De Certeau, *The Practice of Everyday Life*, xix.

**For the Record:**

**An Antiwar Protest in Jakarta**

**Days before the Bali Bomb Attacks (A Photo-Essay)**

Sumit K. Mandal

*positions* 13:1 © 2005 by Duke University Press

**Figure 1**
On October 8, 2002, members of different nongovernmental organizations and student groups met at the headquarters of the modernist Muslim organization Muhammadiyah in central Jakarta to conduct an antiwar demonstration outside the U.S. Embassy. The numbers trickled in. While concern mounted in the preceding weeks about what appeared to be an impending U.S. attack on Iraq, antiwar protests were just getting started. (All photographs by the author.)

**Figure 2**
Nong Darol Mahmada, a member of the Liberal Islam Network (*Jaringan Islam Liberal*), was a key organizer of the demonstration. She endured a wait of a few hours, unsure if the expected interreligious coalition would come together as she hoped and if the busloads of students already on their way would make it through the city's notorious jams. While the interreligious representation was not as strong as it could have been, in the end the students did arrive and the march on the U.S. Embassy began.

**Figure 3**
The demonstration enjoyed a police escort during its journey of some forty minutes through some of Jakarta's busiest districts. More than two hundred people came together as the marchers approached the U.S. Embassy and were funneled through a line consisting of police officers on one side and journalists and onlookers on the other.

**Figure 4**
The protesters made clear their indignation at the Bush White House and their affection for Americans as a people. Peaceful resolutions rest more firmly on greater numbers of Muslims seeing the difference between regimes such as the Bush White House and a diverse citizenry.

**Figure 5**
The U.S. Embassy was heavily guarded. Traffic was diverted to some twenty meters away from its front gates; police officers and armored vehicles were placed in strategic locations. Throughout the initial stages of the protest, the police maintained a tight defensive line. The police nevertheless handled the demonstrators with professionalism and even curiosity if not friendliness, a clear product of the democratization processes at work since 1998.

**Figure 6**
Luluk Hamidah, an activist from Nahdhatul Ulama, read Islam Network's Universal Awareness Declaration, which had been prepared in advance. Women constituted a substantial share, if not the majority, of the intellectual leadership of the protest.

**Figure 7**
The police appeared interested, and thus increased the number of attentive listeners, rather than taking an aggressively defensive posture.

**Figure 8**
A small delegation led by the Muslim leader and writer Ulil Abshar Abdalla presented the declaration to embassy officials. Ulil is seen here crossing the street on his way back to the gathering, flanked by some of the leaders of the protest, including Luluk Hamidah.

**Figure 9**
The protests were marked by a measured and focused anger, and what might even be described as lightness, against the heavy defenses on the perimeter of the embassy.

Just over four days later Bali was shaken by bombs, and 202 people were killed. Soon afterward, security was intensified in unprecedented ways. Even now, as I write this, a trip to the shopping mall requires baggage checks for pedestrians and vehicle inspections for those who drive. The bombing in Bali did not help efforts by Indonesians to fight U.S. aggression by peaceful means, nor did it mitigate the terribly poor opinion of the Bush administration held by many in the country. The war in Iraq merely fueled more and angrier protests. The small demonstration documented here is noteworthy, if for nothing else, for preserving in memory the capacity of indignant and intelligent Indonesians of different faiths to seek peaceful options and resolutions to the violent path taken by the Bush regime.

## Declaration of Universal Humanity

Liberal Islam Network

All the statements and official documents from the U.S. government about the plan to attack Iraq are illogical, full of contradictions, and seething with hatred and desire for war; they have no connection with the tragedy of September 11, al Qaeda, or the so-called war on terror.

The plan to overthrow Iraq is in conflict with the U.N. charter, which established that one of the United Nations' goals was to "safeguard future generations from the catastrophes of war"[1] and that the organization was founded to "take effective collective steps in the effort to prevent and remove threats against peace."[2]

The excuse put forward in the official document called the Bush doctrine that established the so-called preemptive attack policy opposes international law because the U.N. charter also condemns unilateral action against the borders of another state unless such action is taken for reasons of self-defense. In this case, there is no excuse whatsoever for the U.S. government to defend

*positions* 13:1 © 2005 by Duke University Press

itself against Iraq. Resolution 678 of the U.N. Security Council also forbids any country from attacking another country without the consent of the Security Council.

This crushing of Iraq has been carried out even after that country has endured ten years of economic sanctions, which have already caused suffering for millions of Iraqi civilians, especially children and women, because those sanctions included the destruction of facilities that made access to clean water possible. The enforcement of the economic sanctions itself directly contradicts the supplementary protocols of the 1977 Geneva Conventions on the rules of war, which forbid economic penalties for civilians as a method of war. These economic sanctions have probably caused the deaths of more Iraqis than the deaths that have been caused by what are called the weapons of mass destruction.[3]

Now the indescribable suffering of the Iraqi people will increase with the devastation of that country by the most destructive weapons ever known to mankind. The excuse put forward by the American government states that the Iraqi regime has been developing weapons of mass destruction (chemical, biological, and nuclear weapons) that threaten international peace. This excuse continues to be used despite the fact that those very weapons of mass destruction date from the past, from the time of the Iran-Iraq war, and were developed with the full support of the American government, which provided raw materials, a means of storing them, and expert advisers. These facts have already been exposed by members of the United Nations, international NGOs, and even by members of the U.S. Congress.

Now what are called the weapons of mass destruction that Iraq is supposed to possess cannot be found, even though the American government persists in attacking in the name of that excuse. Even if it were true that Iraq possessed such weapons, America still would not have the right to attack, just as Iraq does not have the right to attack America, even though America does possess weapons of mass destruction in quantity and on a very large scale.

It is thus clear that this war is being waged only to fulfill the hegemonic ambitions of an imperialistic America, as has been clearly indicated by the Bush doctrine. This war is being waged in order to integrate all other nations into an American world order, as participants in what might be called a Pax Americana.

When viewed from the perspective of possible threats, it is the American ambition to form a global empire that represents a clear and present danger to peace, world security, and universal humanity. Thus:

1 We oppose the plan to destroy the country and people of Iraq, and we oppose it to the strongest and highest degree with this statement. This in no way means that we support in any form the dictatorship of President Saddam Hussein, which over the past quarter of a century it has been in power has been to blame for the suffering of a large section of the Iraqi people.

2 We appeal to the leaders of America and the world to take an explicit lesson from history, that war will bring nothing to the world community except misfortune and suffering. It will not prove useful in any way and will only cause further desolation in these critical times. War will only cause a deep civilizational wound, because war not only causes suffering for its victims but also diminishes the heart and the humanity of those who wage it.

We believe that in war, in the certain destruction of one country by another, there will not be any winner; that the two sides will take the fight as far as they can, only to end up in defeat—a defeat for humanity, and also a defeat because civilization will have been left behind.

We believe that war is not the best way to begin the twenty-first century, in which we must—after the experience of the preceding twenty centuries—try ever harder to improve the entire world community by becoming more and more aware that all peoples are united by a common human spirit. Therefore it is a logical necessity that we must cooperate with, and not confront, all the inhabitants who share this earth.

We also join with the American people in inviting their leaders to return to the path of peace and not to engage in the reckless adventure of war.

We ask that the compassionate Lord guide and accompany us on our sincere journey on the undeviating path to peace.

Jakarta, October 8, 2002

Translated by Laurie Sears

## Notes

This is the text of the declaration read at the October 8, 2002, Jakarta protest. Thanks to Nong Daral Mahmada for providing the text.

1   Preamble of the U.N. charter, www.un.org/aboutun/charter/.

2   U.N. charter, Article 1, Clause 1.

3   John Mueller and Karl Mueller, "Sanctions of Mass Destruction," *Foreign Affairs* 78, no. 3 (1999): 43–54.

## Three Deities

Joy Kogawa

I feel it is no coincidence—after all my intentions not to be here—that I should be speaking on this particular day about a particular event that happened some years ago. I refer to the atomic bombing of Nagasaki on August 9, 1945.

Arundhati Roy is asked these days, as the unthinkable is being thought and the talk of nuclear war swirls around her, "Why don't you leave Delhi?" She answers,

If I go away, and everything and everyone—every friend, every tree, every home, every dog, squirrel and bird that I have known and loved— is incinerated, how shall I live on? Who shall I love? My friends and I discuss *Prophecy*, the documentary about the bombing of Hiroshima and Nagasaki. The fireball. The dead bodies choking the river. The living stripped of skin and hair. The singed, bald children, still alive, their clothes

*positions* 13:1 © 2005 by Duke University Press

burned into their bodies. The thick, black, toxic water. The scorched, burning air. The cancers implanted genetically, a malignant letter to the unborn. We remember especially the man who just melted into the steps of a building. We imagine ourselves like that. As stains on staircases. I imagine future generations of hushed schoolchildren pointing at my stain . . . that was a writer. Not She or He. That.

She adds, "The very notion that war is an acceptable solution to terrorism has ensured that terrorists in the subcontinent now have the power to trigger a nuclear war."

World War I, dubbed the "war to end all wars," gave way to another world war. And today we are faced with the numbing thought that the last "bomb to end all bombs" at Nagasaki may yet give way to the bomb to end all life. Roy says that whether nuclear bombs are used or not, "they violate everything that is humane. They alter the meaning of life itself. Why do we tolerate them? Why do we tolerate these men who use nuclear weapons to blackmail the entire human race?"

I was in Nagasaki in June this year and thought of the pilot who flew overhead that day in 1945. In an interview, Captain Sweeney used the word *pretty* to describe Nagasaki. One novelist, calling it the "Naples of the Orient," wrote, "Nagasaki overwhelms one with its beauty and serenity. It is a town of stone roads, mud walls, old temples, cemeteries and giant trees." Captain Sweeney said it was the greatest thrill of his life when he dropped the bomb.

There is a thrill in murder. There is a thrill in war. It is not just the certifiably insane who feel this. The lust for blood continues unabated in the human condition. But like parents of murdered children being faced after years with the release of their murderers, we must face again the appetite for war, the fears that feed it, the hunger for vengeance. It is fresh blood the dogs of war demand. At what point do we come to know that the blood we taste and drink is our own and that of those we love?

Hans Kung states that in our striving for peace, we should begin with religion. "Peace among the religions" he says, "is the prerequisite for peace among the nations." In our religious mythologies, we find sources of both violence and peace.

The three deities of this talk are, first, the god who demands all; second, the goddess who grants mercy; and, third, the deity who promises abundance.

The religion in which I grew up was Christianity. The god of my childhood was the god of Abraham, the god of the patriarchs, a god who demanded all. Like us, Abraham found himself in a world of death and suffering. In such a world, his god promised him abundance—as many descendants as there are stars in the sky. This was to be through Abraham's two main sons—Ishmael, his eldest, born of the servant Hagar, and Isaac, the child of his wife, Sarah. Although Ishmael and Isaac lived as rivals, when Abraham died they buried their father together, as brothers.

Today, three great faiths—Judaism, Islam, and Christianity—claim Abraham as father. His descendants are, indeed, as the stars of the sky—Jews and Arabs, by right of birth, and Christians, by adoption and faith. Muhammad, the founder of Islam, traced his lineage through Ishmael. Jews claim their lineage through Isaac. All three faiths are bound together as siblings.

The foundational myth of Abraham's great test has confounded people through the ages. In Genesis 22, we are told that Abraham was ordered to do the unthinkable.

The time came when God put Abraham to the test. "Abraham," he called, and Abraham replied, "Here I am." God said, "Take your son Isaac, your only son, whom you love, and go to the land of Moriah. There you shall offer him as a sacrifice on one of the hills which I will show you." . . . So Abraham took the wood for the sacrifice and laid it on his son Isaac's shoulder; he himself carried the fire and the knife, and the two of them went on together. Isaac said to Abraham, "Father," and he answered, "What is it, my son?" Isaac said, "Here are the fire and the wood, but where is the young beast for the sacrifice?" Abraham answered, "God will provide himself with a young beast for a sacrifice, my son." And the two of them went on together and came to the place of which God had spoken. There Abraham built an altar and arranged the wood. He bound his son Isaac and laid him on the altar on top of the wood. Then he stretched out his hand and took the knife to kill his son; but the angel of the Lord called to him from heaven, "Abraham, Abraham." He answered, "Here I am." The angel of the Lord said, "Do not raise your hand against the boy; do not touch him. Now I know that you are a God-fearing man. You have not withheld from me your son, your only son." Abraham looked up and there he saw a ram caught by its horns in a thicket. So he went and took the ram and offered it as a sacrifice instead of his son.

Until I read Carol Delaney's book *The Trial of Abraham*, I did not know that for most Muslims, it is Ishmael and not Isaac who was the intended sacrifice. But for all three faith communities, one of the main values that is gleaned from the story is that of obedience, of complete submission to the will of God. Mohammed Atta, before his flight into the World Trade Center on September 11, 2001, is said to have written or said, "I must be like my father Abraham willing to sacrifice all." And he did.

Delaney asks us, "Why is the willingness to sacrifice the child, rather than the passionate protection of the child, at the foundation of faith?" She suggests that we need a new myth and says, "I ask that people imagine how our society would have evolved if protection of the child had been the model of faith."

Today, the children of Abraham in the West and the Middle East—Christians, Jews, and Muslims—are speaking about justice, freedom, and submission to God. Their words translate into violence and a growing dread that the fearful forces at play will propel us into a reckless abandonment of constraint and a catastrophic worldwide conflagration that will end life as we know it.

There are other voices in the world—voices that come from traditions of mercy and peace. To begin, there is a certain small island in the East, where the world's longest living and most intensely peaceable people live.

My brother, a retired Episcopalian priest, was in Okinawa for a few years in the 1990s. He told me that in 1815, Captain Basil Hall of the British navy steamed into Naha, Okinawa, and was amazed at what he found. The story goes that on his way back to England, he dropped in at the island of St. Helena and had a chat with Napoleon.

"I have been to an island of peace," the captain reported. "The island has no soldiers and no weapons."

"No weapons? Oh, but there must be a few swords around," Napoleon remarked.

"No. Even the swords have been embargoed by the king."

Napoleon, we're told, was astonished. "No soldiers, no weapons, no swords! It must be heaven."

Okinawa must surely have had a culture as close to heaven as this planet has managed. We might well wonder about the spiritual heritage of such a people. Today, they boast not just the longest-living human beings in the world—the number of centenarians per one hundred thousand people is six times that of the United States—but also the world's longest disability-free life expectancy.

According to *The Okinawa Program* by Bradley Willcox, Craig Willcox, and Makoto Suzuki, Okinawan society

> reflects a cultural cosmology where the female embodies and transmits sacred forces (*shiji*). Most Okinawan villages still have "divine priestesses," called *noro* or *nuru*, whose job it is to commune with the gods and ancestors and serve as spiritual advisers. In fact, until the late nineteenth century, the king's well-being and success as ruler depended on the spiritual sustenance granted by the high priestess (*kikoe ogimi*), who was of equivalent social standing. This is a unique cultural phenomenon. Although women act as religious functionaries in other societies, there is no other modern society in the world where women hold title as the main providers of religious services.

When Japan, that once-warring nation, took over the kingdom, there was an entirely bloodless coup. No soldiers were found to help later with the invasion of Korea. A disobedient people, Japan concluded. A kingdom without soldiers was clearly impossible.

On Easter Day 1945, on the day of triumph for the Prince of Peace, Okinawa became a special target for the forces of hate. The Battle of Okinawa was the biggest land battle in history to that point. In twelve weeks, over 234,000 people died, more than the total number killed that August in the two atomic bombings.

My brother was in Okinawa in 1995 on the fiftieth anniversary of the battle. Beginning at Easter, and for twelve weeks thereafter, a breathtaking action of speech took place. For two hours at noon and two hours at night, with a pastoral candle lit, the dead were recalled, and their names were read.

These were not prayers for the Okinawan victims alone—grandparents, schoolchildren, the familiar members of the community. The prayerful embrace included the naming of Japanese and American soldiers, those who had brought this disaster upon the most gentle of peoples. Here was mercy quietly demonstrated. It did not make headline news. But the Prince of Peace, mocked and murdered on Easter Day 1945, was powerfully alive on Easter fifty years later.

In Okinawa's Peace Park, the names of the dead are engraved on row upon row of granite slabs, which resemble the waves of the ocean nearby. A white towering structure encloses a huge statue of Kannon, the goddess of mercy in Japanese Buddhism. She is described as an Asian symbol (with no deification) and is the central figure in the structure, where each year on August 15 an interfaith service is held.

There is something surreal about the Christian calendar and the dates of war atrocities. Was dropping the world's first atomic bomb on the Day of the Transfiguration, the day when Christ's face became glistening white, a deliberately conscious act? The word for *transfiguration* in Japanese, *hen-yo-bo*, also means *disfiguration*. In Okinawa, the day of resurrection was the day of death. In Hiroshima, the day of transfiguration was the day of disfiguration.

A Christian military chaplain prayed over the bomb before it set out on its journey.

> Almighty God, Father of grace, we pray you, let your grace come down upon the men who will fly in this night. Guard and protect those of us who will venture forth into the darkness of your heaven. Lead them on your wings. Guard their bodies and their souls and bring them back to us. Give us all courage and strength for the hours that lie before us, and reward us according to the hardships they will bring. But above all, my Father, give your world peace. Let us go our way trusting in you and secure in the knowledge that you are near to us now and for all eternity. Amen.

While this prayer was being said, prayers to the same god were rising to heaven in Nagasaki, from Urakami Cathedral, the preeminent presence of Christianity in all of East Asia. Nagasaki, visited by Francis Xavier in the 1500s and later by renowned European physicians, was Japan's window to the West. It became the primary medical center and the primary center for European studies, to be visited by the top students of Japan.

Although Christianity had begun to take root in Japan in the sixteenth century, within a hundred years the country was closed to outsiders and Christianity was banned; for the next two hundred years, Japanese Christians, known as the "hidden Christians," were hunted down to be crucified, hung over sulfur pits, or otherwise tortured and killed.

In 1873, the 235-year ban on Christianity was lifted, and survivors joyfully headed back to Nagasaki, settling in the Urakami district. Urakami Cathedral was built there brick by brick by believers; it was completed in 1914, the year that the war to end all wars began. At 11:02 a.m. on August 9, 1945, it was precisely at this spot, over Urakami Cathedral, over Christians, that the atomic bomb exploded.

Father George Zabelka was the Catholic chaplain on Tinian Island, in the Northern Marianas, at the time, and was, as he put it, "the last possible official spokesman for the Church before the fire of hell was let loose." He lived to regret his approval of the actions that day. "There is no state of corporate evil that is not the result of personal sinfulness," he said in an interview in 1984.

> In August of 1945, I, as a Christian and as a priest, served not as an agent of reconciliation but as an instrument of retaliations, revenge and homicide. . . . I chose nationalism over Catholicism, Caesar over Christ, as the "Great Artist" manned by Christians in my care, took off to evaporate the oldest and largest Christian community in Japan—Nagasaki. . . . I played an important and necessary role in this sacrilege—and I played it meticulously. I mean it literally. . . . A sacrilege is the desecration of what is considered holy. For the Christian, the ultimate place of the holy is the human person. . . . Therefore every act of violence toward a human being is an act of desecration of the temple of God in this world. War for the Christian is always a sacrilege. There is no such absurdity as a Christian ethic of justified sacrilege. I am a priest who played a role in a sacrilege and that must be said by me and others like me without equivocation or else the future is a nightmare. . . . I want to expose the lie of killing as a Christian social method, the lie of disposable people, the lie of Christian liturgy in the service of the homicidal gods of nationalism and militarism, the lie of nuclear security.

For Father Zabelka, it was an act of mercy and grace that in his old age, he was able to make a pilgrimage to Hiroshima and Nagasaki, to his calvaries. He wished to look into the faces of the bomb victims and say, "Brother, forgive me for bringing you death instead of the fullness of life. Sister, forgive me for bringing you misery instead of mercy."

Dr. Takashi Nagai was a bomb victim who did not live long enough to welcome Father Zabelka. He was a nuclear physicist, dean of the radiology department at the medical school of the University of Nagasaki, a medical doctor, scientist, researcher, artist, and scholar, knowledgeable about atomic energy. He was also a Christian convert, one of Abraham's children, and his beloved wife, Midori, was a descendant of Christian martyrs.

He had his own understanding of the holocaust. It was not an accident. The particular place the bomb fell was not done by human design alone. That morning, according to *A Journey to Nagasaki*, a booklet published by the Nagasaki Testimonial Society, three B29s left Tinian Island, with the lead plane, *Bock's Car*, carrying a plutonium bomb. One of the planes missed the initial rendezvous point. The two remaining planes then headed for Kokura, the second target destination. This time, smoke obscured the view. The backup was Nagasaki. Tokiwa Bridge, the target in Nagasaki, was covered by clouds. Captain Sweeney, the pilot, continued northward. An hour before noon, there was a break in the clouds.

In his book *The Bells of Nagasaki*, Dr. Nagai shares his anguish in graphic detail. The children in the many schools in the area, the nuns in prayer, his wife with the rosary melted beside her bones, the faithful Christians who had been purified by such intense suffering for so long—all these deaths were not accidental. Nagasaki's hell was a sacred offering for peace. Its meaning was that this was not to happen again. Not to anyone.

Dr. Nagai believed that the bomb was carried by the wind and by God precisely to Urakami. The grammar checker on my computer rejects the words "the bomb was carried by the wind and by God" and offers instead, "God carried by the wind and the bomb." Father Zabelka would have agreed with the computer. He says it was God who suffered at Hiroshima and Nagasaki. "Calvary, the place where Christ suffered and died . . . is the holiest shrine in Christianity. Hiroshima and Nagasaki are Calvaries. For here Christ in the bodies of the 'least' was put to death by exactly the same dark and deceitful spirit of organized lovelessness that roamed Jerusalem two thousand years ago." The cry of the ancient psalmist, and the cry of Christ, "My God my God, why hast Thou forsaken me?" translates in this context to "My God, my god, why have we forsaken Thee?"

We forsake each other, and we kill, partly because, like Father Zabelka on Tinian Island, we do not know what we are doing. We do not realize that when we kill, we are killing our own. What I understood this year, as I walked the few blocks of that sacred place from Dr. Nagai's museum to the cathedral, to the Peace Park, and to the monument of the hypocenter was that when we murder the other, we are murdering our own family, our Isaac, our Ishmael, our Jesus, our children, our futures. The enemy whose face is hidden from us is our friend, our close relative, someone we love.

Could the catastrophe at Nagasaki have been prevented? Einstein, without whom the bomb could not have been made, did not know what his discoveries would unleash. He would rather have been born a peddler, he said, or a plumber. Two thousand years ago, there was one who prayed that his killers would be forgiven because they did not know what they were doing. But today we know what our weaponry is capable of doing.

On the walls of the museum commemorating Dr. Nagai's life was his question. Who had done this? Who had brought this catastrophe to Nagasaki? His answer was that we had done it ourselves. We humans had created hell. We were responsible. These were not words of hatred. He was a follower of the man who said, "Love your enemy." The tiny one-room house in which he wrote his books was called Nyokodo—"as yourself, house," from "Love your neighbor as yourself."

"I have my mind," he said as he lay dying. "I have my eyes, I have my hands." With these tools still left to him, the bedridden Nagai, in the extremity of his suffering, poured his passion for peace into his books, a line at a time. Exhausted after writing a line, he would pray, then continue with the next line.

Dr. Nagai's words, "I have my eyes, I have my hands," remind me of a legend of the goddess of mercy. It is said that she was manifest in a compassionate princess, Miao Shan, the third daughter of a king of ancient China. Miao Shan's fervent desire was to be a Buddhist nun. The king, however, wished her to marry. At length, the king relented, and Miao Shan entered a convent, where at the order of the king, she suffered grave hardship. But Miao Shan remained steadfast. Enraged that she would not relent, her father ordered the convent destroyed. Shortly afterward, the king became ill and was informed that only medicine made from an arm and an eye of a person without anger could save him. Miao Shan gladly sacrificed both arms and both eyes for her father's health. When the king went to give thanks to his benefactor, he was horrified to discover it was his own daughter. She became the goddess of mercy. Like Miao Shan, Dr. Nagai offered his hands and his eyes in an act of sacrificial love.

There is another story that connects the Buddhist goddess of mercy with Christianity. Between roughly the sixth and the tenth centuries, as Buddhism spread eastward, the male Buddhist deity of compassion became known in China as Kuan Yin, the goddess of mercy. Nestorian Christians traveling the silk road south and east from Persia were carrying statues of Mary, the mother of Christ. People, seeing these, took them to be images of the Buddhist goddess of mercy. In Japan, during the ongoing persecution of the hidden Christians, the presence of these statues in Christian homes signified to the authorities that these were Buddhist homes. But unseen by the persecutors were crosses and crucifixes, symbols of Christianity, hidden within the Madonnas. Here is an instance, thanks to a confusion in the minds of persecuting authorities, that the mother of Jesus and the goddess of mercy stayed the hand of murder.

My first encounter with the goddess of mercy was in a dream in a Buddhist temple when I was visiting Japan in the early 1990s. Before that dream, I had not given a thought to her and knew nothing at all about her. I described the experience in *The Rain Ascends*, as the narrator, Millicent Shelby, begins her journey saying, "She came to me that spring in a dream and touched me in her evanescent way, saying that she, the Goddess of Mercy, was the Goddess of Abundance. Mercy and Abundance. One and the same. The statement shone in my mind with the luminosity of an altogether new moon."

It is about a decade later now, and the "altogether new moon" of that dream still shines in my mind, but even more strongly today. The goddess of mercy is the goddess of abundance. I did not understand what the dream meant at the time, but today I recognize that both mercy and abundance are aspects of the same god of Abraham who demands our all. Today, in our slavish devotion to our dream of abundance, we have forgotten that without mercy there can be no abundance, and without abundance there can be no mercy. The market fundamentalists of our day, like Christian fundamentalists, Islamic fundamentalists, and Jewish fundamentalists, are willing and able to wage war, to sacrifice our collective children and the future. Without obedience to the voice of mercy, our worship of abundance is a nightmare, Isaac and Ishmael lie murdered, and we have a bloodthirsty deity reigning over a planet of ashes and dust.

According to *Kuan Yin: Myths and Revelations of the Chinese Goddess of Compassion*,

> She, who has been worshipped for centuries on the island Pu To in China, is also unheeded these days. Today the sacred island of the goddess is ablaze with neon, resounds to karaoke and disco bars and has become a major place of prostitution. It is as if the secular has declared war on the divine feminine. This is not the work of Communism but the consequence of the pursuit of consumerism. This seems to be the lowest ebb the sacred island has ever reached and we fear for the future of this unique place. Maybe Kuan Yin will have to perform a miracle on her own island—for little else seems possible in the face of such denigration.

How do we rediscover the power of mercy in our day? Is it, as Carol Delaney asks, that we need a new myth? Or is the "passionate protection of the child" already present in the original story? It was the presence of mercy that stopped Abraham's hand. She also empowered the hands of Dr. Nagai. I believe she continues to be active throughout the world, in distant unheralded islands, on street corners, in homes, and in the towers. Hapless creatures though we are, I believe as we give her our all, she will lead us into the abundant way.

**Note**

This text was originally presented at a conference of the Nordic Association of Canadian Studies in Stockholm on August 9, 2002.

# The Black Cat in the Dark Room

Harry Harootunian

## Learning to See in the Dark

In a now famous article published in the *American Historical Review* in 1979, the historian Gilbert Allardyce believed he was delivering the final death blow to the category of fascism and its utility in historical and social science scholarship. Allardyce appealed to the metaphor of a black cat in a dark room to convey the proper description of fascism's actual insubstantiality and invisibility as a reliable historical category, openly declaring the certain conviction that there was nothing to it at all, nothing to find in the dark, empty room. But Allardyce may have stumbled (in the dark) over the cat in question, without actually knowing there was one there. He may have quite inadvertently bumped up against fascism in the dark void and tripped over its role in historical analysis had he not been so prepossessed with cursing the dark rather than feeling his way around. He may have found the

*positions* 13:1 © 2005 by Duke University Press

importance of fascism as a historical category without quite knowing that his confident denunciation was actually introducing a way to identify what he had announced barely existed.

It will be my principal purpose to try to show the importance of learning to see in the dark, which means seeing fascism precisely where its silhouette is indistinguishable from the surrounding shadows. By this I mean seeing the object less as a manifestation of an explicitly defined arrangement of institutions and social movements filled with marching Blackshirts or Brownshirts than as a form itself, behaving very much like the value form produced by a society structured by the commodity fetish. While I will return to this question in the latter part of this paper, I want first to consider some of the scenarios that might help explain why fascism has been so roundly dismissed and discounted, why it has been banished to darkness and has provoked even leftist historians like Perry Anderson to advise against any effort to "conjure up renewed dangers of a fascism, a lazy exercise of right and left alike today."[1] Although Anderson wrote these lines some years before the current crisis, he might now want to revise his judgment as somewhat premature. The reason we need to learn how to see in the dark is because since 9/11, the question of fascist politics has surfaced once more and pushed its way to the front of our contemporary intellectual agenda. What consumer of daily events today, even as those events are mediated by newspapers and television sympathetically reporting only what they receive from the state, would not be able to see in them signs of how everyday life is becoming progressively fascistic? Specifically, I am referring to the appearance of a new initiative to promote an American imperium (resembling a similar impulse during the Cold War), which not even the most determined nominalist can deny without looking foolish. We must, at the same time, recognize in this initiative the active role of the state, with its mobilization for total war in the wake of 9/11, in preparing the population for the prospect of an infinite war against terrorism. Readers of Japan's modern history will recognize the locus classicus of the familiar concept of *total war*, but many may not know that when philosophers of the Kyoto School in 1942 turned to recharging the concept with meaning—they then called it a *philosophy of total war*—they saw in it the promise of not merely the mobilization of society for war but the template for society's complete reorganization as Japan's answer to the country's modernizing historical experience, which was based on slavish imitation of Euro-America. As Kosaka Masaaki put it: "In reality, it is the problem of contemporary total war to surpass previous ideas of war. . . . Total war is at that place where modernity has reached a complete impasse; in a word, total war is the overcoming of the modern."[2]

Any discussion of imperialism—as Nicos Poulantzas, altering an observation by Max Horkheimer, once said—requires also addressing the question of fascism.[3] But the formula must today be supplemented with the statement that no discussion of modernity, defined as the accumulation of capital and its reproduction, can afford to avoid addressing the subject of fascism since fascism was the distinctive product of the same historical conditions that generated and shaped modern society and is thus inscribed in its interstices. The recent appeal by Richard Pearle, former advisor to the Department of Defense and neoconservative adventurer, to total war brings to mind Japan's military adventures in East Asia and World War II and its membership in the fascist axis. Hence the contemporary conjuncture overdetermining the reemergence of fascism in our present moment demands an accounting of the reasons for its effacement in the immediate postwar period, an effacement whose effects reverberate today with self-serving but anxious announcements that we cannot use fascism to describe the path on which American political society has embarked. The dark room housing Allardyce's black cat referred to the Cold War itself, without his ever acknowledging it; since he, like so many, was implanted in the very ideological system that represented a struggle pitting the United States against the Soviet Union as a contest between objective scientific truth and distortion, he was in no position to see outside of his own occluded angle of vision. During the Cold War years, the subject of fascism had been thoroughly discounted and was seen merely as the opposite of objective truth and equated with communism, conveying the associations of distortion, false consciousness, and even worse. By the time the vaunted *American Historical Review* published it, Allardyce's article had become a kind of common sense, a truism so unimpeachable that not even the editors of that professional journal could question its veracity. We can only assume they were driven by the manifest truth of its content rather than by its scholarship and mode of argumentation, since the latter were so poorly articulated that the combined jumble of assertions would barely pass as an undergraduate paper today. It was precisely this kind of argumentation that led to Holocaust denial, and it is hardly surprising that Allardyce was one of many who approved Ernst Nolte's historicist whitewashing of fascism. This example of how fascism's conceptual utility was trivialized also showed the willingness of professional organizations like the American Historical Association and its scholarly journal to support Cold War politics and ideology, which, in retrospect, it paraded as science and objectivity.

What was at the heart of this profound orchestration of forgetfulness was, in fact, the Cold War. The massive polarization staged by the contest between the so-called free world and the totalitarian dictatorships—between democracy and Marxist-Leninist communism—narrowed the compass of competing alternatives, forcing them out of the field of contention or encouraging their assimilation into one pole or the other. This Manichean transmutation was a momentous event, inasmuch as its effect was to repress much of the history of the twentieth century. But it was also paradoxical because fascism, by most accounts, was seen as the most characteristic political form of the twentieth century, owing to its deep imbrication with capitalist modernity and its mission to remove conflict-producing conceptions of the social (liberalism, communism) in order to make capitalism work better. It is, by any measure, an astonishing spectacle to see how easily the history of this struggle—"our history," as Jean-Luc Nancy once put it—was so easily and rapidly erased from the historical screen.[4] It should be remembered that fascism appeared in all industrializing societies, having less to do with late development, as once believed by social scientists, than with the crises generated by capitalism and accumulation and its capacity for producing the conditions of social conflict. In this regard, fascism, with its promise to end the rule of private property and its own conception of revolutionary upheaval, was perceived as an obvious alternative to communism, and it was also seen as an alternative to liberalism, from which it drew more than either were willing to acknowledge, in its distrust of possessive individualism, interest, and institutions devoted to political pluralism. In its resolute effort to save capitalism from itself, from the excesses of civil society, and from the class conflict it was capable of producing, fascism was able to successfully transmute the subject of class into a communal or collective subject of the folk by rearticulating ideological components like the democratic popular into the national popular, by actually appearing to eliminate precisely those aspects of liberalism that could solidify the people, but at the same time removing them from conflict-producing identities.[5] Fascism promised to rid society of politically destabilizing forces, but to retain capitalism—the reign of private property—which is precisely what was initiated by the classic historical examples we have before us. (This desire to repair unstable political societies, today called "regime change," was also, I should add, the purpose of both modernization development during the Cold War and the current American military occupation of Iraq.) Moreover, virtually everywhere it tried to establish a beachhead in the interwar period, fascism called into question the utility of all forms of political representation (sharing with modernism a comparable distrust of the claims of artistic and cultural representation), demanding in many cases a moratorium on political representation altogether and proposing in its place the installation of some sort of structure informed by a principle of organic communitarianism and its appropriate principal of authority, usually vested in the figure of what Slavoj Žižek has called the master. The master's function would be to regulate and restore balance, fending off the excesses inevitably produced by capitalism and their propensity for causing antagonism. But an essential condition of this arrangement demands the termination of subjective autonomy, which underlies the claims of individualism, and its replacement by the "restoration" of new forms of communitarianism, which supposedly constitute repetitions of prior history lived by the folk. As we look back on this moment, there was nothing mysterious about fascism's purposes, despite its own romance with spectacle and public performance (Bush's strutting on an aircraft carrier announcing "mission accomplished" might qualify as a reminder of this tradition); it was as ideologically meaningful as any other claim of the time, and it certainly forces us today to confront the use of terms like democracy and freedom and question their substantive content if not their ideological utility in justifying the conduct of imperial war. But this particular assault on political society in the interwar period, and the recommendation to redesign it, is not confined to a particular historical moment, but rather reveals to us a necessary (if not sufficient) condition of preparing for and embarking on a course of total war aimed at regime change. We are still in the epoch of capitalism, regardless of how advanced, late, or post it is, and this means we have not yet exorcised the fascism that has remained inscribed in capitalism—like a ghost in the machine—as a condition of capitalist modernization.

Since Hannah Arendt's epochal book *The Origins of Totalitarianism* (1951), at least, there has been a tendency to reduce fascism and communism to their shared dimensions by referring to both as expressions of totalizing regimes—different sides of the same coin. This was a favorite reflex of the Cold War era and helped to clarify the polarized positions represented by the United States and the Soviet Union. In the scholarly world, this powerful intervention licensed the widespread practice, especially among historians and political scientists, of envisaging fascism as a variant of Marxism, an offshoot or outgrowth, sharing similar properties and similar political, economic and social emblems, ideas and goals. This particular intellectual impulse actually served to encourage the incorporation of fascism into Marxism, plunging it into a dissolving agent, so to speak, in order to sharpen the positions of the West's struggle with Soviet communism during the Cold War era. Stalin was simply a more successful Hitler, for the time being, since both had implemented nihilistic policies aimed at eliminating whole populations. What was forgotten in this rush to rename both fascism and communism as totalitarianism was the Soviet contribution to the victory over Germany in World War II and the Soviet Union's incalculable, indeed unimaginable, loss of life, which recent estimates put at nearly 50 million people—up from earlier, more modest estimates of 20 million to 25 million. The effect of this stunning tactic of twining or superimposition was to both remove fascism from contemporary considerations by sweeping it under the carpet of communism and confine its effectiveness to a specific historical period that had long passed. Once fascism's specific configurations of political and social organization, arrangement of authority, and social movement had played out their productivity on a historical stage, the process of forgetfulness began to rapidly set in, since there appeared to be no good reason to fear a return now that it was safely tucked away in a past epoch, done and over with in the present. Social science during the Cold War period, especially in the form of modernization theory, contributed to the effacement of fascism from contemporary consciousness by substituting modernity for capitalism and anticipating the realization of evenly developed modernization of all societies. In many ways, modernization represented a sleight of hand (if not a scam) since it was forever transmuting all of those residues Marxists had identified as feudalistic and contributory to fascism into powerful traditional values that survive evolutionary growth to mediate a society's momentous transition to modernity. Societies once considered as fascist became instances of the modernizing process. Historians settled on the minutiae of historical examples, occurrences, and instants, the definitions of which, in their generality or narrowness, were designed to limit the utility of the category and its broader applicability. In fact, the favorite historical approach was the compilation of a checklist of attributes whose presence or absence would determine the suitability of fascism as a proper description. With this drive for classification came the comparative method, usually favored by social scientists, and the further diminution of the object of analysis to the contours of either Germany or Italy, or, even more dramatically, to those of Italy alone because Mussolini was once quoted as saying that fascism was "our thing." The consequence of all this activity was to privilege the search for the pure form of fascism and, as with any attempt at purification, reduce the object to its point of disappearance under the weighted necessity of excluding all impurities. I have seen all kinds of eliminations in the name of purifying the category or defining it more rigorously, some, surprisingly, including Franco's Spain, Salazar's Portugal, and Hirohito's Japan. In fact, historians have made this form of debunking into a cottage industry, producing large books to show how the subject of fascism virtually vanishes once critical standards are tightened. In the realm of Asia, Chiang Kai-shek and his nationalists seem to have escaped the historical onus of being labeled fascists, despite the New Life Movement's program to discipline Chinese society and the circulation of thuggish blue-shirt gangs to keep people in line, while specialists have tripped over each other in the rush to register their agreement on the worthlessness of fascism to describe what was going on in Japan in the 1930s, appealing to supposedly concrete criteria such as the extent of tenancy (improved conditions in the countryside), the role of veterans' associations, the persistence of landlordism, the development of something called "civil society," the numerical count of Brownshirts filling the streets and misrecognizing the figure and role of the emperor. (Some have even "proved" their case empirically by announcing they have never seen the word *fascism* used in documents of the period.) While this approach has easily specified some

of the properties embraced by fascist groups and regimes, it is based on
the primacy of historical knowledge that is aimed at dispelling ideological
illusions at the expense of a conception of ideology—Žižek's social fantasy—
that has already structured social reality. In other words, the comparative
approach, driven by an obsessional nominalism privileging the normativeness of definition, proceeds to construct a checklist that acts to eliminate
and purify in order to show that while societies like Japan may have been
corporatist, militarist, authoritarian, and absolutist, they were not fascist.
The tactic is reminiscent of the debate over comparative feudalism that took
place at about the same time fascism was being deposited in the trash heap
of discarded historical categories. This debate also revealed a similar desire
to distill the category of unwanted impurities—which, in this case, referred
to non-European claimants to the experience wanting to ram their way into
what clearly was the exclusive club of European feudalism. In retrospect,
this controversy over feudalism was as much a culturally driven struggle as
it was a problem of historical scholarship and interpretation. Japan, China,
Byzantium, and whatever else were seen as belonging to the so-called outside
and were thus considered ineligible to qualify as societies that, at one time
or another, had developed a form of feudalism. Its purest form was reduced
to a short existence in some indeterminate region between present-day Germany and the Netherlands. In other words, historicization itself has led to
the banishment from historical memory of the category of feudalism. When
we look more closely, we are able to see that this banishing act has depended
on identifying the forms of historical fascism and thus establishing the al-
lowable margin permitted by the operative definition and its permissible
criteria.

What seems to have been denied in this banishment is the force of the
present in determining and choosing its past. In its place there has been an
overdetermined effort to assert the primacy of a historical order that runs
from past to present, which means that the past leads to the present or prefig-
ures it and the present constitutes an identity with it that defines the movement of continuity. Here, the past chooses its future, which is our present.
When Ernst Nolte famously consigned fascism ("fascism in its epoch") to a
past bounded by 1919 and 1945, he was effectively arguing that the present is
now different and has no need to fear the past's return (or its reprisals), even

though the societies most involved remain basically the same as those that had earlier produced fascism.[6] (Actually, this is, in a strange way, the logical consequence of the argument put forth by Daniel Goldhagen.[7]) By the wave of a wand, the period 1919 to 1945, the time of fascist regimes and war, was now over, as if declaring an ending was guarantee that the past was no longer capable of taking reprisals on our present. If a period is passed, that means it is ready for historical reconstruction. In the reconstruction, the lessons of the past are supposed to guide the present and make it different. Usually, as we've recently seen, this kind of historical practice opens the way to badly conceptualized analogies. But it is important to recognize that the lesson of history is how the past chooses and controls the present by making sure it—the present—avoids the mistakes of the past as the principal condition of its claim to difference. In this regard, the present always appears, ipso facto, as an improvement and thus an advance over the past, its putative overcoming satisfying the narrative demand for continuity, progressive development, and difference. If, however, we imagine an alternative perspective that allows us to choose our pasts in the present, we are offered another possibility, based on the act of construction. There is nothing revolutionary about this recommendation once we acknowledge that any attempt to reconstruct the past takes place in the present. Instead of smuggling repetition into a linear, continuist narrative through the instrumentalization of the lesson and analogy, it should be possible to establish a genuine continuity through the operation of repetition signaling difference. Such an operation would not be constrained by the necessity to look for a repeat performance of similar events, but rather of forms reappearing in new and different registers of the historical experience that recall for us the past in present. If every age, as Primo Levi claimed, can expect the return of fascism in new and different registers, what he described in *The Drowned and the Saved* as the continuation of the "silent Nazi diaspora," I think he was clearly convinced that even fascism need not always take the form of violence and coercion associated with its historical experience, polluting the judicial process and poisoning the educational system—but only by encouraging in innumerable ways nostalgia for a world in which order supposedly prevailed.[8] Such nostalgia easily leads back to precisely those devices employed to maintain both the illusory fear of disorder and those new disciplines devoted to maintaining order. Not long ago, Samir Amin warned against the reappearance of neofascism in our time, not as a repetitive replica of a past historical episode but as a form capable of carrying charged and "abusive connotations from experiences of another era, which is different from our own." What he was pointing to was the sharing of "anti-democratic characteristics and common methods" that would find expression in different political registers in the developed centers of the center and periphery.[9]

Even today, when there is an attempt to raise the possibility that perhaps fascism existed in Japan during the 1930s, the reaction has usually been swiftly dismissive, as if one were speaking a foreign language in a crowd unable to understand it. Yet no such reservation inhibited those who lived through it and left us the record of their experience. Among those, none was more consistently insistent than Tosaka Jun, whose last book, *Japan as a Link in the World*, sought to explain how what was happening in Japan during his lifetime was actually no different from what was occurring elsewhere throughout the capitalist world. In this sense, the word *link* undoubtedly referred to the metaphor of the imperial chain and its uneven development, as had already been proposed by Lenin to represent the arrangement of capitalist countries heading for global conflict and revolution and reflected within Russia's weakness. Tosaka clearly saw fascism in the 1930s as part of an international movement and Japan as bonded to its imperialist momentum. Although Japan's fascism represented a reiteration of what was occurring globally, possessing its own irreducible characteristics, the formation of a "Japanese-style fascism" could not be attributed simply to self-production but rather to the direct "initiative of military and civilian bureaucrats" acting against the bourgeoisie and finance capital.[10] When looking at Japanese society in 1937, he explained, "the object of increased fascist oppression was the general population. . . . As for increasing oppression, it stemmed from the Japanese-type subject of leadership but resistance to it came from the people."[11] Just as Tosaka saw in the contemporary conjuncture the signs of a fascist gathering, so it is precisely the eventfulness of our present that necessitates a renewed interest in the question of fascism in both its first coming, in the pre–World War II era, and its reappearance—a second coming—in a new and different historical register in the postwar epoch. Moreover, the signs and signals emitted by the current situation already show how the very language once used by social scientists to either displace fascism or bury it altogether can no longer effectively conceal its presence. At the same time, this recognition of eventfulness need not send us looking for a matching repetition of events between then and now or committing ourselves to foolish historical analogies that, in fact, are based on the presumed repetition of events. But the recent manifestation of telling punctual events should sensitize us to the current situation and, more importantly, to the relationship between punctuality itself and duration in the life history of certain political, ideological, and cultural phenomena.

## On the Track of the Cat

It is precisely the eventfulness of the present that necessitates a renewed interest in the question of fascism, in both its prewar inaugural moment and its reappearance in a new and different register in the postwar epoch. What I am referring to is the capacity of the contemporary configuration we are currently experiencing to recall the example of past conjunctural analyses of fascism, like the one that drove Tosaka, to reintroduce into our everyday lives the specter of fascism. This ghostly reminder demands the figuring of an ontology of the present capable of identifying what has come to hold us in its thrall, and naming it for what it is. Such an ontology might be based on a conception of the event as envisaged by Alain Badiou,[12] or it might constitute the elements of a theory of historical repetition that still needs to be worked out. One of the obvious problems plaguing scholarly discourse since the earliest days of the Cold War has been the dismissal of the term ideology from social scientific lexicons and its rapid demotion to the status of a pejorative. Since the 1950s, social science—and by extension the humanities—has relegated ideology to the backwaters of discredited terms (with the help of seriously politicized misreadings of Karl Mannheim's *Ideology and Utopia* and the hegemony of Parsonian systems theory) denoting nothing more than faulty or false cognitions, distortions, untruths. Social science replaced ideology with categories like social values, core values, ethos, and political culture (usually signifying consensus)—values that were shared by a group and that defined the group's putative solidarity, that is, what brings people together as a group—which claimed both the authority of normativeness regulating

conduct and behavior, and the veracity of a truer reflection of what and
why people thought. In our time, Slavoj Žižek has revisited this scene and
described it as pure ideology precisely because today "people know it but still
do it," unlike those who commanded Marx's attention, who "don't know it
and do it."[13] With the banishment of ideology went fascism, so common-
place and meaningful during the period of World War II but rapidly found
unacceptable once the fascist regimes of Germany, Italy, and Japan were
defeated. Its identifying emblems were easily subsumed by terms like totalitarianism, authoritarianism, and even corporatism, not necessarily terms of
equivalence since the latter—the currency of social science—was often used
more as an analytic category in a narrative classification system.

In scholarship, then, fascism was seen specifically as a historical, now
passed episode in Germany and Italy, even though Spain and Portugal were
still around after the war to remind us of its capacity to survive, owing to those
countries' newfound relationship with the so-called free world and their
elevation in the cold war as prescient fighters against communist conquest.
With Japan, scholarship soon forgot that the United States had fought a war
with a society that was seen, at the time, as no less fascist. After all, Germany,
Italy, and Japan actually constituted the first axis of evil. By the time Steven
Spielberg made *Saving Private Ryan* (1998), the struggle in World War II was
no longer seen as having been over fascism, which the film never bothers to
mention, but over the value of male bonding—homosociality—and social
reproduction. Scholarship on Japan fast-forwarded to forget about fascism
and focus on democratization, and when, from time to time, fascism was
whispered about in articles, it was done so to reassure us not only that it had
vanished but also that it had never really existed. For their part, the Japanese also engaged in a similar silence to rid historical memory of the fascist
interlude, except for Marxists who tirelessly and monotonously banged the
drums of what they called emperor-system fascism. Even an independent
and courageous intellectual like Takeuchi Yoshimi managed to discount the
obvious fascist dimension to the *kindai no chokoku* (overcoming the modern)
discussion and its eponymous label because it had no thought content, as
such, misrecognizing precisely the point of a fascist ideological form. Just
as the banishment of fascism (and ideology) from the scholarly and political
lexicon has made it difficult to call a spade a spade, or see a black cat in

a dark room, and has encouraged scholars to find other names to describe the history of the 1930s, so the larger implications of its removal mean that we cannot put a name to what has been happening in the United States. Since the Supreme Court, acting very much like Nazi juridical institutions, enabled George Bush to steal the 2000 election, and events like 9/11 supplied the new leadership with immeasurable political capital and access to power, our everyday lives have been transformed by media-induced fears and improbable narratives linking patently obvious incommensurables to figures of imminent threat justifying immediate action. Who could deny that recent revelations (and photographs) disclosing the depths of depravity committed by American soldiers in Iraq against alleged prisoners and, worse, the justifications offered on the basis of a capacious threat to national security are really so different from the Nazi appeal to emergency measures, backed by German jurists, in the 1930s?

I have often wondered about the recent academic fad of resuscitating the writings of Carl Schmitt and the popularity of self-appointed amanuenses like Giorgio Agamben (not to forget Marxists like Etienne Balibar) who have been at the forefront of this philosophical revival. But I have yet to see the same enthusiasts actually envisage the current situation in industrial societies through the optic of the political theory of emergency. We can recognize how damage is being inflicted today—very much as it was in the 1930s—by policies that diminish dissent and criticism, police language and behavior under threat of arrest, interrogation, and even loss of citizenship (the latter if Patriot II is enacted). Clearly we are experiencing the reemergence of fascism in a new manifestation, yet we can also acknowledge the historical force of an earlier episode that had already forged the link between fascism, a new political organization, and an imperial ideology, an immense chain in which states seek hegemony at the global level. But as the historical example of the 1930s amply shows, the current situation recharges and redramatizes this imperialist impulse with important consequences for national formation.

Fascism, both in the 1930s and today, is intimately bonded to the imperialist logic of capitalism, whether in the desire to seize territories for colonial expropriation or to carry out "regime change" as a condition for subsequent regional reorganization and the platform for further interventions. In its classic historical form, it was devoted to saving capitalism, while imperialism and colonial expropriation had already been implemented to resolve accumulation crises of overproduction through what David Harvey has called the spatial-fix. The Japanese philosopher Miki Kiyoshi saw co-operativism as a way of reworking capitalism to make it Asian and solve both the temporal and spatial crisis Euro-American capitalism had already inflicted with a worldwide depression and aggressive imperial monopoliza-tion. What has changed is the role of hegemony and competition. Today only the United States seems bent on expanding its hegemony into empire, or is capable and willing to do so; some, like "old Europe," are determined to check this trend, while others, like "new Asia"—Japan and South Korea—willingly supply assistance and cash. Notwithstanding Hardt and Negri's refusal to name their empire, and their neo-Walserian animadversions on the question of sovereignty, what seems to be occurring today suggests a replay, in a different register, of course, of what happened in the 1930s. It is interesting to note how historical analogies are inevitably dragged out to justify precisely what such a repetition signifies, even though they are, in fact, deployed to warn against and prevent its recurrence. Amin, once more, reminds us that the "danger of the rehabilitation of fascism should not be underestimated."[14] The developed countries have already shown an immense propensity for unilaterally imposing policies that both favor and enhance big capital, and invariably in a way that continues the crisis and "the management of marginalization in the form of an economy of mul-tiple speeds."[15] Despite promoting the jargon of freedom and democracy, the center has not failed to conceal the fact that preservation of the forms of democracy relate only to procedural, not substantive, practices, which are inevitably manipulated and emptied of all content.

What an ontology of the present thus requires is a theory of historical repetition not weighted by the familiar narrative of tragedy and comedy. I have already suggested that it is precisely the recognition of this relation-ship between an imperialist chain and its ideology, and its diverse national inflections, that prompted Tosaka in the 1930s to see Japan as simply one link (*ikkan*) in a global network and Japan's fascism as one among a num-ber of local experiences. More important, Tosaka, unburdened by Second International economism, recognized the importance of the role played by ideology in the formation of the imperialist chain and its relationship to uneven development. In fact, Tosaka accorded ideology a primary role of articulation in Japan's capitalist system once imperialism began to modify the economic domain. This was the principal purpose of his book on the Japanese ideology, which raised the question of not just the manifest content fascism expressed (Japanism, Asianism, archaism) but rather the latent mystery of fascism as form itself, what he referred to in his *Shiso to fuzoku* (*Thought and Custom*) (1936) as the process of how "thought is able to acquire bodily reality in society according to grasping the form of custom."[16] This identity of fascism with ideology, Japan, and the broader conjuncture is also the message of *Nihon ideorogiron* (*The Japanese Ideology*), in which Tosaka explicitly identified the ground shared by Italian fascism, German Nazism, and a Japanese type whose echoes can still be heard today.[17] By proposing this grouping, Tosaka was recognizing that it was form, as such, that characterized the fascist experience of his time, not either or simply political organization, the ensemble of economic forces, or the claims of a social movement. It is here, I think, that we need to see how the easy invocation of terms like corporatism and even militarism, with their supposedly scientific and neutral charge, reveal an immense will for misrecognition driven by the desire to displace fascism and domesticate its obvious excess. These terms and others belong to the vocabulary of political science and all of the fantasies it has conjured up to defend and justify the state and the political status of the present and thus satisfy what, in effect, is its principal vocation and the object of its "discipline." What we need to see is that terms like *corporatism* fulfill some sort of political and organizational requirement but do not address the question of what happens to the status and stakes of subjectivity under fascism. We know that the content of this ideological form appealed to the figure of archaism, mediated by philology, as the optic through which to grasp contemporary reality and relied on the narrative of national history to convey its Japanist message. "Japanism," Tosaka wrote, "is one kind of Japanese fascism. If not seen in this manner, it would be impossible to understand this fascism as one link of an international phenomenon or to explain the special circumstances of how Japanese employ diverse fascist philosophers of Europe."[18]

We must, I believe, pay close attention to this privileging of form, as against simply social structure or organization, a thematic, or content, as an obvious declension of the value form that had already constituted global capital's self-mediating ground of the social and the lens through which we grasp the world. Such a move permits us to call attention to the structuring capacity of the social formation by the value form, with its enormous vocation for providing "a kind of matrix enabling us to generate all other forms of the 'fetishistic inversion.'"[19] In the case of fascism, it took the form of thought, as such, not simply thought and thinking, whose invocation demanded subservience for no other reason than its own that would lead to the fetishistic disavowal of knowledge: "I know . . . but all the same." In Japan, the emperor—not the system that rules in his name—has been the sign of this imperative, as he still is. It was precisely this sense of the form of custom Tosaka wished to extract from conduct and habitual practice, second nature, that promised to reveal the extent to which custom itself, in his thinking, behaved very much like the commodity and its demand for unquestioned assent, even though it might be outmoded. Custom's "special characteristic," he observed, should be called the "skin of society," and buried within it is thought.[20]

With this observation, Tosaka was in a position to recognize the commanding role played by the commodity form in social relationships on the scale of global capital and how the locus of activity had actually shifted from state domination to the powers of the market. Moreover, this recognition was at the heart of his difference with Kobayashi Hideo, whose vision of a timeless and static everyday life, what he referred to as the experience of commonness, simply appeared to obey the repetitive rhythms of the value form, even though he once described this operation as *statics*, a history that does not move. Moreover, the form authorized an arrangement, according to Ernesto Laclau, whereby "ideological elements taken in isolation have no necessary class connotation, and that connotation is only the result of the articulation of ideological discourse."[21] This entailed not a dismissal of class or its social basis, as such, but rather the identification of the preconditions for its analysis through a prior inquiry that constitutes the distinctive unity of an ideological discourse or narrative. With Tosaka, there was, more often than not, an appeal to the masses and the people, to offset the ahistorical and organismic category of the folk—a subject that eliminated the very possibility of class conflict and struggle and elevated the communal body to what

Nancy called "being in common."[22] The tactic of appealing to archaisms not only drew attention to the question of unevenness and the contemporary noncontemporaneousness by underscoring the coexistence of different pasts in the present but also supplied the so-called folk with a continuous unitary identity that exceeded all history. The importance of Tosaka's conception of a critique of fascism as ideological form is its direct challenge to a model of analysis that has envisaged ideology as merely a product of class belonging and the mediations of the larger social structure. Yet this was precisely how it was imagined after the war in a number of influential articles produced by Masao Maruyama and his school.

I do not want to flog a dead horse, but I do think it is important to acknowledge the difference between Tosaka and Maruyama in our understanding of fascism. Despite recent claims in Japan seeking to show the similarity between the two thinkers in their respective analyses of fascism, Maruyama brought its analysis back to the question and role of social movements and class basis and what they presumably reflected in the domain of political economy. Just as important to this approach was the imperative to compare Japanese fascism with fascism in Germany and Italy in order to emphasize a crucial divergence.[23] Accordingly, the decisive divergence with Nazi Germany was the role played by the agricultural sector. Even though the Nazis attached great importance to the farmer, theirs was still a workers' party. The "formation of the Japanese radical movement had no mass organization" and no zeal for organizing one. Even when Maruyama turned to the place occupied by the lower-middle class and intellectuals in the fascist movements of Germany and Japan, the Japanese case diverged significantly since in Japan fascism recruited small-factory owners, building contractors, shop owners, and small landowners, the core of what he called the pseudointellectuals who vocalized the aspirations of the people. Whatever else the case exemplifies, with its cascade of qualifying classifications, Maruyama fixed fascism and ideology to an identifiable class base to conclude that Japanese fascism never took the form of a revolution (but was rather, as he described it, a pseudorevolution) with a mass organization occupying the state apparatus. In fact, it was the "historical circumstance that Japan had not undergone the experience of a bourgeois revolution that determined (the) character of the fascist movement."[24]

The importance of this perspective is that it attributed an exceptionalist fascism to specific conditions of historical deficiency as a precondition for reassuring a postwar Japan that once those conditions were surpassed, there would be no need to fear the return of fascism, an argument made later by the German historian Ernst Nolte. For Maruyama, it opened the way for a second start, unimpeded by the historical baggage of an incomplete past, while for Nolte it virtually heroized Germans and Italians for their prescience in staving off communism, which he called the Asiatic threat, a struggle taken over by the United States. The principal benefit of this approach is that it encourages the dismissal of fascism as nothing more than a historical curiosity and, in time, an overstated and exaggerated description, a form of left-wing, infantile lunacy. But no such immunity can be claimed for a conception of fascism bonded to form, whose signifiers might be shuffled like a deck of cards but whose structuring agency—at least in capitalism—will not disappear. The importance of this identity between fascism and ideological form is that its power is not based on knowledge, like the supposed historical realities associated with narrative, which always promises that a moment will be surpassed. But ideological form, like the value form, the principal of social mediation on a global level, is never really exceeded, but only reproduced in new and different registers, the new in the ever same, as Walter Benjamin remarked long ago. This is why the writer Yukio Mishima reminded his countrymen and countrywomen that the emperor was not a thing but rather resembled an enduring form that followed the rules of repetition. As Emile Zola once said: "'Form.' Form is the great Crime."[25] The reason, as subsequently explained by the critic Peter Szondi: "The formal . . . always contains the possibility of its future tradition within itself."[26]

## Notes

Unless otherwise noted, all translations are my own.

1  Perry Anderson, *The Origin of Postmodernity* (London: Verso, 1998), 112.

2  Suzuki Naritaka, Koyama Iwao, Kosaka Masaaki, and Nishitani Keiji, *Sekaishiteki tachiba to Nihon* (*The World Historical Position and Japan*) (Tokyo: Chuo Koronsha, 1943), 275.

3  Nikos Poulantzas, *Fascism and Dictatorship* (London: Verso, 1974), 17.

4  Jean-Luc Nancy, "Our History," *diacritics* 20, no. 3 (1990): 96–115.

5  This is a well-known argument from the 1930s that also seems to have disappeared in the Cold War, along with the figure of fascism. See Herbert Marcuse, *Negations*, trans. Jeremy J. Shapiro (Boston: Beacon, 1968), 10–11; Mark Neocleous, *Fascism* (Minneapolis: University of Minnesota Press, 1997), 44; and Harry Harootunian, "The Postwar Genealogy of Fascism and Tosaka Jun's Prewar Critique of Liberalism," *Journal of Pacific Asia* (1994): 95–112.

6  Ernst Nolte, *Three Faces of Fascism*, trans. Leila Vennewitz (New York: Holt Rinehart and Winston, 1966).

7  Daniel Goldhagen, *Hitler's Willing Executioners* (New York: Knopf, 1996).

8  Primo Levi, *The Drowned and the Saved*, trans. Raymond Rosenthal (New York: Vintage, 1989), 20; and Levi, *The Reawakening*, trans. Stuart Woolf (New York: Collier, 1965), 204–31. See also *L'assymetrie de la vie*, trans. Nathalie Bauer (Paris: Robert Laffont, 2004), 70, for Levi's declaration that every age produces its own form of fascism.

9  Samir Amin, *Capitalism in the Age of Globalization* (New York: Zed, 2000), 102–3.

10  Tosaka Jun, *Zenshu* (*Collected Works*), vol. 5 (Tokyo: Keisosha, 1966), 44.

11  Ibid., vol. 5, 43.

12  See Alain Badiou, *Theoretical Writings*, trans. Ray Brassier and Alberto Toscano (London: Continuum, 2004), 97–102.

13  Slavoj Žižek, *The Sublime Object of Ideology* (London: Verso, 1989), 21.

14  Amin, *Capitalism in the Age of Globalization*, 103.

15  Ibid., 102.

16  Tosaka Jun, *Shiso to fuzoku* (*Thought and Custom*) (Tokyo: Heibonsha, 2001), 6.

17  Tosaka Jun, *Zenshu*, vol. 2, 227–438.

18  Ibid., vol. 2, 232.

19  Žižek, *Sublime Object of Ideology*, 16.

20  Tosaka, *Shiso to fuzoku*, 6.

21  Ernesto Laclau, *Politics and Marxist Theory* (London: Verso, 1979), 99.

22  Jean-Luc Nancy, *The Inoperative Community*, trans. Peter Connor, Lisa Garbus, Michael Holland, and Simona Sawhney (Minneapolis: University of Minnesota Press, 1991), xxxviii, 11–80.

23  Masao Maruyama, *Thought and Behavior in Modern Japanese Politics*, ed. Ivan Morris (London: Oxford University Press, 1963), 25–83.

24  Ibid., 80.

25  Quoted in Geoff Waite, *Nietzsche's Corpse* (Durham, NC: Duke University Press, 1996), 83.

26  Ibid.

# Preemptive War and a World Out of Control

Kuang Xinnian

Disregarding the opposition of France, Germany, and Russia, as well as an unprecedented tide of global antiwar protests, the Bush administration brazenly launched its invasion of Iraq without U.N. authorization. President Bush—in a display of arrogance and self-righteousness—labeled the Iraq war "Operation Iraqi Freedom," while his Secretary of Defense, Donald Rumsfeld, proclaimed that the inhabitants of Iraq could be expected to offer the invading army a jubilant welcome of fresh-cut flowers and music. But the outcome of the invasion was only the provocation of more violence and even greater chaos. Surveys of world popular opinion show that most people, including those of America's most slavish ally, England, have only contempt for America's warmongering. America, not Iraq, is perceived as the greatest threat to global security.

> Thanks to the blessing and curse of fate
> I've already lost track of who I am,

*positions* 13:1 © 2005 by Duke University Press

Am I an angel or a devil,
strong or weak,
a hero or a rogue.[1]

The flames of war that have ignited across Iraq have brought to mind these lines of verse written on one of the brick walls of the Babylonian Hanging Gardens. What is most bitterly ironic is that this land, now ravaged by barbaric artillery fire, is one of the sources of ancient human civilization and the birthplace of the world's first legal classic, *The Code of Hammurabi*.

Lian Qingchuan, a reporter and assistant editor of *21 Shiji huanqiu baodao* (*Twenty-First Century Global Report*) in Guangzhou, describes the consequences of the war in Iraq in his essay "The Shattered Present" ("Posui de xiandai"). He writes,

As the first precision guided cruise missiles skimmed over the waters of the Persian Gulf and smashed into their targets in the south of Baghdad, the curtain was lifted on the second Gulf War and the world—the present as we knew it—began to disintegrate. This was a war whose launch had long been suggested. So, the start of the war held no suspense, and the results of the war were not unexpected; it is the postwar story that will bring the most surprises. Before the war, this world, this present, functioned with a semblance of order; although this order carried with it a degree of uncertainty, every nation and all international actions were governed by a set of behavioral norms. That is, within the framework of the U.N., America acted as a superpower, commenting with due diligence on all aspects of international policy, while nations of the Third World, regardless of their strength, were able to use the U.N. as a medium through which to have their voices heard. But the Iraq war changed all of this. . . . One premeditated war changed our present entirely.[2]

Following the collapse of the Soviet bloc, the world lost its balance. Just before the end of the twentieth century, humanity's path forward suddenly appeared uncertain.

Many consider the twentieth century a period of tragedy. In the second half of the century, the world lived on the verge of annihilation. The United States and the Soviet Union were prepared to make use of nuclear armaments large enough to obliterate the world several times over. For many, the end of the Cold War confirmed what Francis Fukuyama predicted would be the end of history, and many dreamed of the emergence of a post–Cold War golden era. Others were less optimistic. Giovanni Arrighi, in the conclusion of his book *The Long Twentieth Century*, paraphrases Joseph Schumpeter:

> Before humanity chokes (or basks) in the dungeon (or paradise) of a post-capitalist world empire or of a post-capitalist world market society, it may well burn up in the horrors (or glories) of the escalating violence that has accompanied the liquidation of the Cold War world order. In this case, capitalist history would also come to an end but by reverting permanently to the systemic chaos from which it began six hundred years ago and which has been reproduced on an ever-increasing scale with each transition. Whether this would mean the end just of capitalist history or of all human history, it is impossible to tell.[3]

The Iraq War lifted the curtain on the twenty-first century. This war should not be considered in purely military terms, but rather as a significant political incident that will produce far-reaching changes in international politics. The Iraq War can be seen as a sort of experiment in military strategy, an opportunity to implement a policy of preemption as proposed in "The National Security Strategy of the United States of America" (September 17, 2002). Unfortunately, the adoption of this strategy in Iraq has led to the disintegration of international political order and has caused many long-respected policies to be rendered ineffectual overnight. It is difficult to imagine or estimate what the ultimate consequences of this strategy will be. However, as British Prime Minister Tony Blair once stated, the Iraq War is certain to play a determining role in politics for the next several decades. As for what sort of political consequences will be produced, opinions differ dramatically.

The existing world order was constructed under the leadership of the United States following World War II. The United Nations, the representative of this order, is certainly not an entirely democratic organization. Since its inception, the United Nations has been controlled by two superpowers, the United States and the Soviet Union. These two superpowers used the United Nations as a stage on which to vie for power. But it is important to note that neither the United States nor the Soviet Union doubted the significance or efficacy of the United Nations—and the United States, in particular, used the United Nations to export its values to the rest of the world. Both their confrontations and their mutual hold on power gave the second half of the twentieth century a long peace. However, after the collapse of the U.S.S.R., the surviving hegemon, the United States, no longer had the patience to use the United Nations to put forward its own values, but rather pursued what might be referred to as peace under imperial domination (*diguo tongzhi xia de heping*).

America's invasion of Iraq has damaged the authority of the United Nations and the principle of the inviolability of national sovereignty. Before the war broke out, Bush repeatedly sent out warnings in which he stated that if the Security Council refused to pass a resolution authorizing the use of force, the United Nations would become irrelevant. Some hawks in the administration and conservative newspapers even threatened that the United States could withdraw from the United Nations, bringing it to an ignominious end. The strategy of preemption as espoused by American neoconservatism, along with new interpretations of sovereignty, will bring about a revolution in the twenty-first century, and the war in Iraq will serve as a model. The United States will use its neo-imperialist imagination in an attempt to recreate the so-called rogue states and restore world order. The strategy of preemption is a sign of America's abandonment of both traditional Western international regulatory systems and the principle of rule by law as established under the U.N. charter. Instead, America is bringing about the return to an era where naked power takes preeminence. At a press conference held June 27, 2003, after talks with the French minister of foreign affairs, Dominique de Villepin, Nelson Mandela commented on this shift: "Since the establishment of the U.N., there have been no world wars; therefore, anybody, and particularly the leaders of the superpowers, who takes unilateral action outside the frame of the U.N. must receive the condemnation of all who love peace." On a visit to Ireland on June 20, 2003, he went on to say, "Any organization, any country, any movement that now decides to sideline the United Nations, that country and its leader are a danger to the world. We cannot allow the world to again degenerate into a place where the will of the powerful dominates over all other considerations."[4]

The strategy of preemption is not simply a military strategy, but is, in fact, a kind of barbaric politics, a serious attack against civilized humanity. It is ultimately tied to the question of whether the world is seeking civilization and order, or whether it is entering into a period of violence and chaos. The United States' adoption of this strategy provoked the intense opposition of Europe and, indeed, the entire world because many believe that a strategy of preemption would take the world in the latter direction. As a result of the Iraq War, a deep rift was opened up between America and its western European allies, to which the media now frequently affix the label "Old Europe."

Modern history, beginning in 1492, has been a Eurocentric history of colonialism, imperialism, and expansion. However, the United States has replaced Europe as imperialist colonizer. The imagination of American neoconservative politics has inspired the United States to become a tyrannical and self-appointed hegemon, willfully changing global boundaries, and a particularly intense force for the destruction of world order. Europe, on the other hand, has become a force for rationality and civilization. The dispute that arose between Europe and America during the Iraq War was both a conflict of potential profit and a sign of civilizational disparity.

To a large extent, this disparity can be traced to historical difference—in Europe, protracted and bitter ethnic wars and class conflicts, including the two world wars with their massive death tolls and widespread devastation, have made a deep imprint on Europeans' historical memory. From the perspective of civilizational history, the United States's old Europe has been transformed through these experiences into a new Europe. American political scientist Robert Kagan suggests that it is no longer necessary to pretend that America and Europe remain allies.[5] After the end of the Cold War, the values of the United States and Europe began to diverge; the divide over the question of the war in Iraq only marks the early stages of what will be a long-term process. Kagan uses Fukuyama's concept to argue that Europe is already at the end of history and can look forward to a peaceful and stable future; traditional power politics have given way to consultations between equals as a supranational organization gradually takes the place of independent nations. However, the United States is still in a state of historical progress and must utilize traditional power politics (military) to deal with Iraq and other threats.

It should be made clear that the U.S. strategy of preemptive strikes did not begin with the war in Iraq. At a gathering of the American Society of International Law in 1963, one of the Kennedy administration's respected advisers on foreign affairs, former Secretary of State Dean Acheson, delivered a speech in which he attempted to justify the potential bombing of Cuba, saying that when U.S. power, prestige, and position in the world were placed in danger, there could be no issues of legality in evaluating the U.S. response. In the past twenty years, the U.S. government has shown disregard for international law and the U.N. charter—undertaking military action in Grenada, Panama, Haiti, Kosovo, Libya, and the Sudan, among other nations. However, before the disappearance of the Soviet Union, the White House did not dare to make the invasion of sovereign states and the overthrow of legal governments an overt national policy. With the collapse of the Soviet Union and the concomitant loss of a power that could counteract U.S. hegemony, the balance of power that had undergirded global stability was lost. It was only then that American neoconservatives clearly expressed their support for preemption as a national policy. Now America's hegemony is founded on unprecedented and unsurpassed military strength; its military expenditures, equal to the total amount spent by the rest of the world, ensure that this position will be maintained.

America's embrace of preemption and unilateralism is evidence of a paradox in American politics: on the one hand, democracy is held up as a universal value, on the other, the United Nations is looked on with contempt, international law is violated, and hegemony is pursued—a policy of peace under imperial domination is advocated. The Bush administration has based itself on a narrow vision of national profit, and it is only with threats, bribes, intimidation, and coercion that it manages to garner the support of others. As a result, it fails to gain popular support and remains in a state of isolation. Joseph Nye, the dean of the Kennedy School of Government at Harvard University, in an article titled "U.S. Power and Strategy After Iraq," writes,

> By devaluing soft power and institutions, the new unilateralist coalition of Jacksonians and neo-Wilsonians is depriving Washington of some of its most important instruments for the implementation of the new national security strategy. If they manage to continue with the tack, the United

States could fail what Henry Kissinger called the historical test for this generation of American leaders: to use current preponderant U.S. power to achieve an international consensus behind widely accepted norms that will protect American values in a more uncertain future. Fortunately, this outcome is not preordained.[6]

The Iraq War has brought America into an unprecedented state of political isolation. The norms, morality, and legality of American hegemony were toppled along with the statue of Saddam Hussein. Only forty-eight of the nearly two hundred countries in the world supported America's invasion of Iraq, and fifteen of these countries were unwilling to openly state their support. In his essay "Arrogant Empire," Fareed Zakaria writes, "In its campaign against Iraq, America is virtually alone. Never will it have waged a war in such isolation. Never have so many of its allies been so firmly opposed to its policies. Never has it provoked so much public opposition, resentment and mistrust. And all this before the first shot has been fired. . . . A war with Iraq, even if successful, might solve the Iraq problem. It doesn't solve the America problem."[7] Robert C. Byrd, an eighty-five-year-old Democratic senator from West Virginia, made the following comments in March 2003: "Today I weep for my country. . . . No more is the image of America one of a strong, yet benevolent peacekeeper. The image of America has changed. Around the globe, our friends mistrust us, our word is disputed, our intentions are questioned."[8]

The possession of unlimited hegemonic power that takes the pursuit of its own benefit as a primary aim cannot but threaten other nations. North Korea's decision to withdraw from the Nuclear Non-Proliferation Treaty is only one of the consequences of the Iraq War. Korea is a relatively small and weak nation whose modern history is composed entirely of colonial domination, military occupation, and political division; given this past, it is not surprising that the North Koreans are extremely proud and sensitive. However, as soon as the Bush administration assumed power, it brought to an end the so-called sunshine policy, launched by former South Korean President Kim Dae-jung, and destroyed the process of North-South Korean reunification. Bush's labeling of North Korea, Syria, Iran, and several other countries as the axis of evil and rogue states not only left North Korea staring down the barrel of America's gun but also pushed forward the schedule for invasion. The Bush administration's pursuit of absolute security for America demonstrates an absolute disregard for the anxiety of North Korea and many other weak states in regard to their own security.

North Korea is pressing for a promise of security from America, but America has refused to sign a treaty of mutual nonaggression with North Korea and has not abandoned its threats of military action. America's actions in Iraq provide ample evidence that the acceptance of weapons inspectors not only provides no guarantee of immunity from attack but also actually proves to be the fuse that can touch off a war. In the view of third-world nations, America is an unreliable superpower, a country that will wantonly trample on regulations in pursuit of its own profit; it is, in fact, the greatest rogue state of all. The North Korean response to U.S. Deputy Secretary of State Richard Armitage's comments that "prospects are fair for eventual multilateral talks [with North Korea]" may be some indication of this widely held view.[9] As the North Korean Official News Agency put it, "America has declared that it has no interest in attacking North Korea, and has actually pursued a plan for peaceful resolution, but, in the background of all the dialogue there is a preparation for a war intended to make fools of us."[10] America's policy of preemptive strike has contributed to the reemergence of the nuclear threat in North Korea, and the Bush administration has taken advantage of this threat to mislead and deceive the American public, preparing little by little to move toward a military conclusion.

America absolutely refused the requests of France and several other nations to give the U.N. weapons inspectors more time to continue their work in Iraq. Several months after the occupation of Iraq, the generous time limit to weapons inspections proposed by France and others has been long surpassed. Yet America has still not discovered any weapons of mass destruction, nor has it yet uncovered any evidence of cooperation between Saddam and Osama bin Laden. All the reasons and excuses offered for the invasion of Iraq have come to nothing. After the occupation of Baghdad, on May 15, 2003, Secretary of Defense Rumsfeld proclaimed that Iraq's weapons of mass destruction would "probably never be found." The reality was increasingly clear—the American and British governments had intentionally used false intelligence to mislead Congress, Parliament, and the people with the ultimate aim of launching the war against Iraq.

President Bush's excessive self-confidence has raised deep doubts among many people. If the entire world were controlled by only one hegemon, and this hegemon was a Hitleresque character, then who could guarantee or exercise restraints on his misuse of power? Japan used the Zhongcun Incident as an excuse for engineering the Mukden Incident (1931), thus beginning the Japanese invasion of China in the 1930s–1940s. Germany used the killing of Germanic peoples in the Sudetenland area as a pretense for its 1938 occupation of Czechoslovakia, thus leading to the outbreak of World War II. America takes pride in its democratic system, but we must not forget that Hitler came to power within a democratic system. Particularly noteworthy is an event of July 12, 2003: immediately on taking office, Belgium's new government announced that it had already abolished the so-called genocide law in order to avoid the possibility of having to prosecute American President Bush and Israeli President Sharon for war crimes. America had warned that if President Bush were charged with war crimes in a Belgian court, then Belgium's position in the EU, NATO, and other international organizations would be threatened. We can see that America was using its status as the sole hegemonic power to get rid of a series of international constraints.

America's strategic shift has not only led to the disintegration of the world order, but has also prompted deep changes in American internal politics. Just as Hitler used the burning of the Reichstag for his own ends, President Bush manipulated and took advantage of the fear created by the 9/11 terrorist attacks, causing the American people to accept the dangerous policies of neoconservatism. The Bush administration's use of the 9/11 terrorist attacks and antiterrorist ideology has brought about a series of changes to American national law. Limits to the rights of its citizens—from freedom of the person to freedom of speech—mean that the American democratic system is facing a crisis.

The unilateral policies implemented by America, particularly its use of preemptive strike against self-defined threats, can only intensify the disorder of the crumbling system left behind after the Cold War. Saddam's power has been taken away, and most of those wanted by the Americans for their role in Saddam's government have been arrested or killed. However, the surprise attacks aimed at ending America's occupation have increased rather than decreased. Since Iraqi political power has been crushed by illegal force, Iraq will inevitably continue to suffer from violence, chaos, and terrorist attacks. Islamic terrorists and their suicide bombs burst like roses blooming in summer, becoming a frightening spectacle of the new millennium. If we say that nuclear weapons are the fruition of the evil of modern civilization, then suicide bombs (literally, "body bombs," *renti zhadan*) are unique to postmodern civilization. In the new millennium, the body (*renti*) is mysteriously transformed into a bomb (*zhadan*), at once soft and violent. America's cruise missiles and precision guided bombs are called "precision guided"; however, during the war in Kosovo, five of America's cruise missiles "mistakenly" struck the Chinese embassy in Belgrade. No matter how highly developed Western civilization may be, can there be any weapon with an aim more precise than the one that has been rejected by this very civilization—the Islamic warrior's suicide bomb? The suicide bomb, then, is the ultimate product and curse of modern civilization. If preemptive strike is a politics of excessive self-confidence, suicide bombers are a politics of lost hope, a necessary supplement to the politics of preemption.

The consequences of a preemptive policy are impossible to predict. Because of its dismantling of regulations and order, this policy may result in the appearance of destructive forces that will be neither restrained nor limited, that carry an inexhaustible potential for violence. There is a popular Chinese saying: "Releasing a demon is easy, catching a demon is hard." Americans should not forget that the designer of the 9/11 terrorist attacks, Osama bin Laden, was once propped up by the United States; he is a purely American product. The United States used illegal violence to destroy the existing order, and it is likely that this will lead to even more illegal violence and even greater chaos. The danger of preemption lies in the fact that its demonstrated uses and the chain reactions that it sets in motion can neither be determined beforehand nor be controlled. America is not simply following along this dangerous route in isolation; rather, its strategies will arouse other latent powers that will use any means necessary to overcome existing taboos. That is, the strategy of preemptive strike leads down a road of unlimited violence. On the one hand, this strategy signals profound political change. But, more than this, the adoption of this strategy leads to the destruction of humanity's ethical foundations and moral boundaries and to the rise of a deep and widespread spirit of disbelief and fear.

More than two thousand years ago, Confucius said: "That which I do not want done to me, I should not do to others." Unlike Samuel P. Huntington's concept of "the clash of civilizations," the foundational wisdom of five thousand years of Chinese civilization is based on the concepts of the way of the mean (*zhongyong zhi dao*), tolerance for civilizational difference and diversity, and the ideal of a harmony of civilizational similarities—the concept of harmony with difference. Unfortunately, Western civilization often takes the presence of different perspectives as an evil. America not only believes in the universality of its values, but has also adopted the strategy of preemptive strike as a way to spread these values. The potentially widespread reliance on preemptive deterrence is a serious test to human civilization.

Translated by Jim Bonk

## Notes

1  Iraqi song used by Phoenix TV (Hong Kong) in its "Live Broadcast from the Iraqi War," March 20, 2003.

2  Lian Qingchuan, "Posui de xiandai" ("The Shattered Present"), *Zhonnguo baodao dianzi zazhi* (*China Report: Electronic Magazine*), no. 272, mlcool.com/info/if002846.htm.

3  Giovanni Arrighi, *The Long Twentieth Century: Money, Power, and the Origins of Our Times* (New York: Verso, 1994), 356.

4  "Mandela Does Not Want to See Bush, Moreover Refers to Him as the 'World's Greatest Threat,'" *Xinhua Wang* (*Xinhua Online*), June 29, 2003.

5  Robert Kagan, "Power and Weakness," *Policy Review* 113 (June 2, 2003), 3.

6  Joseph Nye, "U.S. Power and Strategy After Iraq," *Foreign Affairs* (July-August 2003), 74.

7  Fareed Zakaria, "Arrogant Empire," *Newsweek*, March 24, 2003, 19.

8  Speech found at byrd.senate.gov.

9  "Assistant Secretary of State Declares that America Is Willing to Enter into Direct Dialogue with North Korea," *Lianhe Zaobao* (*United Report* [Singapore]), February 6, 2003.

10  Ibid.

# A Letter from Europe

Edoarda Masi

All over the world, incomparable numbers of people have participated in protests against the U.S. war in Iraq. Protestors of every social, national, and ideological category share an awareness that our destructive potential is now so dangerous, we must reject absolutely the idea of war if we are to safeguard the human race. Species survival is a motivation of such vast and profound resonance that it appeals to every human being who is not insane or criminal.

At the root of the collective opposition, however, is the acceptance of values proposed by the structures currently in power and their uncritical and voluntary application to the current state of international affairs. Thus, the shared sense of the absurdity of this war also takes shape within the ideological apparatus broadcast by the very aggressors who enjoy an almost total monopoly of conventional information: the self-determination of peoples, the possibility to live together in peace, democracy, respect for human rights and the rights of the individual, respect for international law, the primacy of legality.

*positions* 13:1 © 2005 by Duke University Press

One example among many: from the day of the attack, the expression "illegal war" has been used extensively. Yet as every jurist knows, legality in the sphere of international relations is a contradiction in terms. While at the institutional level legality has an instrumental function, since institutions operate by definition on the terrain of legality, in the sphere of a popular movement legality issues a countercommand to the reiterated commitment against preemptive war. In addition to the folly of applying criteria of legality or illegality to war, the concept of illegal war implies, in this specific case, that no opposition would be admissible if the U.S. government had succeeded (or should now succeed) in obtaining the approval of the Security Council of the United Nations—the semblance of so-called international legality. The use of this expression implies a profound conformism according to which legality and the compliance with codified rules should be the measure of behavior at the levels of states, nations, classes, and individuals. According to this criterion, personalities like Thomas Münzer, George Washington, Giuseppe Garibaldi, and Mao Zedong would all be bandits, and as such they were indeed labeled. Similarly, Picasso's *Les demoiselles d'Avignon* caused a scandal because it violated what were then the rules of painting. We forget, to the peril of a politically creative and effective opposition, that every creative act—in science, philosophy, and art, as well as in politics—shatters existing structures.

The basic features of an imposed ideological apparatus passively accepted—the *pensée unique*—are the omission of social conflict and the substitution of ethical and psychological judgments for political ones. Contradiction and class conflict are replaced by the notion (extended internationally) of rich and poor. These categories are proposed to be outside of history. They are presented as natural phenomena, and as such, appear attenuable and combatable only as we combat an (inevitable) physical illness. As the space of nations is replaced by that of international, imperial, or religious organizations (that govern, or fail to govern, tribes and ethnic groups), countries are arbitrarily imagined as absolutely different from other countries and as having no *internal* differences, contradictions, or conflicts. Significant attention to internal differences has facilitated, in the last two centuries, a recognition of oppressive structures that have tended to cross national borders (even if they did not reach the globality of our time) and, as a consequence, facilitated the formation of solidarity groups with deep and transversal ideologies. First proclaimed in 1848 and blossoming with the Paris Commune until the end of World War I, this solidarity burst into the *universal* (socialist) consciousness of the *common interests of the workers*, which was opposed to the interests of the capitalists, who were also the colonizers.[1]

Through the current ideological lens, the conflicts racking the world appear dimly, as unintelligible, desperate chaos. Every instance of struggle is regarded as either senseless violence or a conspiracy of perverse individuals. Alongside messages that seem potentially universal, a distortion of the historical consciousness and a fragmentation of the world into illusive aggregations (based on superstition, traditional usage, deviations of religious fanaticism) present themselves as the return to an imagined past that history has destroyed.

Under such ideological domination, the power elite's clear betrayal of the principles it itself imposes and disseminates tends, paradoxically, to facilitate the surge of aware opposition in a confluence of political, ideological, moral, and religious orientations in reciprocal contrast with one another. From this amorphous convergence emerges the great moral force and practical impotence of the antiwar movement. There is no one in charge of the movement, so to speak, and it is thus unable to do more than bear witness. Indeed, the opposition has done little to clarify its various motivations, for fear of dissolving its bonds in the inevitable debate such clarification would demand. Perhaps out of inexperience, it has been forgotten that alliances formed to achieve a common goal are only as strong as the terms and borders that define them. As long as the opposition comes in the sphere of the ideological context imposed by power, it can be as broad and technically unconquerable as it likes, but it will remain impotent.

There is further confusion, perhaps easier to overcome on the theoretical plane if not on the practical one. It comes from the antiwar stance of some European governments, which appears to represent the (real or presumed) interests of the individual countries—actually neither more nor less legitimate than the (real or presumed) interests of the United States. The antiwar stance of the French and German governments, most notably, has created the impression of a generalized European resistance to the imperialistic aims of the United States. This presumed (or hoped-for) European resistance has

been further confounded with the popular protest, to which has been attributed an anti-American content (with varied connotations and without
definition of the term). This is the path taken by many great intellectuals
recently, such as Jürgen Habermas and Jacques Derrida, who attribute to
the European masses the duty of a sort of defense of the identity of European
civilization against the United States. But even some of the critics of this
position have headed off directly into a blind alley. For example, the American philosopher Iris Marion Young rightly accuses the real conflicts existing
today in every society of being sources of destructive disorder and war, but
then goes on to see these conflicts essentially as a struggle between rich and
poor, especially between the countries of the "rich North" and "poor South"
of the world.[2] Until we investigate why the United States and Europe are simultaneously allies (against whom?) and competitors, we do not have strong
enough arguments to combat this ideological chaos. In addition to making
the obvious distinction between governments and peoples, we would have
to examine the economic, social, and military forces that are currently con-
cealed behind these governments and why they force their governments to
pursue an imperialistic and warmongering policy.

At the beginning of the nineteenth century, capital was found to be a
system of control of the social metabolism through its mode of production.
For the entire nineteenth century and part of the twentieth, capital was
incarnated, so to speak, in the bourgeoisie that, at the peak of its rise, became
the ruling class of the nation-state. During this period, the opposite poles of
capital and labor were represented on the political and social scene as the
domination of the bourgeoisie over the industrial proletariat, and on the
international scene as the domination of the bourgeois nation-state, through
colonization, over the nonindustrial proletariat of the noncapitalistic world.
In the course of history, labor has tended to liberate itself in part, and later
entirely, from its subordinate role and demand a role of self-government. As
long as the bourgeoisie was able to control capital and, as the ruling class, was
able to control the nation-state, it enacted a number of compromises with the
representatives of organized labor—through policies that were sometimes
reforming and other times repressive—in order to enable the two poles to
endure in reciprocal struggle and integration. The compromises that ensured
the survival of the two antagonists for a certain time (the last, most important

one, was the Keynesian compromise) lost strength in the measure to which the existence of one of the two contenders radically threatened the existence of the other. Thus, capital increasingly needed to restrict the space allotted to labor.[3]

By defeating the attempts at socialism and effectively dissolving the politically organized labor proletariat, capital devoured labor as a political entity. At the same time, the mechanism of accumulation and expanded reproduction enabled the formation of enormous structures of capital as organisms of global domination—the transnational corporations—that aim for total and direct control of the nation-states and for creation of their own concentrated political power (without fully succeeding, in the current stage, due to the internal competition within the very sphere of capital).[4] During the twentieth century, we have thus reached a situation in which the passage of power from the political-military domain to the power of the economic giants at all levels is complete. The bourgeoisie no longer exists as the ruling and mediating class, and the breakup of the nation-state is imminent, not in the sense—as has been repeatedly observed, by Noam Chomsky, for one—that the state no longer participates in the economy in support of capital, but, on the contrary, in the sense that the state is the absolute agent of capital, and less and less an autonomous subject. When political power ceases to be an autonomous entity, politics loses its reality.

The organisms of global domination are oriented toward the elimination not only of politically organized labor, but also of labor altogether. The new proletariat is scattered in atomized, flexible particles, potentially lacking in any human autonomy, as maneuverable as objects and reduced to the status of pure merchandise. At the same time, the growing weight of the financial structures and, in the last few decades, of the tendency to substitute financial speculation for the profits deriving from production has proved capable of influencing the world economy and could be further abetted by rapid universal communications technologies instrumentalized for purposes of domination. These changes, however, are nearly suicidal: speculation, which claims to feed on itself, must touch the capital accumulated in production; and the apparent elimination of the labor factor will necessarily lead, sooner or later, to the self-destruction of capital and the entire economic system.

The self-destructive process appears to find a remedy in spheres of labor that are newly exploitable and subject to a high degree of control. There is a return to forms of banditry that are worse than those of the nineteenth century, to direct and indirect recolonization of huge masses of workers, even nonindustrial workers, who populate the nonmetropolitan areas of the world. On the political and military terrain, this recolonization reproduces an updated and corrected version of the older form of colonialism. On the economic plane, however, the innovations are vast and are capable of altering the early configuration of capital-labor, when there was an indirect domination of the nonindustrial proletariat. In the current system—which conjoins so-called intellectual property and patents with agribusiness's rape of agricultural and livestock-breeding resources and managerial control of genetic manipulation—a direct relationship has been created between large capital and nonindustrial labor in both the "northern" and "southern" agricultural zones of the world.[5] The management of the system is partly entrusted to such organizations as the WTO and is guaranteed by a series of international treatises that have been stipulated, one after the other, in the last ten years and are still in the process of completion. Once codified, these treatises will efface any residual illusion of independence for individual countries, including legislative independence, democracy, and civil freedoms. The concentration of control of mass communications and the large number of experts in that sector are indispensable for the completion of this program of tyranny.

Clearly this colonialist solution only extends the destructive and self-destructive process. The war without end is merely its most explicit and immediately terrifying aspect. As a pretext for the development of weapons, for waging war, and for the exercise of its own form of terrorism, the government of the United States now declares that terrorism (rather than communism) is the new absolute evil to be crushed. This development, with its concomitant assignment of international policing tasks to NATO states and the label *axis of evil* to any country that does not accept these tasks, clearly specifies the new enemy as any form of opposition or resistance to the global domination of capital—whether it is presented as a nation-state structure or as the aggregate opposition of individuals (defined as terrorists or friends of terrorists for the sole fact of their opposition).

The antagonist to the present system of domination seems to be humanity as a whole. But as a gigantic counterpart of capital on the planetary plane, it appears evident that the proletarian condition will be extended and that it will eventually coincide with the universal condition of colonized countries. This leads to the need to transform and integrate the labor movement into a movement for decolonization and against every form of destruction, starting with war.

## Notes

1 On the contrary, current radical information media like the Web site "Rebelion—informacion alternativa" (www.rebelion.org) find it natural to suggest, as a means of protest against the war, a generic boycott of American, British, Spanish, and Italian products, a boycott that would affect 80 percent of people everywhere, including those who oppose the war with active protests. Worse is the phenomenon, well known to all of us who, in the final analysis, participate out of impotence, of the new version of solidarity with the proletariat, a sort of generalized charitable association dispensing alms to "poor" individuals or countries.

2 See "Europa, provincia del mondo" ("Europe, Province of the World"), *Il Manifesto*, August 7, 2003, 12.

3 See especially the considerations of David Kotz ("Neoliberalism and the U.C. Economic Expansion of the '90s," *Monthly Review* 54, no. 11 [2003], 15–33) regarding the passage from Keynesianism to neoliberalism in the second half of the 1970s. According to the article, we can argue that the oligopolistic and financial evolution of capital is incompatible with the state, which is a dispenser of welfare and settler of conflicts *supra partes*; that the welfare system was unable to preserve the domination of capital in the face of the growing advance of labor and its demands; that Keynesianism ultimately revealed its weakness as a possible means of conciliation between capital and labor; and that in the deepening conflict, either capital or labor appeared destined to prevail.

4 See the repeated analyses of István Mészáros on the subject of the American empire as the expression of global capital without the ability to actualize that expression because, in spite of globalization, global capital is not unified and therefore cannot be incarnated in a single state.

5 For a very keen discussion of this theme, with extensive bibliographical references, see George Liodakis, "The Role of Biotechnology in the Agro-Food System and the Socialist Horizon," *Historical Materialism* 11, no. 1 (2003), 37–74.

# Permanent War

Marilyn Young

If we have to use force it is because we are America. We are the indispensable nation. We stand tall. We see farther into the future. —Madeline Albright, Secretary of State, February 19, 1998

I recall all too well the nightmare of Vietnam. . . . I am determined to do everything in my power to prevent this country from becoming involved in another Vietnam nightmare. —Senator Robert Byrd, June 29, 2002

It is possible that the destruction of September 11 uncovered the suppressed remains of Vietnam. —Wolfgang Schivelbusch, *The Culture of Defeat*

We're going to get better over time. We've always thought of post-hostilities as a phase distinct from combat. . . . The future of war is that these things are going to be much more of a continuum. . . . This is the future for the world we're in at the moment. We'll get better as we do it more often. —Lawrence Di Rita, special assistant to Secretary of Defense Donald Rumsfeld, July 18, 2003

*positions* 13:1 © 2005 by Duke University Press

There seem to be only two kinds of war the United States can fight: World War II or Vietnam. The conviction on the part of some Americans and many politicians that the United States could (or should or would) have won the war in Vietnam is a convenient mechanism for getting around a remembered reality of defeat. An alternate strategy is to concentrate the national mind on World War II, skipping not only Vietnam but also Korea. In recent movies and television serials, World War II is depicted as a long, valiant struggle that the United States fought pretty much on its own, winning an exceptionally clean victory that continues to redeem all Americans under arms anywhere, at any point in history.[1] In virtually every military action since 1975, the administration in charge has tried to appropriate the images and language of World War II. Thus, Manuel Noriega, Mohamed Farrah Aidid, Slobodan Milosevic, and Saddam Hussein (twice) were roundly denounced as the Adolph Hitler du jour; September 11, 2001, of course, is the twenty-first-century Pearl Harbor. Nevertheless, in each of these wars or warlike events, some journalist or politician was bound to ask the fearful question: is this another Vietnam?

What is it that people fear in a repetition of Vietnam? Military and political defeat, of course, but, beyond that, the daily experience of an apparently endless war, one that registered on the home front not in calls for sacrifice and heroism but rather in domestic division, resistance to the draft, high desertion rates, urban riots, popular suspicion of the government, a steadily rising number of U.S. dead and wounded, the shame-inducing images of napalmed Vietnamese children, the reluctant knowledge of American atrocities like My Lai. In his speech in June 2002, Senator Robert Byrd listed his own nightmare images: "the antiwar protests and demonstrations, the campus riots, and the tragic deaths at Kent State, as well as the resignation of a president. And I remember all too well the gruesome daily body counts."[2]

Because the Vietnam War cannot be assimilated to a triumphal American narrative, presidents must regularly pick their way around it. They have done so mainly by taking its public relations failings to heart rather than by contemplating its history or meaning. Despite calling Vietnam a noble crusade, Ronald Reagan was in no mood to risk repeating other aspects of the conflict. Money and arms substituted for U.S. combat troops in both Nicaragua and El Salvador, and when a suicide bomber killed over two hundred U.S. marines in Lebanon, Reagan quickly withdrew the rest. At the same time, to demonstrate that the world's mightiest military power was not afraid to use its power directly (and to justify a military budget that never responded to the end of any war, including the Cold War), small, predictably winnable mini-wars were waged against small, largely defenseless countries. Operation Urgent Fury made it clear to all Grenadians, and most particularly the island nation's left-leaning government, that neither the United States nor those students who went abroad to get medical degrees could be pushed around. Six years later, the first Bush administration taught General Noriega and the people of Panama a similar lesson in Operation Just Cause.

The victories in Operations Urgent Fury and Just Cause were useful and their titles ambitious enough. Yet they were painted on too small a canvas to take the sting out of defeat in Vietnam. For that, more troops would have to travel longer distances, use greater firepower, and engage a real army. When Saddam Hussein seized more of Kuwait than the administration of the first President Bush thought necessary, the stage was set for a military extravaganza that might indeed mean, as the president so fervently hoped, that "we've kicked the Vietnam syndrome once and for all."[3] Vietnam, by negative example, had taught the civil and military branches of the government how to market a war as well as how to fight one. It was all in the timing: enough time to engage the easily distractable imagination of the public but not so much time that boredom set in, or worse, anxiety. Operation Desert Shield, the period from August 1990 to mid-January 1991, served to create a steadily intensifying crisis atmosphere. Network TV and its cable rival, CNN, used the time to settle on appropriate logos and their musical accompaniment. Operation Desert Storm, first as thirty-nine days of sustained and furious bombing and then in the form of a massive ground invasion, was the longed-for release. The desert theme—modest, descriptive—worked so well that some years later, Clinton, without regard for its World War II invocation of the German enemy, named one of his attacks on Iraq Desert Fox.

Media cooperation was essential if Desert Storm and Desert Shield were to successfully overcome memories of Vietnam. Early in the war, General Norman Schwarzkopf pointed out that inflated body-count figures had led many Americans to distrust military press briefings. Alternatively, when the figures were believed, they had upset people. Therefore there would be no body counts in the Gulf War. Thus, through over a month of bombing and a week of ground fighting, no estimates of Iraqi losses were ever offered, nor did the press demand them. The result was a televised war relatively innocent of dead bodies, a war that, except for images of the bombing of a Baghdad air-raid shelter and repeated shots of desperate oil-soaked cormorants, would not spoil one's dinner. Indeed, the wildlife allegedly destroyed by Saddam Hussein's ecological terrorism substituted for images of humans wounded by American bombs. After the war, CBS revealed that one particularly sad cormorant, whose struggle for life was shown over and over again on TV, had actually been the victim of an oil spill caused not by Iraqi sabotage but by Allied bombing.

By the end of the war, it had become possible to take the enemy not as people, but as machines; the tanks, buses, and cars that jammed the highway out of Kuwait City seemed to have fled on their own, their charred hulks containing no human remains. There was thus an apparent, visual purity to the U.S. victory that successfully masked its savagery.

The sense of purity was conveyed by a cooperative press, but the administration took no chances: the press was tightly controlled as well. In Vietnam, reporters learned to treat military press briefings with the respect they deserved, widely mocking what they called the five o'clock follies. Reporters understood that it was the task of the military to report victory and that it was the reporters' task to find out what was going on. This is not to romanticize the role of the press in Vietnam. The overwhelming majority of reporters supported the war, and their criticisms were rarely based on principle but rather on tactics. Even so, the reporters made clear the cavernous abyss between what the U.S. military and State Department wished the public to believe and what seemed to the press to be the case. The abyss was called the credibility gap, and it meant that people began to treat government handouts with an unprecedented degree of skepticism. Since Vietnam, the military has been careful not to allow this process to repeat itself. "Three Pentagon press officers," James LeMoyne reported during the first Gulf War, "said that they spent significant time analyzing reporters' stories in order to make recommendations on how to sway coverage in the Pentagon's favor." Reporters who asked hard questions were warned that their antimilitary attitude would count against them. On-camera TV interviews were halted in the middle if the press officer did not like what was being said, reporters who filed stories on troop doubts about the war found their access to senior military men curtailed, and the soldiers themselves were subjected to close questioning by their officers.[4] The troops were also carefully briefed on how to talk to the press. "Say you are highly trained," Anthony Swofford, a Marine sniper in the first Gulf War, was told. "Say you're excited to be here and you believe in the mission and that we'll annihilate the Iraqis." When a marine in the company argues that it is un-American to censor speech, the staff sergeant responds: "You are Marines. There is no such thing as speech that is free. You must pay for everything you say. Especially the unauthorized crap."[5]

Throughout the first Gulf War, generals and retired generals, admirals and retired admirals were given hours of TV time to speculate, point with pointers, describe in sensuous detail the operation of this or that weapon. The Middle East experts of choice, like the military men, supported the president's policy. The peace side received air time, but in proportions that effectively marginalized it. Peace demonstrations in Europe went uncovered, and demonstrations and marches in the United States did not fare much better. Told by Vietnam revisionists that the media had created the peace movement by showing it on TV, the networks exercised due caution.

In the war against terrorism as waged in Afghanistan, there was a similar unanimity of expert opinion but far fewer visuals. No generals instructed the public on the fine points of the map of Afghanistan; no reporters accompanied the troops. When a reporter for the *Washington Post* tried to reach the site of a missile attack on an alleged al Qaeda target, he was stopped at gunpoint.[6] But a press too tightly controlled becomes restive, and the Pentagon has been alert to invent other means of containing the media. During the first Gulf War, the entire population had the experience of seeing the view from the nose cone of a missile as it descended toward its target, but not the view from the ground looking up. It was difficult to imagine what greater service the news media could offer a warring state. But that was before the television show *Survivor* offered a new model. According to the *New York Times*, the Pentagon planned to "promote its war effort through television's genre of the moment, the reality series." Over the protests of its news division, the ABC entertainment division would produce a thirteen-part series offering, according to the press release, "compelling personal stories" of America's fighting men and women. "There's a lot of other ways to convey information to the American people than through news organizations," Rear Admiral Craig R. Quigley pointed out. "That's the principal means," the admiral went on, "but if there is an opportunity to tell about the courage and professionalism of our men and women in uniform on prime time television for 13 straight weeks, we're going to do it. That's an opportunity not to be missed."[7]

By the second Gulf War, the military had arrived at a more perfect form: the embedded press corps, which has, by and large, fulfilled its punning name. At one point in the war, TV talk-show host Charlie Rose conducted a telephone interview with Frederik Balfour, a *Business Week* correspondent who was embedded in the Third Infantry Division. Balfour had opposed the war before it began, but now riding along with the troops, dependent on them for his protection, he found it was impossible not to feel part of their "cause." Rose next asked Colin Soloway, *Newsweek* correspondent with the 101st Airborne Division, if he had been able to go along on any Apache helicopter missions. No, Soloway explained regretfully, Apache helicopters only have seats for the two pilots. Still, he was able to view the videotape when the helicopters returned to base, and the pilots were glad to "walk him through" whatever engagement they had conducted. The TV audience did not get to see the tapes—any more than they had during the first Gulf War.

Looking back on the first Gulf War, it would seem the first President Bush had done everything right. In addition to avoiding that which must not be done—conscription, an uncontrolled press, body counts, gradual escalation—Bush had done that which should be done: sent a massive force immediately; accused the enemy of atrocities before such an accusation could be made against the United States; kept American casualties to an absolute minimum; given the victorious troops a victory parade. Yet the Vietnam syndrome lingered. If the first test of the political success of a war is the reelection of those who made it, then despite all these preparations, the administration had failed. If the second test is how the war is represented in popular culture, the failure proved even greater. The only notable movie to come out of the war, *Three Kings*, depicted the conflict as Vietnam on speed: a war of multiple betrayals and massacres; a war without honor or sense.

For all the efforts of the administration to recreate World War II, the first Gulf War never achieved the necessary majesty. It remained a punitive war against an oil ally that had gotten out of hand and had to be punished. The first President Bush chose to retain a presumably chastened Saddam Hussein in power. American troops did not march triumphantly through the streets of Baghdad, as they had in Berlin and Tokyo. The Gulf War planners, many of whom, like Colin Powell, had fought in Vietnam, put great thought and energy into avoiding the dangers of that war, and they succeeded. Still, they could not make war good again.

Clinton's military expeditions, undertaken with a clear memory of what the Vietnam War had been about and why he had opposed it, fared no better. In Somalia, the Clinton administration worked toward the World War II formula by naming one of that country's many warlords as its Hitler and proceeding to hunt him and his lieutenants down. In the course of those unsuccessful efforts, a famine-stricken population, which had initially welcomed U.S. intervention, turned famously ugly. Eighteen dead Americans and one thousand dead Somalis later, Clinton withdrew U.S. forces. For most of the public, the lesson drawn was that if you could not have World War II and did not want Vietnam, it was best to stay home or to participate from thirty thousand feet up. Thus, in Kosovo, safe in the skies, the U.S. Air Force played its part, prevailing over a "pint-sized nation whose entire gross national product amounted to one-sixteenth of the Pentagon's budget."[8] It was a model intervention: no Americans were hurt, and the stock market soared.

Clinton's use of military force was one response to the ghost of Vietnam; George H. W. Bush's more robust resort to arms was another. But neither could meet the contradictory need of the country to see itself as both supremely powerful *and* forever an underdog, as both the only redeemer and the preeminent victim. In Vietnam, its power had not prevailed, it was not the underdog, it had redeemed no one and nothing, and however frequently Vietnam veterans were called upon for surrogate-victim duty, it was difficult to avoid the sense that Vietnam itself remained the main victim. And then came September 11.

For a time, it seemed that terrible event would succeed in burying the ghost of Vietnam. It gave the United States a moral authority it had not had since Franklin Delano Roosevelt was president. In addition, once Bush had declared war on terrorism (a recurring declaration starting with the presidency of Ronald Reagan), the rhetoric of both World War II and the Cold War returned. In the manner of the Cold War, the war against terrorism was perforce endless; in the manner of World War II, it was a struggle against enemies of consummate wickedness, an axis of evil. Best of all, this particular endless war against evil would require little home-front effort beyond continuing to consume at normal or preferably exorbitant levels. The first battle in the new war, overthrowing the Taliban, proved to be only a minor challenge to the military. What happened in Afghanistan thereafter—warlord rule, a possible revivification of the Taliban, devastation of the countryside—detained neither the Bush administration nor the general public. The relentless march to war against Iraq, long urged by the second President Bush's close advisers, could now begin.

Yet at a narrative level, the combination of Cold War and World War II stumbled. The most important institutional legacy of World War II, the United Nations, for a time almost brought the march to a complete halt. The grand coalition of the first Gulf War would not reenlist, and the administration was reduced to recruiting international support through highly publicized bribery and threats, only to achieve a "coalition of the willing" made up of, among others, Eritreans and Solomon Islanders. Administration insistence that Saddam Hussein had weapons of mass destruction, up to and including nuclear weapons, joined a collective memory of how World War II ended with the dominant fears of the Cold War era, but convincing proof of the existence of the weapons was never assembled. Not only was the World War II template elusive, but the Vietnam War returned in the form of a mass antiwar movement, global in scope, broadly inclusive, spontaneously organized, clearly and repeatedly saying no to war.

Nothing could have deflected the administration from having its war. Yet the sharp outlines of a victorious war story quickly blurred. Instead of the orderly march into the defeated capital past the cheering thousands, there was looting, arson, anarchy, the shooting and killing of peaceful demonstrators, and shouts of "down with America." Instead of a ceremonial turning over of power to the new rulers, historically the moment that legitimized the new order, senior American officers sat alone on the plush sofas of an empty palace. A historian, Wolfgang Schivelbusch, observed that the "absence of the vanquished from their place at the table of surrender resonated as a sinister silence, like a tragedy ending without a dying hero's last words." The scene of the generals in the palace was a "scene of ersatz surrender, for the simple reason that the defeated regime had vanished without a trace."[9]

The most famous surrender scene in twentieth-century U.S. history took place on the deck of the battleship USS *Missouri* on September 2, 1945. It was a ceremony, John Dower has written, "laden with symbolism." The ship bore the name of President Truman's home state; it flew the flag that had flown from the White House on Pearl Harbor Day, as well as the one that Commodore Perry had flown as he sailed into Tokyo Bay in 1853. Japan's "utter subjugation was reinforced by the dramatic setting of the surrender ceremony itself."[10] During the second Gulf War, George W. Bush, appropriately costumed, copiloted a navy jet onto the deck of the aircraft carrier *Abraham Lincoln*, which had had to put out to sea a bit in order to make the landing feasible. There were no Iraqis there, of course, only cheering American sailors and a largely admiring press corps. But if the surrender was ersatz, so was the victory speech, for to openly declare victory would require the release of Iraqi prisoners of war, and no one wanted to do that. Nor, for that matter, did the president wish to announce the return of peace, as General MacArthur had on board the *Missouri*. Instead, in a great mix of historical references, Bush called upon the spirits of war presidents past (Roosevelt, Truman, Kennedy, and Reagan)[11] in the course of announcing a victory in "one battle" in the ongoing war against terrorism, a victory comparable to the allied landings in Normandy and the battle of Iwo Jima.[12] But what neither Bush nor the press had foreseen was the ongoing resistance to U.S. occupation on the part of various Iraqi groups, a resistance that takes a daily toll in American and Iraqi dead.

Initially, the Vietnam syndrome referred to the reluctance of the public to engage in war. Now, it seems clear, it is the U.S. government that is caught in Vietnam's grip, convinced that the only cure for that long-ago defeat is yet more war. But redeeming Vietnam is only one function of the wars the United States has fought since September 11, 2001. The other, perhaps more significant purpose, is to extend, selectively, the benefits the Cold War had brought to the United States over its forty-five-year life span, benefits that were regrettably lost due to the Soviet Union's withdrawal from the field and its subsequent disappearance.

In the summer of 1950, the majority of Americans (some 57 percent, according to a Gallup poll) believed that with the police action in Korea, World War III had begun.[13] Writing shortly after the fall of the Taliban government in Afghanistan, Eliot Cohen, director of strategic studies at Johns Hopkins' School of Advanced International Studies, made the same calculation in an important op-ed piece for the *Wall Street Journal*.[14] It was crucial, Cohen argued, to call things by their right name. The "less palatable but more accurate name" for the war on terrorism is "World War IV." "The Cold War was World War III," Cohen wrote, and World War IV resembles it in many ways: it is global; it will require "a mixture of violent and nonviolent efforts"; it will last a very long time; and "it has ideological roots." The enemy now is "militant Islam," and Afghanistan was "just one front in World War IV, and the battles there just one campaign." Cohen envisioned at least two others: in Iraq and Iran.

Norman Podhoretz pursued this theme several months later in a long essay titled "How to Win World War IV," and former CIA director James Woolsey embraced the same idea, predicting that World War IV was likely to last longer than World War I or World War II but "hopefully not the full four-plus decades of the Cold War."[15] Notable among all three commentators was their evident zest for war. Podhoretz was explicit: "I fully realize," he wrote, "that we are judged both by others and by ourselves, as lacking the stomach and the skills to play even so limited an imperial role as we did in occupying Germany and Japan after World War II." He sometimes doubted the country's capabilities in this regard and worried about the long history of national inattention and passivity. "Yet," he concluded, "given the transfiguring impact of major wars on the victors no less than on the vanquished, who can tell what we may wind up doing and becoming as we fight our way through World War IV?" The prospect of what the United States (or any other warring state) might become as it fought its way through the twenty-first century did not give Podhoretz pause. He was confident everybody in the world would be better off and that victory in World War IV would mean, as President Bush proclaimed, "an age of liberty here and across the world."[16] In terms of public rhetoric, domestic security policies, militarization of foreign policy and of culture, curtailment of civil liberties, a pervasive sense of fear and threat, the war on terrorism is the Cold War redux. It takes little historical imagination to see in the permanent war against terrorism a continuation of what was initially imagined as a permanent war against communism. The world that had seemed to crumble with the Berlin wall in 1989 reappeared, a little dusty: good and evil, us and them, enemies everywhere. This view was bipartisan. Senator Joseph Lieberman, who could have been vice president on September 11, described the war on terrorism as "the medieval zealotry and religious fanaticism of a holy war against the universalistic, humanitarian, democratic and tolerant ideals of America." The country's fundamental principles were "as much on the line in this war against terrorism as they were in our battles with Nazism and communism."[17]

Along with the Manichaean language came a revivification of a number of Cold War tactics, such as psychological warfare, embodied in the short-lived Office of Strategic Influence, whose open goal was to spread disinformation abroad. Washington and Hollywood fell into each other's arms. In late October 2001, forty Hollywood executives met with Chris Henick, then deputy assistant to the president, and Adam Goldman, associate director of the Office of Public Liaison. Leslie Moonves, president of CBS, explained their mission: "I think you have a bunch of people here who were just saying, 'Tell us what to do. We don't fly jet planes, but there are skill sets that can be put to use here.'" There was a clear need, both "domestically and internationally to tell the story that is our story."[18]

The government acted quickly to blunt any questioning of administration policy, passing the Uniting and Strengthening America by Providing Appropriate Tools Required to Intercept and Obstruct Terrorism Act. Known for short as the U.S.A. Patriot Act, it provides for an unprecedented peacetime abrogation of civil liberties in a piece of legislation whose name itself discourages dissent.[19] Nine months after its passage, in a move that makes the FBI Cold War informant network look benign, the administration launched Operation TIPS, whose acronym must also have preceded its full naming. Through a pilot project in ten cities, the Terrorism Information and Prevention System would enable 1 million letter carriers, train conductors, utility employees, and ship captains to report "suspicious activity" by calling a toll-free number that would connect them "directly to a hotline routing calls to the proper law enforcement agency."[20] The post office declined to participate, congressmen protested, and Operation TIPS quietly closed its Web site and disappeared. But Operation TIPS was the formalization of a system already in place, the Neighborhood Watch Program, whose original anticrime mandate was now expanded: "With the help of the National Sheriffs' Association, the Neighborhood Watch Program will be taking on a new significance. Community residents will be provided with information which will enable them to recognize signs of potential terrorist activity, and to know how to report that activity, making these residents a critical element in the detection, prevention and disruption of terrorism." One alert citizen in Williamsburg, Virginia, John Chwaszczewski, shot at a helicopter as it landed in his neighborhood to pick up a local businessman. "Maybe I overreacted," Mr. Chwaszczewski said.[21] A Federal Express driver working in a Middle Eastern neighborhood in Brooklyn told a reporter: "Whenever I would go to a place where there was a lot of them [Arab Americans], I would tell the landlord, hey, you got nine people living up there or whatever, and they would call the F.B.I. and get them checked out."[22] Raymond Arnold, a field-service representative for a local gas company, made the Cold War connection explicit, recalling his earlier effort on behalf of patriotic observation: "A long time ago, I saw a Communist flag [*sic*] in someone's basement."[23]

After the demise of Operation TIPS, the Department of Defense Advanced Research Project Agency established the Total Information Awareness program (TIA). Some uneasiness about the Orwellian ring of the title led to a cosmetic change shortly after the program was announced; henceforth it was to be known as Terrorism Information Awareness (TIA). Headed by Ronald Reagan's national security adviser and convicted Iran-Contra felon, Admiral John Poindexter,[24] the TIA planned to gather all available public and private electronic records—financial, media, Internet, phone, fax, etc.—into a centralized database in order to discover and then track potential terrorists. Despite the change in name, and also a change in logo,[25] there was growing bipartisan opposition to TIA and a move in Congress to restrict both its scope and its funding. But the greatest blow to Poindexter's plans was self-inflicted. As reported in the press, the admiral had designed an online futures market in terrorism. The Web site, www.policyanalysismarket.org, invited investors to join in a process of "group prediction which should prove engaging and may prove profitable." The Pentagon staunchly defended the plan: "Research indicates that markets are extremely efficient, effective and timely aggregators of dispersed and even hidden information. Futures markets have proven themselves to be good at predicting such things as elections results; they are often better than expert opinion."[26] Few were convinced; shortly after the story broke, Poindexter resigned.

The use the Bush administration has made of September 11 echoes the use the Truman administration made of the North Korean attack against South Korea. The stated goal was to drive the North Koreans out of the South in what was at first an unnamed military effort, later a police action, but never a declared war. Having driven the North Koreans back, Truman went on to make war against North Korea, as Bush, who set out to capture Osama bin Laden "dead or alive," went on to make war on the Taliban and then Iraq. After the Chinese joined the North Koreans, Truman denounced them, at an informal lunch with reporters, as "the inheritors of Genghis Khan and Tamerlane, who were the greatest murderers in world history." Truman explained that Western jurisprudence had "originated with Hammurabi in the Mesopotamian Valley, [was] propounded by Moses and 'elaborated on by Jesus Christ, whose Sermon on the Mount is the best ethical program by which to live.'" Led by the United States, others could join the battle: "I have been trying to mobilize the moral force of the world—Catholics, Protestants, Jews, the eastern church, the Grand Lama of Tibet, the Indian Sanskrit code—I have been trying to organize all these people to the understanding that their welfare and the existence of decency and honor in the world depends on our working together, and not trying to cut each other's throats."[27] The idiom, even the grammar, has a contemporary ring. Then, as now, working together meant working toward a world order defined by the United States. The enemy then, as now, was a vast, amoebic "ism" that could take up residence in any number of surprising places, instantly deterritorializing them.

Out of the ashes of the Korean War and Ground Zero came analogous convictions about the efficacy of force, the fear that compromise or concession signaled weakness, and the irrelevance of the local causes of conflict.

The Korean War enabled the United States to fund the remilitarization of Europe and Japan, create an expanded alliance system, build a chain of military bases that spanned the globe (Japan, South Korea, Taiwan, the Philippines, Thailand, Australia, Diego Garcia, Saudi Arabia, Ethiopia, Turkey, Greece, Italy, Spain, Portugal, Germany, England, Iceland), and establish an ever-expanding nuclear arsenal. Out of September 11 and the war against Iraq, the United States has dismantled an alliance system it declared overly constricting and expanded its chain of military bases into new areas of the world: Iraq, Afghanistan, Uzbekistan, Djibouti, Pakistan, Georgia, Kazakhstan, Bulgaria, Yugoslavia (former), in addition to expanding existing base facilities in Kuwait, Saudi Arabia, and Turkey. The combination effectively embraces the richest areas in the world for oil exploration and development.[28]

Ominously, the administration has pressed for and received funding to renew nuclear weapons research and testing, in disregard of the Comprehensive Test Ban and the Nuclear Non-Proliferation treaties. The Pentagon's Nuclear Posture Review argues for a "new triad" approach to nuclear planning: "New capabilities must be developed to defeat emerging threats such as hard and deeply buried targets, to find and attack mobile and relocatable targets, to defeat chemical or biological agents and to improve accuracy and limit collateral damage." The need for these new weapons is based on "classified intelligence" indicating that more than seventy countries have underground facilities of which "at least 1,100" are thought to be "strategic command centers or weapons bases." The administration is committed to useable nuclear weapons as a means of deterring "smaller countries" from developing nuclear weapons systems. "Under this theory," the *New York Times* reports, "those countries may now believe that the stigma of using a large nuclear weapon against them is so great that the United States would never do so." A "less devastating weapon" would thus be a more credible threat.[29]

Inherent in the Cold War was the possibility it could end through the evolution of the Soviet Union into one of "us." Although the Soviet Union never formally surrendered and several communist states remain at large, much of the American public was persuaded that the United States had won the Cold War, and even that peace, with its expected dividends, had arrived.

But terrorism is a tactic (not an ideology) that the weak will always have available for use against the strong. In the war on terrorism, the administration of the second President Bush may have discovered the model for permanent war in a unipolar world.

## Notes

An earlier version of this essay appeared in Ellen Schrecker, *Cold War Triumphalism: The Misuse of History after the Fall of Communism* (New York: New Press, 2004).

1  More daringly, Hollywood revisited the Vietnam War in the 2002 movie *We Were Soldiers* (dir. Randall Wallace), which portrayed a battlefield victory early in the war that obscured the ultimate defeat. For more on this, see Marilyn B. Young, "In the Combat Zone," *Radical History Review*, no. 85 (2003): 253–64.

2  Paul J. Nyden, "Byrd Challenges Bush's Ideas on War; West Virginia Senator Warns of Another Vietnam," *West Virginia Gazette*, June 29, 2002, www.truthout.com.

3  George H. W. Bush, quoted in Maureen Dowd, "War Introduces a Tougher Bush to the Nation," *New York Times*, March 3, 1991.

4  James LeMoyne, "Pentagon's Strategy for the Press: Good News or No News," *New York Times*, February 17, 1991. The relationship between the press and the military is scathingly caricatured in the movie *Three Kings* (dir. David O. Russell, 1999).

5  Anthony Swofford, *Jarhead: A Marine's Chronicle of the Gulf War and Other Battles* (New York: Scribners, 2003), 14–15.

6  Felicity Barringer, "'Reality TV' About GIs on War Duty," *New York Times*, February 21, 2002.

7  Ibid.

8  See Andrew J. Bacevich, *The American Empire* (Cambridge, MA: Harvard University Press, 2002), 92; see 181-95 for a succinct critique of U.S. policy in Kosovo.

9  Wolfgang Schivelbusch, "The Loneliest Victors," *New York Times*, April 22, 2003. In his book on the culture of defeat, Schivelbusch asks whether "America's post–September 11 war fever is really a response to an earlier and unresolved defeat." His alternative suggestion is not much more comforting: "Could it be that the decades of relative American peacefulness and readiness to cooperate that followed the defeat in Vietnam were merely an interim period, akin to the Weimar Republic?" *The Culture of Defeat: On National Trauma, Mourning, and Recovery*, trans. Jefferson Chase (New York: Metropolitan Books, 2003), 294.

10  John Dower, *Embracing Defeat: Japan in the Wake of World War II* (New York: W. W. Norton, 1999), 40–41.

11  See John Prados's analysis of the speech on www.tompaine.com, May 2, 2003.

12  For a transcript of Bush's speech, see www.americanrhetoric.com/wariniraq/gwbushiraq5103.htm.

13  Paul G. Pierpaoli, Jr., *Truman and Korea: The Political Culture of the Early Cold War* (Columbia: University of Missouri Press, 1999), 29.

14  Eliot Cohen, "This is World War IV," *Wall Street Journal*, November 20, 2001. In an interview Cohen said he used the phrase *World War IV* "tongue-in-cheek as a way of getting people to think about the current conflict as something bigger than the Afghanistan war." See Stephen Goode, "The Character of Wartime Statesmen," www.insightmag.com, May 27, 2003.

15  Norman Podhoretz, "How to Win World War IV," *Commentary* 11 (2002): 19–29; Charles Feldman, Stan Wilson, CNN, "Ex-CIA Director: U.S. Faces 'World War IV,'" April 3, 2003, www.cnn.com.

16  George W. Bush, address to Joint Session of Congress, September 20, 2001, www .whitehouse.gov/news/releases/2001/09/.

17  David Lightman, "Lieberman's Foreign Policy: Propagate U.S. Values," *Hartford Courant* online service, www.ctnow.com/about/hc-archives.htmlstory, January 14, 2002.

18  Jim Rutenberg, "Hollywood Seeks Role in the War," *New York Times*, October 20, 2001.

19  Provisions include indefinite detention of noncitizens for minor visa violations, reduced judicial supervision of telephone and Internet communication, granting to the attorney general and secretary of state the power to label domestic groups terrorist organizations and deport noncitizen members. In general, the act "significantly boosted the government's law enforcement powers while continuing a trend to cut back on the checks and balances that Americans have traditionally relied on to protect individual liberty." See "USA Patriot Act Boosts Government Powers," www.aclu.org.

20  See Andy Newman, "Citizen Snoops Wanted (Call Toll-Free)," *New York Times*, July 21, 2002. See also www.citizencorps.gov. Protest against Operation TIPS has been vigorous. "Ashcroft's informant corps is a vile idea. . . . Operation TIPS should be stopped because it is utterly anti-American. It would give Stalin and the KGB a delayed triumph in the Cold War." Editorial, *Boston Globe*, July 17, 2002.

21  Associated Press, "Citing Fear, Man Shoots at Helicopter," *New York Times*, July 21, 2002.

22  Newman, "Citizen Snoops Wanted."

23  Ibid. In New York, a plane carrying an Indian movie star and her family to the city for a tour was accompanied to La Guardia Airport by fighter jets and the family was detained after passengers reported their "suspicious behavior" to the airline stewards. Apparently family competition for the window seat frightened their fellow passengers. Lydia Polgreen, "Bollywood Farce: Indian Actress and Family are Detained," *New York Times*, July 18, 2002.

24  He was later acquitted on a technicality.

25  From an omniscient eye, atop a pyramid, scanning an illuminated globe to a circle combined with an inverted Nike sneaker swoosh.

26  Carl Hulse, "Pentagon Prepares a Futures Market on Terror Attacks," *New York Times*, July 29, 2003. The focus of trade would be on the "civil and military futures of Egypt, Jordan, Iran, Iraq, Israel, Saudi Arabia, Syria and Turkey." A congressman who had learned about

the scheme explained how it worked: "You may think that Prime Minister X is going to be assassinated. So you buy the futures contracts for 5 cents each. As more people begin to think the person's going to be assassinated, the cost of the contract could go up, to 50 cents. The payoff if he's assassinated is $1 per future." In a letter to Poindexter protesting the scheme, two senators pointed out that the scheme would appear "to encourage terrorists to participate, either to profit from their terrorist activities or to bet against them in order to mislead U.S. intelligence authorities."

27  Paul R. Kennedy, "Truman Calls Reds Present-Day Heirs of Mongol Killers," *New York Times*, December 24, 1950. Wordier than President Bush, Truman drew the line of global division as sharply: "Those people who believe in ethics, morals and right associate themselves together to meet those who do not believe in ethics, morals and right, who have no idea of honor or truth."

28  See Paul Rogers, "Permanent Occupation?" www.opendemocracy.net, April 24, 2003. Rogers writes that the combination of new and old bases marks a "major military investment in . . . the Persian Gulf and Central Asia . . . that are the primary and secondary regions of the world for new oil exploration and development."

29  All quotations in this paragraph are from Carl Hulse and James Dao, "Cold War Long Over, Bush Administration Examines Steps to a Revamped Arsenal," *New York Times*, May 29, 2003. The House of Representatives removed bans on research into "smaller" nuclear weapons, provided funding for the development of "turning existing nuclear warheads into weapons capable of piercing underground bunkers," paved the way for renewed underground testing, and provided funds for research into "'advanced' concepts."

**This Is a True Story**

Carel Moiseiwitsch

*positions* 13:1 © 2005 by Duke University Press

## THIS IS A TRUE STORY
(NOT SUITABLE FOR CHILDREN)

NOT SO LONG AGO IN A LAND CALLED PALESTINE
THERE LIVED AN OLD MAN CALLED ABU KHALID.
HE HAD AN OLD GREY DONKEY CALLED HILWEH
(WHICH MEANS SWEET IN ARABIC) WHO WORKED
WITH HIM EVERY DAY IN THE OLIVE GROVES.

١

EACH MORNING AS THE SUN ROSE
ABU KHALID AND HILWEH THE DONKEY
COULD BE SEEN WALKING SLOWLY UP
THE SIDE OF THE HILL TO THE OLD STONE
TERRACES WHERE THE OLIVE TREES GREW.
TREES THAT HAD BEEN CARED FOR BY
ABU KHALID'S FAMILY FOR COUNTLESS
GENERATIONS

٢

ABU KHALID WOULD TALK TO HILWEH ALL THE TIME. THEY WERE VERY GOOD FRIENDS, THEY WERE WORK BUDDIES. "YA HILWEH, LET'S GO!" ABU KHALID WOULD SAY, AND HILWEH WOULD WIGGLE HER BIG FURRY EARS.
THEY UNDERSTOOD EACH OTHER PERFECTLY.

ON THIS PARTICULAR DAY, THE SUN WAS RISING OVER THE TOPS OF THE GNARLED OLIVE TREES. THE BIRDS WERE SINGING AND RED POPPIES DANCED IN THE GREEN GRASS.

ABU KHALID WAS TELLING HILWEH
THAT THEY WERE GOING TO WALK INTO
NABLUS AFTER THEY HAD FINISHED
MENDING A BROKEN BIT OF STONE TERRACE

IN THE KASBAH OF THE OLD CITY OF NABLUS
ABU KHALID WOULD SIT IN A CAFÉ, DRINK TINY
CUPS OF SWEET COFFEE, SMOKE A NERGILA
PIPE AND TALK TO HIS FRIEND MUSTAPHA
WHO OWNED THE CAFÉ.

ABU KHALID AND HILWEH WERE TAKING MUSTAPHA A BOTTLE OF THE FINEST OLIVE OIL FROM LAST YEARS OLIVE HARVEST

JUST AS ABU KHALID WAS TALKING ABOUT THIS AND HILWEH'S EARS WERE WIGGLING IN ANTICIPATION OF THE SOUK WITH IT'S LOVELY SMELLS AND EXCITING TASTES - - - - - - - - - - - -

..... THE TWO CAME TO A HALT. IN FRONT OF
THEM THE RED EARTH HAD BEEN PILED UP
ACROSS THE ROAD. THREE SOLDIERS AND A HUGE
BULLDOZER THE SIZE OF MUSTAPHA'S CAFÉ
STOOD BESIDE THE ROAD BLOCK.

\|.

"STOP! WHAT ARE YOU DOING HERE?"
ONE OF THE SOLDIERS SAID POINTING HIS GUN
AT THE 2 FRIENDS.

"WE ARE GOING TO WORK IN THE OLIVE GROVES"
EXPLAINED ABU KHALID
"AND WHEN WE ARE FINISHED WE WILL GO TO
NABLUS TO TAKE SOME OLIVE OIL TO A FRIEND."
"GIVE ME THE OIL" SAID THE SOLDIER
"YOU ARE NOT ALLOWED TO TAKE IT TO NABLUS!"

\|\|

"BUT IT'S SUCH A SMALL AMOUNT"
PROTESTED ABU KHALID
"AND IT'S A GIFT FOR A FRIEND"

"NEVER MIND" SAID THE SOLDIER
AND HE TOOK THE BOTTLE OF OLIVE OIL OUT
OF THE PANNIER ON HILWEH'S BACK
AND THREW IT ONTO THE GROUND,
THE GLASS SMASHED ON THE STONES
AND THE OIL SEEPED ONTO THE RED EARTH.

HILWEH TURNED AND LOOKED AT
ABU KHALID, SHE TOOK A STEP TOWARDS
HIM, KNOWING HER FRIEND WOULD BE UPSET.

"MOVE BACK!" SCREAMED THE SOLDIER AT HER
"NO DONKEYS ARE ALLOWED HERE!"

"BUT WE WORK TOGETHER IN THE OLIVE GROVES"
SAID ABU KHALID, TRYING TO CALM THE SOLDIER
DOWN.

"YOU HAVE A CHOICE" THE SOLDIER REPLIED,
POINTING HIS GUN AND KICKING A STONE.

١٤

"WE CAN EITHER SHOOT THE DONKEY
OR CRUSH IT WITH A BULLDOZER"

ABU KHALID WAS SO SHOCKED
HE SAT DOWN UNABLE TO SPEAK.

10

HILWEH WALKED OVER TO HIM AND PUT HER
ROUGH FURRY FACE AGAINST ABU KHALID'S
                            WET CHEEK.
THE SOLDIER SCREAMED AGAIN
"DON'T MOVE! I TOLD YOU NOT TO MOVE!"
BUT HILWEH CONTINUED TO TRY AND
COMFORT HER WEEPING FRIEND.

17

A LOUD BANG ECHOED THROUGH THE
OLIVE GROVE AND HILWEH FELL TO THE
GROUND, A GAPING WOUND IN HER NECK
SPILLING HER RED BLOOD ALL OVER
                             THE ROAD.

IV

THE SOLDIERS LAUGHED AT THE SIGHT
OF THE OLD MAN HOLDING HIS DYING DONKEY,
THEY CLIMBED INTO THEIR HUGE BULLDOZER
AND DROVE AWAY.

18

ABU KHALID STAYED WITH HILWEH
UNTIL SHE DIED. THEN HE WALKED SLOWLY
HOME.
HE HAS NEVER RETURNED TO HIS BELOVED
OLIVE GROVES TO THIS DAY.

19

# After the Invasion of Iraq

Claudia Pozzana and Alessandro Russo

With the occupation of Iraq by the American and British armies, a completely new stage has been reached in international relations and in individual states' internal relationships; it is dominated by powerful destructive forces disintegrating civil functions within the states and by hypertrophic military functions. Both the sphere of politics and the state gravely risk being governed by an ever-growing warmongering tendency. The wars in Afghanistan and Iraq have shown that the American government is capable of deploying an immense destructive power without any principle of moderation, either internal or external, and that this will be the general pattern of its strategy for a long time to come. Due to a series of historical circumstances, which should be considered attentively, a technical-military elite without rivals has concentrated in the United States and has convinced the U.S. government that it can act exclusively on the basis of pure, uncontested power.

*positions* 13:1 © 2005 by Duke University Press

In reality, no unconditional power does exist: everything can be transformed into its contrary, and all pretence to omnipotence has its equivalent in absolute impotence.[1] However, if this tendency continues to be uncontested, in the next few years U.S. strategy will be a succession of military campaigns to deploy its power without any specific aim except that very same deployment. At present—notwithstanding every explicitly or implicitly declared aim, such as exporting democracy or controlling sources of energy—the deployment of American military power is not a means to obtain specific ends, but rather an end in itself. In other words, for the U.S. administration, war is not a means to impose a peace but a means to produce more war.

The gravity of the situation requires efforts for new thinking, both in analytical skills and in modes and forms of political organization, capable of confronting the dominant tendency, of circumscribing it, and, in the end, of completely transforming it. This work needs to be seen as a long-term task, with a political vision solid in principles and capable of grasping the singularity of each situation.

## The Extremism and Adventurism of the U.S. Government

The main objectives of the Iraq war have been not only the elimination of an unruly ex-vassal—let all vassals beware of how easy this is—but also the total destruction of the Iraqi state apparatus and the installation of a regime of foreign military domination, which, with regard to its brutality, competes with the worst colonial traditions. The destructive rage against the life of the common people (their markets and housing) and against symbols of the state's civil functions (its museums and hospitals) has been infinitely greater than the rage directed against the military threat that Iraq supposedly posed, at least according to the bellicose propaganda of the invaders.[2]

The war against Iraq achieves the deregulation of the interstate international relationships established after World War II, which had become more and more precarious since the end of the 1980s. Principles such as the self-determination of peoples or nonintervention in the internal affairs of other states had already been trampled down by the wars of the 1990s—especially the "humanitarian" war against Serbia—and are now being annihilated by the deployment of the pure power of the U.S. military apparatus. Democracy, prostituted at the service of this destructive aggression, now signifies the decomposition of contemporary statehood. The winner can even promise reprisals against those who have obstructed its plans and threaten those who it thinks might not agree with it in the future.

Today, interstate relations are dominated by the fear created by American military power and by the determination proclaimed by the U.S. government with impunity to use this power against whomsoever it decides is its enemy without any justification outside its own decision. In this situation, any connivance with the military occupation—whether to provide humanitarian aid or peacekeeping, or to secure business advantages and oil profits—endorses the extremist and adventurist strategy of the Bush administration. The alleged astuteness of agreeing with it in order to influence it and to moderate its successive moves is both illusory and ruinous. Those who today are vassals of the unlimited American war sooner or later risk suffering the same destruction that is being inflicted today on the state of Iraq.

## Who Is the Real Target of the Unlimited American War?

The document on national security strategy published by the U.S. government in September 2002 proclaims unlimited deployment of its military power as a guide for the state's action but is unable to openly identify its real and true antagonist. This is not because the declared enemy, terrorism, is by nature both ubiquitous and evasive, but because it constitutes an occasional and, finally, inessential enemy.

Since September 11, 2001, in its propaganda the American government has portrayed its action as a response to the criminal attacks on the twin towers of the World Trade Center; however, it is clear that it is pursuing a plan that in no way addresses either the punishment of the authors of that crime or the prevention of similar terrorist activities. Neither the war against Afghanistan nor that against Iraq has any connection with September 11, but both are the result of the plan that the current U.S. power elite (those of the sinister Project for a New American Century) has fully elaborated for over a decade and that has now met the conditions to be implemented.

Such a plan contains a fundamental strategic change. In contrast to previous American military imperialism, whose objective was to extend the influence of the U.S. state and economic model, in opposition to the Soviet one, and to construct subaltern forms of dependent statehood, the present American military intervention has qualitatively new characteristics. It aims to destroy any cohesiveness of the state and to replace it with a combination of direct military occupation and economic corruption. As the philosopher Alain Badiou has recently argued in a lecture at the University of Bologna,[3] the objective of the American military intervention is to create plebeian masses everywhere deprived of any capacity of collective cohesion.[4]

It could be argued that the aim of American military interventionism is the dislocation and disarticulation of the state's civil functions and that the present military campaigns are only the first steps in a plan to fully militarize the state. Actually, considering that the American war is not a means but rather an end in itself, an essential obstacle to the integral deployment of military power is constituted, in the very same field of statehood, by its civil functions. In the modern era, such civil functions fundamentally include the potentialities and the institutional capacities of the state to act and intervene in order to limit inequalities and, by taking this route, resolve the conflicts generated by them, in a pacific manner. In this sense, the strategy of pure power is above all addressed against the civil functions of statehood in general and includes the civil functions of statehood in the U.S., well known to be the object of a frontal attack by the Bush administration. In fact, this administration's objective is to create plebeian masses everywhere, above all in its own country. If it proceeds uncontested, the strategy of pure power will have disruptive effects on American society: the immense civil potentialities will more and more be suffocated, and the country will be pushed toward an unprecedented social and spiritual crisis.

Inevitably, the strategy of pure power will meet obstacles in various regions of the world and will therefore extend well beyond the areas affected by the present American military campaigns. Although the civil functions of statehood, in the sense specified above, have experienced a profound crisis at least since the 1980s, they nonetheless remain operative in vast areas of the world, including Europe and China. The very permanence of these functions makes it inevitable that these regions will be viewed with hostility by U.S.

pure power, which will sooner or later try to exploit every weakness of those states in order to carry out warmongering and disruptive plans against them.

## Two Converging Historical Conditions in the Present Military Conjuncture

The compulsion of the U.S. administration to act exclusively in the name of pure power is the result of two converging historical conditions, both related to the formations of statehood in the twentieth century. One condition has been the fall of the Soviet Union, which left in the U.S. government's hands a military power without any moderating mechanism. The other condition, much less evident, is the crisis of parties as specific constituent apparatuses in twentieth-century forms of statehood.

### The End of the Cold War

With regard to U.S. military power, the existence of two camps of statehood—socialist and capitalist—constituted, both externally and internally, a civil and military mechanism of moderation. The Cold War was not only the military opposition between the two most powerful armed forces in the world but also the opposition of two forms of statehood. Above all, the two vied for world primacy of their civil functions while increasing their military capabilities, making them both efficient and clearly visible.

Beyond the enormous ambiguity this produced and the encompassing glow of empty propaganda issued by both sides, the opposition brought an intrinsically civil element that ultimately concerned the question of which of the two systems was better equipped to bring about egalitarian conditions. On this level, the reciprocal accusations were, in fact, that in the opposite camp equality was not real but merely a simulacrum. The capitalists claimed socialist equality was purely bureaucratic and left out freedom and democracy. The socialists argued that bourgeois equality was a purely formal equality that masked the substantial inequalities of capitalist exploitation.

The main reason the military conflict between the two fronts remained only potential and confined to a series of localized wars was that interstate relationships contained an element of civil opposition—and, in the last analysis, properly political opposition—and so were not exclusively military. Usually cited as the principal factor of the relatively pacific situation in the decades following World War II, the so-called equilibrium of terror, reciprocal nuclear blackmail—in brief, the simple balance of military power, without any civil and political opposition—by itself not only could not have prevented a frontal battle between the two sides but also inevitably would have produced a bellicose outcome worldwide.[5]

During the Cold War, American military power was therefore subject to a double element of limitation, civil and military, internal and external. In other words, at the military level there was an opposing power, which prevented the deployment of a strategy of pure power by the United States, and this constituted an external factor of moderation. But this also translated into a factor of internal moderation because the actions of the U.S. government had to include interventions to limit inequalities—i.e., it had to promote the civil functions of the state—in order to prove its own superiority to the Soviet model. This produced infinite ambiguities and contradictions, but it led to an internal restriction on American militarism. Let us think of figures like Kennedy and Johnson, oscillating between the most obtuse military adventurism in Vietnam and a series of specific policies (such as the war on poverty and affirmative action) for reducing inequalities, for example, black poverty.

## The End of the Party-State

Far more opaque is the other historical condition of the present military conjuncture: it concerns the crisis of parties as state apparatuses. This crisis is strictly connected to the fall of the Soviet system, and the connection needs to be investigated fully, bearing in mind that the three state forms of the twentieth century—parliamentary, nazi-fascist, and socialist—have all formed, albeit in different modes, specific institutional apparatuses internal to the state or, in other terms, the party-state. In the parliamentary case, there were two or more parties, while in the case of fascism and of socialism, there was only one party. There are certainly fundamental differences among these three state forms, which it would be absurd to deny, but it can be seen that throughout the twentieth century, the party apparatuses were essential because they carried out peculiar functions in moderating the ritual-militaristic nature of the state. In other words, whereas the state, left to its own objective law, retains custody of social hierarchies on the basis of its military monopoly of violence, the party-state system has provided an element of subjective limitation because it maintains, within the ambit of state action, the possibility of creating policies to reduce social inequalities. These policies have, in turn, limited the intrinsic spontaneous militaristic and ritualistic inclinations of the state itself.[6]

For now, all these questions are only the titles of recently initiated but absolutely indispensable research.[7] The end of the party-state marks the closure of these egalitarian possibilities, and what is replacing this exhaustion urgently needs to be identified. The crisis of the Soviet-type party-state appears to be the most evident (even if the destiny of China's party-state remains unknown), but equally grave is the pathology of the parliamentary system.

In Italy, upon the general breakup of the party system, an alliance of adventurer businessmen has emerged alongside a fringe of fascists and racists (whose planned objective is the collapse of the state and the secession of several regions). In France, the plebiscite for the election of Jacques Chirac, with a majority that once would have been said to be typical of socialist countries, is a sign of instability and marks the end of the previous party system. In almost complete parallel, the American election was resolved with a travesty of the legal system, revealing an extremely serious institutional fragility, the consequence of which has been almost complete parliamentary unanimity on the military operations proposed by the Bush administration. In England, the decomposition of the distinctions between the parliamentary parties is represented by the figure of the present prime minister himself.

The United States, because of its very preeminence, embodies in concentrated form the terms of this crisis: the maximum of military power accompanied by the maximum of political impotence. The Bush administration possesses destructive capabilities infinitely greater than any other state in history but cannot rely on any moderating principle, either internally or externally: its war has no peace. In the long run, a strategy of pure power, if uncontested, will lead to the self-destruction of the state and society in the United States. On a global scale, it is equally predictable that besides producing grave spiritual and material destruction, this will further aggravate the crisis facing the civil functions of statehood, both in international relations and within individual countries.

In this respect, the Italian case is exemplary, and it can be said that it anticipated the general tendency by more than a decade. This immediately manifested itself in the first great crisis of the parliamentary system after the fall of the Soviet Union, with the parallel undoing of the Italian Communist Party and the Christian Democrats. Present conjuncture in Italy shows that the bureaucratic struggle for state power favors those who aim at the dissolution of the civil functions of the state and treat the parliamentary residuals from the previous era with disdain and cynicism. However, those who aim at gaining or maintaining positions in the terms of a parliamentary party-state are penalized.

## What Is to Be Done?

The breakup of the party-state initiates a radical crisis that urgently demands an intervention of new ideas and new forms of political experimentation. The movements that for a few months in Italy created belief in a reawakening of the horizon of politics today reveal all its intrinsic weaknesses. Many cherished notions of regenerating the parties of the left from the bottom up, and even of conditioning Italian foreign policy on the basis of a pacifistic requirement, have been exposed as illusory under these political circumstances. Despite the fact that millions of people mobilized themselves with great conviction to demonstrate against the war, the rainbow flags that today fade ever more away on balconies throughout Italy are a testimony to failure.

Notwithstanding the enthusiasm and the personal generosity of those who have participated, the depth of thought has been nowhere near sufficient to deal with the grave crisis affecting the parliamentary system. Equally insufficient in the face of the nature of this war has been the pacifist vision, even if justly animated by indignation. Today, the foreign policy of Italy has become blindly subaltern to the militarism of the United States. The parties that should have been regenerated by the movements have approved the Italian military involvement in the occupation of Iraq (of course, as a "peace force"), as had already been the case in Afghanistan.

Reflection on these failures is necessary because there is a risk that they will be translated into fatalism. To avoid transforming the subjective energies that manifested themselves in recent months into their contrary, i.e., into a further annihilation of politics in Italy, it is urgent to reinvent places, forms, and modes of politics.

The idea that a right and left dialectics still exists, which will sooner or later rehabilitate the civil functions of the party-state, is not only illusory but also damaging. It is necessary to invent new places for politics, at a distance from the parliament, that are capable of independently analyzing the conjuncture; to publicly state and argue new political prescriptions; and to find a civil solution for today's crisis in statehood. It is indispensable that a new vision of equality be elaborated in order to prescribe the functions of statehood with new ways of reducing inequalities. Finally, an essential prerequisite of new political places must be their multiplicity. To use an ancient Chinese saying, let us hope that one hundred flowers bloom and one hundred schools contend.

## Notes

This essay was written in Italian in 2003 and was published as an open letter in *Note per un club politico indipendente* (*Notes for a Political Independent Club*), No. 2, May 2003. It was translated into English by the authors.

1 This is like what occurs in the psychic condition of earliest infancy. All the same, the psychoanalytical analogy is strictly limited to the structure of paranoid delirium, which is implied by every subjective proclamation of omnipotence, and to its inevitable destructive and self-destructive consequences. One would be tempted to compare the behavior of the American administration to the delirious form of massacre perpetrated by the two teenagers in Columbine (the documentary film *Bowling for Columbine* is a meditation on this topic) or to the homicide-suicide of the colonel at the end of the film *American Beauty*. However, the question is evidently much graver and goes beyond forms of private criminality. In fact, both the destiny of the United States and that of the forms of modern statehood are at stake.

2 The ransacking of the museum in Baghdad, carried out with the full connivance of the Anglo-American occupants in order to humiliate the Iraqis, has the same signs of barbaric colonialism as that perpetrated in China in 1860 by Anglo-French troops who destroyed the splendid imperial residence of the Yuanmingyuan, in the outskirts of Peking, in the course of a war undertaken by the colonial powers to secure the freedom to export opium to China.

3   Alain Badiou, "La philosophie peut-elle dire quelque chose de la guerre?" ("Can Philosophy Say Something about War?") (lecture presented at Bologna University, Bologna, April 15, 2003).

4   The existence of warlords in Afghanistan supposedly allied with the American army (the celebrated Northern Alliance) forms the model for the subjugation of local populations through armed gangs of unscrupulous predators. The same model was applied in the early days of the occupation of Baghdad, with the protection of the gangs of raiders provided by the American army. These episodes, far from being collateral effects of the occupation—or even the "first step in the reconquest of liberty," as one American general had the impudence to say—are all consequences of the destructive American strategy toward every civil organization.

5   It must be remembered that the decisive role of containing these warmongering tendencies was carried out by the internal and external politics of China, from its creation of a nonaligned front to its criticism of Soviet social imperialism, and ending with its mediation with the United States in the early 1970s to find a solution to the war in Vietnam.

6   In this sense, the Fascist and Nazi parties were a very weak factor of limitation: they were quickly reabsorbed into the ritual-militaristic functions and ruined.

7   The theses of Sylvain Lazarus should be mentioned, particularly those in the recent *Les trois régimes du siècle* (*The Three Regimes of the Century*) (paper presented at "Les conferences du rouge gorges," held at the Maison des ecrivains, Paris, 2002), which we refer to in order to extend the category of party-state to the entire statehood of the twentieth century.

As for the question of the ritual military nature of the state, we would propose the following path of reflection. Unlike what was believed in the past, the most radical political issue concerning the state, is not how "to extinguish" it, but how, by means of political invention, to limit its inborn, and finally disastrous, compulsion to act exclusively in terms of the monopoly of violence and of the general supervision to ritual hierarchies.

The state in itself is a structurally apolitical entity that has no independent rationality. Only a political rationality decentralized with respect to the state can deal with its objectivity—by itself purely destructive—and transform it into a positive field, restricted but real, of subjective possibilities. In the modern era, such political rationality has equality as its decisive issue. Only by prescribing inventive policies of systematic reduction of social inequalities is it possible to govern and to limit the congenital ritual-military nature of the state, and to value instead its possible technical-administrative capacities in favor of the deployment of the infinite individual potentialities.

The current crisis of the state, resulting from the exhaustion of the previous forms of possible application of egalitarian politics to the state, is in fact manifested both by the hypertrophy of its military and repressive functions and apparatuses, and by the parallel demolition of its civil capacities as well as by their subordination to the hierarchical rituals. The "market," to which, according to the present dominant ideologies, any possible civil egalitarian function of the state should be transferred, far from playing an economical role, is invoked as a guarantee of rituals of the social hierarchy.

# Philippine Wars and the Politics of Memory

Reynaldo C. Ileto

When Anglo-American forces invaded Iraq last year, my immediate reaction was one of déjà vu. It was the Philippines circa 1900 all over again. Of course, many commentators in the United States and the Philippines have been making comparisons between the wars in Iraq and the Philippines, albeit in contrasting ways. Among them is President George W. Bush himself, who evoked the Filipino-American past in his speech last October to the Philippine Congress. "America," he declared, "is proud of its part in the great story of the Filipino people. Together, our soldiers liberated the Philippines from colonial rule. Together, we rescued the islands from invasion and occupation. The names of Bataan, Corregidor, Leyte, Luzon evoke the memories of shared struggle and shared loss and shared victory. Veterans of those battles are here today. I salute your courage and your service."[1]

In other words, America's part in the "great story" of the Filipino people was its participation in the Filipino struggle for liberation. The lesson Bush

*positions* 13:1 © 2005 by Duke University Press

hammered into the heads of his seemingly enthusiastic audience of Filipino lawmakers was that the very existence of their nation-state today is due to the shared Filipino-American struggle against past tyrants and oppressors.

Bush's speech was filled with allusions to war, since his ultimate aim was to secure Filipino participation in the "great war" against terror. A shared history of wars, he argued, makes it natural for Filipinos and Americans to conduct a "joint struggle" today against the forces of totalitarianism and other evils represented by Saddam's Iraq and the terrorists in the southern Philippines. Ironically, however, there was a phase in the Filipino-American relationship when the Filipinos were themselves the distinct object of a preemptive attack and occupation by American forces. The image of a joint struggle, therefore, rests uncomfortably on the historical residues of a conflict that the U.S. colonial state, and to some extent its Filipino offspring, have sought to expunge from the collective memory.

In order to hook the present war into Filipino historical experience, Bush had to move back in time to the first of the Philippines' great wars and reassert the contours of the official narrative leading to the present. He began with a tribute to José Rizal's teachings, paraphrasing Rizal's message that "nations win their freedom by deserving it, by loving what is just, what is good, what is great, to the point of dying for it." This was, of course, demonstrated by Rizal's heroic death during the war against Spain. Bush therefore began with a tribute to "the great patriot, Jose Rizal, [who] said that nations win their freedom by deserving it, by loving what is just, what is good, what is great to the point of dying for it."

Punctuated by applause all around, Bush's speech alluded to three wars that have cemented the common history of the United States and the Philippines. As a professional historian, however, I seem to count not three but five wars in this shared history. So what are these five past wars that maintain their ghostly presence over the nation and the Filipino-American relationship to this day? Permit me to review some key events in modern Philippine history. Sometimes we neglect the basic events and narratives that have dominated the discourses of political leaders and their audiences at critical junctures in the life of a nation. Among them, we can single out narratives of wars for their ability to organize memory and experience in socially comprehensible terms. The present war on terror, with its inbuilt justification of preemptive strikes, is built on a narrative of past wars that we need to scrutinize thoroughly and reconstitute, if the phrase "learn from the past" is to retain any value for future generations.

The first of our Philippine wars was the war of independence from Spain—a very memorable event acknowledged by Bush himself. We all know the story: It began in 1896 when the Katipunan secret society mounted a rebellion against the Spanish authorities in the outskirts of Manila. As the Katipunan grew, this rebellion turned into a major war between a Filipino separatist movement and the government of imperial Spain. A truce was worked out in 1897, however, and Emilio Aguinaldo and his fellow nationalists went into exile in Hong Kong.

In mid-1898, Aguinaldo returned to the islands with U.S. assistance, reorganized his army, and vanquished the Spanish garrisons in Luzon. The republican government he formed, however, was refused recognition by his erstwhile ally, which proceeded to destroy it in 1899. This event, called the Philippine Insurrection then and the Filipino-American War now, is the second great war in Philippine history. It led to the deaths of between 250,000 and 600,000 Filipinos in battle as well as the collateral effects of war. It lasted much longer than the Americans had anticipated, and only officially ended with the U.S. proclamation of victory on July 4, 1902.

Unfortunately, in Bush's speech last October, this second great war was overlooked, and most of our lawmakers, judging from their frenzied applause, seemed to have forgotten it as well. Not surprisingly, though, for when the Americans administered the Philippines from 1902 on, they made sure that this war would become largely a forgotten event. During the forty years of American rule of the islands, educated Filipinos were brought up to think that the future of their country lay in a special, permanent relationship with the United States untarnished by memories of an original war (here used in the same sense as original sin).

The cozy Filipino-American relationship, however, was put to the test when the Japanese army arrived in the Philippines in December 1941 and attempted to purge the country of American influence. So we come to the third great war in Filipino memory, the war with Japan from 1942 to 1945. This consisted of a joint effort by Filipinos and Americans to resist Japanese occupation. This is what Bush considered the high point of America's participation in Philippine history.

In 1947, not long after the war with Japan ended, a rebellion by the Huks, a peasant army in Luzon led by the Communist Party, erupted. The war against the Huks and other movements led by the radical left was part of the global Cold War. This is the fourth great war in the shared Filipino-American history. Bush doesn't call it the Cold War, but this war was present in his speech in many ways—in his allusions to free enterprise, free nations, free Iraq, the protection of religious liberty, and the triumph of democracy over totalitarianism.

So here we have three great wars mentioned in Bush's speech, plus one that he pointedly omitted. If the three wars in Bush's reckoning have made the Philippine nation what it is today, what difference would it make if a fourth war, the Filipino-American War, were factored in? My answer is probably too simple and naive: one cannot build a strong nation on a narrative that is flawed. Many have said this before me: we cannot indefinitely pretend that the second great war—the Filipino-American War—never happened. A national narrative without this crucial event makes us merely an appendage of empire. Bush's speech and the vigorous applause from our senators and congressmen could only have happened because for over a century the memories of our past wars have been shaped by politics. Let me now take a closer look at those wars and the politics of memory surrounding them.

War number one—the war against Spain—is deeply etched in the collective memory. In fact, this war, which is called the Revolution of 1896 in Filipino textbooks, is recognized as the foundational event in the life of the nation-state. Without a collective memory of the first war, the present nation-state would have no meaning to its citizens.

This war is foundational because it was the first time that the term *Filipino* was used to refer to the inhabitants of the islands—not just the Spaniards living there but also, and most importantly, the indigenous peoples. Furthermore, the notion of a Filipino identity was given political form in the sovereign republic of 1898.

Appropriately, Filipino writers have called the intellectuals and military leaders who led the separatist war against Spain "the first Filipinos." Most of the country's national heroes stem from this first war: José Rizal, Apolinario

Mabini, Andres Bonifacio, and Emilio Aguinaldo. They are remembered through their inscription in textbooks as the founding fathers of the nation. To facilitate remembering them, monuments have been built to commemorate their deeds; statues of Rizal, for example are found not just in the Philippines but also in such far-flung places as Honolulu, Madrid, Heidelberg, and Seattle. The birthdays of the heroes of 1896 have been declared national holidays; their images are inscribed on postage stamps, billboards, magazine covers, and town halls.

This is fine, except that another set of heroes has been sidelined in the process, for the way that the collective memory of the war against Spain was shaped during the twentieth century can only be understood in relation to the Filipino-American War that followed it. The first and second wars are closely intertwined, yet the first is remembered while the second is largely forgotten.

The United States became implicated in the first war when it declared war against Spain in May 1898, in what is called the Spanish-American War. Much as the anticommunist Islamic groups such as the Taliban were nurtured to fight America's war against the Soviets in the Middle East, so were the Filipino nationalist exiles in Hong Kong and Singapore invited to be America's allies in this other war against Spain. Commodore George Dewey, commander of the U.S. Navy's Asiatic fleet, helped the Filipino separatists in two ways: first, by destroying the Spanish fleet in Manila Bay, and second, by bringing Aguinaldo back to the Philippines so that he could resume the first war, or revolution against Spain.

In effect, Filipinos won the war of independence from Spain with American help. I expected George Bush to mention this in his speech, but he didn't. When he spoke of Americans liberating the Filipinos from tyranny, he was referring instead to General Douglas MacArthur's return in 1945. Why did Bush avoid mentioning the U.S. role in the 1898 liberation of the Philippines? My feeling is that this would have forced him to bring the Filipino-American War into the picture, and this would have caused some complications for his image of a shared Filipino-American past and destiny.

The Americans were indeed welcomed in mid-1898 as the liberators of the Philippines from the tyranny of Spanish rule. One of Aguinaldo's manifestos states this explicitly: "Wherever you see the American flag, bear in mind that they are our redeemers."[2] And why not? Both the Filipino and the American governments in late 1898 depicted the Spanish colonial past as a dark age. After the victory over Spain, Filipinos hoped that their nation-state would be recognized by the Americans, who, after all, had won their independence from the British not that long ago.

The liberators, however, had other ideas about what to do with the Filipinos. By the 1890s, the United States had recovered fully from its bloody Civil War; its westward expansion across the continent was complete, and so it was keen to join the family of imperial powers consisting of Britain, France, the Netherlands, and others. The Pacific was its zone of expansion, and the Philippine islands were to be its stepping stone—in the form of naval coaling stations and military bases—to the establishment of trade and influence in the Asiatic mainland. There were also profits to be made in the exploitation of Philippine agricultural and mineral resources—not quite oil yet, but other similarly desired substances. The United States wanted, therefore, to wrest control of the Philippines from tyrannical Spain and to keep it for economic and strategic reasons. No leap of the imagination is required to discern the parallels with the vision of a free Iraq serving as a strategic foothold in an oil-rich but hostile environment.

Bush could not mention war number two (the Filipino-American War) because, I suspect, this might have led to disturbing parallels between the Philippines and Iraq after their liberation. In the case of the Philippines, the war of resistance against the United States began in February 1899 when American troops crossed the line separating the U.S. and Filipino armies in Manila. During the first year of the war, the U.S. Army managed to subdue the main Filipino defense forces in central and northern Luzon. The following year, it concentrated on taking southern Luzon and the Visayas, managing to control major towns by the middle of 1900. At that point, Filipino resistance took the form of guerrilla warfare.

After General Aguinaldo was captured in April 1901 and took the oath of allegiance to the United States, a number of his generals did likewise and, in fact, began to assist the U.S. Army in hunting down the leaders of the guerrilla resistance. Driven by their own political motives, a number of prominent Filipinos who had served the fallen republic began to collaborate with their new American overlords, prefiguring the role of former Ba'athists in the current U.S. "pacification" drive. Nevertheless, massive guerrilla re-sistance continued for at least another year. By the end of 1901, in regions such as Samar, Leyte, the Ilocos, and southern Tagalog, the U.S. Army intro-duced all-out measures such as the reconcentration of villagers, the burning of houses and food supplies, the torture of prisoners, and search-and-destroy operations. Most of the remaining guerrilla leaders were forced to surrender owing to battle injuries, hunger, desertions by their troops, and fear of the tremendous firepower that was unleashed by the U.S. Army after and in retaliation for the surprise September 28, 1901 attack by Pulahan nationalist guerrillas (the Redshirts—a so-called fanatical sect) on a U.S. Army camp at Balangiga, Samar, that led to the massacre of fifty-five American GIs.

It takes a bit of persistent research in the archives to rescue fragments of this forgotten second war. Through research in American military records, I discovered, for example, that my wife's grandfather Pedro Carandang became involved in the Filipino-American War when he was appointed mayor of Tanauan, Batangas, after that town was occupied by the Americans in 1900. But Mayor Carandang only served the American commanding officer during office hours. The rest of the time, when his boss was not looking, he provided the guerrilla units of General Miguel Malvar with food, money, information, and secret access to the town. When the Americans discovered this, they arrested Mayor Carandang and imprisoned him until the end of the war.

My own grandfather, Francisco Ileto, participated in the war by providing information about the Americans to his friend General Isidoro Torres, the guerrilla commander of Bulacan Province. The Americans intercepted a letter that my grandfather sent to Torres in 1900 and thus identified him as an enemy spy. This I discovered from the Philippine Insurgent Records. But I do not know whether the Americans arrested him or not.

The reason I do not know what eventually happened to my grandfather is because, remarkably, neither he nor my wife's grandfather passed on their memories of the war to their children and grandchildren. They chose to keep such memories private and to let their children carry on in life as if the war against the United States had never happened. However, they did pass on to their children their memories of the war against Spain. They spoke freely to their children about Rizal, Bonifacio, and the Aguinaldo who declared independence from Spain. But they kept silent about Malvar, Vicente Lukban, and the other Aguinaldo, who had called for a guerrilla war against the Americans in 1900.

How do we explain this selective transmission of the memories of the two wars? After the Americans had pronounced victory on July 4, 1902, they proceeded to reshape the collective memory of those long years of war from 1896 all the way to 1902. The aim of the politics of memory was to encourage the remembering of the war against Spain and the forgetting of the war against the United States. This was conducted through the censored press, civic rituals, and, above all, the colonial school system.

What the American colonial officials wanted Filipinos to "remember," above all, was that the U.S. Army had come as liberators to help free the country from oppressive Spanish rule. This was true at the beginning; the Filipinos indeed hailed the Americans as their redeemers. But how could the liberators justify not recognizing the Filipino republican government? How could they justify their bloody suppression of any resistance to their takeover of the islands? How could liberators justify killing the people they were supposed to have rescued from Spanish tyranny? The other, suppressed, meaning of the coming of the Americans in 1898 was that it was just another foreign invasion, following soon after the Spanish withdrawal.

In order to combat the negative meanings and to establish the official memory of the two wars, the U.S. colonial government did the following:

First, it recognized the liberal aspirations of the leaders of the 1896 war of independence against Spain. The Americans specially promoted the ideas of the nationalist intellectual Rizal, who preferred a gradualist road to self-rule through the education of the populace. The other hero of the first war, Bonifacio, was downplayed by the government because he led a "socialistic" secret society that advocated armed struggle.

Second, the American regime recognized the aspirations of Aguinaldo and the Filipino educated class to form a republican state. However, it insisted that Filipinos in 1898 were not prepared for democracy and self-rule. As "proof" of this lack of readiness, American writings portrayed Aguinaldo as a despotic president and the masses of the people as blind followers of their local bosses. The patron-client, caciquism, and bossism paradigms of local politics originated, in fact, from the war itself and were further developed by

American officials and writers during the "pacification" period from 1902 up to at least 1912. The colonial administration and its local protégés wanted the new generation of Filipinos studying in the public schools to remember the coming of the Americans in 1898 as an act of "benevolent assimilation," wherein the Americans would stay for as long as was needed to help prepare the Filipinos for democracy and responsible self-government. Philippine politics and its academic study followed the contours of, and mutually reinforced, this colonial project.

Third, it follows from the above that the war of resistance to U.S. occupation would be regarded as a great misunderstanding. In fact, these were the very words David Barrows, the superintendent of schools, used in his high school Philippine history textbook to describe the Filipino-American War. If only, he said, the Filipinos had fully understood the noble motives of the United States, and if only the Filipinos had accepted the fact that they were still an underdeveloped people needing to be uplifted by the superior civilization of the Americans, then they would not have resisted the U.S. occupation, and the disastrous war would not have taken place.

Fourth and finally, the American colonial regime decreed in 1902 that anyone who continued to oppose its presence would be arrested for sedition and that armed groups that attacked government forces would be treated as bandit gangs, religious fanatics, and remnants of the defeated guerrilla armies. The decade and a half after the formal end of the Filipino-American War in 1902 is, in fact, one of the most fascinating in Philippine history owing to the many "illicit" forms that memories of the revolution and continued resistance to U.S. occupation took. This was the age of armed militias, holy warriors, kidnappings, assassinations, and joint operations in the Philippines between American soldiers and newly trained native police. I could very well be referring to Iraq, of course. Owing to the official representation of these events, this period would be remembered not as a time of continued resistance to foreign occupation but as one of banditry, religious fanaticism, disorder, and dislocation.

In order to succeed in school, to become employed in the colonial civil service, and to embrace modernity introduced by the Americans, Filipinos were made to remember the Filipino-American War in the terms that the colonial administration dictated. Understandably, then, my grandfather, who came to terms with the occupation when he was recruited as a teacher in the public school system, chose not to transmit his memories of the Filipino-American War to his children.

So as we were growing up, I got to know that my father, Rafael Ileto, had gone to West Point in 1940 and that he had been an officer in the first Filipino infantry regiment that was sent to liberate the Philippines from Japanese rule. This is part of the Ileto family memory, of course. What we never knew, until I, as a historian, discovered the pertinent documents in the U.S. archives, was that my grandfather Francisco Ileto had been a revolutionary spy against the U.S. invasion forces in 1900.

The American colonial grip over the shaping of public memories was most effective in the schools. As the English language spread, so did the official view of the past. The official management of the collective memory, however, did not fully subsume the private memories of the Filipino-American War. After all, countless Filipinos had been involved in the anti-imperial struggle; hundreds of thousands had been killed or injured. Many veterans of the Filipino-American War chose to keep alive these memories through veterans associations, patriotic societies, labor unions, and religio-political sects, just about all of which were illegal. Beneath the official cluster of memories about the two wars, we can identify such alternative modes or channels of memory.

One of the focal points of alternative memories was a veteran of the first and second wars: Artemio Ricarte. Trained as a school teacher, Ricarte was fluent in Ilocano, Tagalog, and Spanish. He became a military commander in battles against the Spaniards and rose to become a general in the war against the Americans. When the war ended, he refused to take the oath of allegiance to the United States and was imprisoned. But he managed to escape, first to Hong Kong, and then later to Yokohama. From these places of exile, Ricarte continued to keep alive memories of both wars, treating them as a continuous and unfinished event. From 1904 up to 1935, he inspired various secret societies and peasant movements that awaited his return from Japan to liberate the country from the Americans.

In order to understand the third war in our series—the Filipino-Japanese War—we need to relate it to the first two. Filipino revolutionists had always sought the help of Japan in their wars against Spain and the United States, but except for small shipments of arms, Japanese involvement in the Philippine revolution was slight. We must remember, though, that the U.S. victory over the Filipino nationalists in 1902 was followed by Japan's momentous victory over Russia in 1905. These two events together signal the beginning of American-Japanese rivalry for dominance in the Asia-Pacific.

The two events also signaled the beginning of American-Japanese rivalry for the attention of Filipino nationalists. For the rise of Japan as an Asian power did not escape the notice of even the new generation of Filipinos learning English in the American schools. The fact that the venerable Ricarte came to be based in Yokohama heightened among Filipino nationalists the consciousness of Japan as an alternative model of development. And so when the Japanese came to occupy the Philippines in 1942, bringing with them Ricarte, there were quite a few Filipinos who welcomed them as liberators. Understandably, there has not been enough research on this phenomenon. What is well known is that the majority of Filipinos in 1940 regarded the Japanese as invaders.

The Filipino-American joint resistance to Japanese occupation, however, did not come naturally. It was premised on the colonial construction of history propagated in the schools since 1903. According to this particular story, the Filipinos had defeated the Spanish government with American help, and the Americans had stayed in order to train the Filipinos for future self-government. Due to the institutional power of this story, by the 1930s the vast majority of Filipinos had forgotten the Filipino-American War. They saw their fate and that of the United States as intertwined. So when the Japanese forces arrived, they were resisted with great persistence, particularly in Bataan and Corregidor. Nowhere else in Southeast Asia did the locals fight so hard on behalf of their colonial rulers.

After the surrender of the Filipino-American forces, a guerrilla war of resistance continued to be waged in various parts of the archipelago. We can detect here the makings of an epic war story, and indeed this is how the period is remembered. From my perspective as a historian, however, the war with Japan was, in reality, pretty much a replay of the war with the United States forty years earlier. The fact that few, if any, dare to state this is pretty much an effect of past memory wars.

The Japanese imperial administration itself became involved in the politics of memory when it encouraged Filipinos to revisit the history of both the first and second wars. No longer was it considered taboo to excavate memories of the Filipino-American War. Veterans of these two wars and their descendants, who had never forgotten that the Americans had come as invaders, were encouraged to speak freely about the past and to play leading roles in organizations supportive of the Japanese administration.

If we examine the backgrounds and ideas of some of the leading "collaborators" with the Japanese, we find connections with the forgotten war against United States occupation. José Laurel, president of the republic of 1943, came from the province of Batangas, a region devastated by U.S. armed operations in 1902. His father had been confined in an American concentration camp and died shortly after his release. A cousin was killed in an encounter with American troops. Claro Recto, Secretary of the Interior, remembered his mother crying while being interrogated by American officers who were hunting down his uncle, a guerrilla leader in Tayabas Province. Veteran General Emilio Aguinaldo was not playing pretend when he graced the independence ceremony in October 1943 and hailed the republic as a fulfillment of the dreams of 1898.

For these leaders of the wartime republic, there was no particular love for their Japanese sponsors, but there wasn't much nostalgia for U.S. rule either. They remembered the war with Spain, the war with the United States, and the war with Japan as variations on the same theme: resistance to foreign domination. Their aim was to ensure the survival of the Filipino nation, which had become sandwiched in a conflict between imperial powers.

I have no doubt that had the Japanese occupation lasted longer, there would have occurred a reprogramming of public memories similar to what the Americans had accomplished. The Filipino-American War would have been resurrected from oblivion and the Americans remembered as invaders, while the Japanese would, perhaps, have come to be perceived as liberators. But this was foiled by the return of General MacArthur in 1945, which he had solemnly promised to do when he left in defeat in 1942. This moment in Philippine history, appropriately celebrated in Bush's speech, is called the liberation.

As soon as the commonwealth government was reinstalled in Manila by the liberators, it proceeded to restore those collective memories of a shared Filipino-American past that the wartime period had begun to erode.

Typically, President Sergio Osmeña, in a 1945 speech, compared General Douglas MacArthur's liberation of the Philippines to the time when his father, General Arthur MacArthur, entered Manila in 1898 to free the Philippines from Spanish rule. Like father, like son—both liberators of the Philippines. What Osmeña conveniently forgot was that General Douglas MacArthur had commanded the American troops who fought and defeated the Filipino republican army in 1900.

The final six months of the war with Japan were very similar to the final six months of the war with the United States forty years earlier. Homes and buildings were razed; civilians suspected of aiding the guerrillas were tortured and executed; disaster accompanied the path of the contending armies. Personal experiences of the final months of the war were, for the most part, sad and tragic. This was the ideal environment for the promotion by postwar Filipino presidents Osmeña, Manuel Roxas, and Elpidio Quirino of the official memory of the war with Japan as a time when Filipino and American soldiers fought and suffered side by side to defend the Philippines. What was the "death march" if not their common *pasyón*, or Christ-like suffering and death? What was Capas, the prison camp in central Luzon and destination of the "death march," if not, said Quirino, the "calvary" of the Filipino-American forces?[3]

The official interpretation of history propagated in public speeches, radio broadcasts, and the school system encouraged the people to remember the American colonial period as a golden age when peace and prosperity reigned: peacetime, as it was fondly called. This age of bliss was shattered when the Japanese came and plunged the country into a dark age. The darkness was only lifted when the liberator MacArthur returned. Liberation meant the recovery of a lost age of happiness under America's tutelage. It was not difficult to establish this official rendering of the past war because it touched a chord with the countless private memories of death and destruction suffered at the hands of the Japanese army.

In this official postwar construction of the past—a crucial component of the nation-building process—again the Filipino-American War was a non-event or, at least, relegated to the fringes of politics. Not everyone, however, could obliterate this war from memory, especially since its remembering had been encouraged during the Japanese occupation. A new generation

of nationalist intellectuals had been nurtured during this wartime period—
they included historians such as Teodoro Agoncillo and Renato Constantino.
For them, both the war against the United States and the war against Japan
were to be remembered equally.

One well-known organization that refused to forget the Filipino-American War was the Hukbalahap. Formed during the war against Japan, the
Huk army saw itself as a successor of the armies that fought the Spaniards and
the Americans. Its commander Luis Taruc insisted that there was a parallel
between the coming of the Americans in 1898, when they "crushed a people's
movement that had come into being in the struggle against Spain," and their
return in 1945, when they tried to "crush another people's movement that
had come into being in the struggle against Japan."[4] The historic role of
the United States as liberator and tutor—so emotionally articulated in the
speeches of presidents Roxas and Quirino, both of whom had been nurtured
by the Americans—was belittled by Taruc as a sham so that the United
States could "make huge profits in our country." Only a minority, he said,
saw through "the performance of the 'independence ceremony' that occurred
on July 4, 1946."[5] After pseudo-independence in 1946, the Hukbalahap, led
by the Communist Party, transformed itself into a national liberation army
opposing U.S. imperialism and its local Filipino clients.

Thus began the fourth great war that swept the Philippines: the Cold
War. But for President Bush in his keynote speech, this was just the third
great war. Forgetting the Filipino-American War enabled him to bypass the
bungled liberation of 1898 and to posit the 1945 liberation of the Philippines
as the event that parallels or inspires the recent events of 2003. "Since the
liberation of Iraq," he declares, "we ended one of the cruelest regimes in
our time.... And we're helping to build a free Iraq." But, he also noted,
"democracy has its skeptics. Some say the culture of the Middle East will not
sustain the institutions of democracy. The same doubts were expressed about
the culture of Asia. These doubts were proven wrong nearly six decades ago,
when the Republic of the Philippines became the first democratic nation
in Asia. Since then, liberty has reached nearly every shore of the Western
Pacific."

Liberation by the United States, followed by its granting of independence
in 1946, have made the Philippines the model for Iraq, says Bush. But what

about the turmoil following 1946? For Bush, of course, this turmoil was an effect of the Cold War, in which freedom had to be defended. Today, the Cold War has its equivalent in the war on terror.

As I stated earlier, the immediate postwar governments of Roxas and Quirino highlighted the joint struggle by Filipinos and Americans against the Japanese. This strategy was aimed at solidifying the alliance between the Philippines and the United States. It was targeted at the Huks and the communists, who, being aligned with the Soviet Union, were critical of U.S. imperialism. However, after Laurel and most of the collaborators with Japan were pardoned in 1948 and as the Cold War intensified in the 1950s, the war with Japan gradually faded from official memory. After all, Japan was a staunch Cold War ally now, and Japanese war reparations were forthcoming. Officially, the war with Japan was to be forgotten during the Cold War, although privately it continued to be remembered as a dark age by those who had lived through it—that is, my father's generation.

The collective memory of the war against Spain certainly became a terrain of conflict during the Cold War. The anticommunist camp, including the Catholic Church hierarchy, continued to endorse the intellectual Rizal as the hero of the revolution. It championed Christianity as the light that would ward off the communist threat in Asia—a trope repeated by Bush when he reminded us of Pope John Paul II's words of praise for our democracy, which, Bush said, was an example for others, the source of the "light" (of freedom) in this part of the world.

The radical nationalists, however, championed Bonifacio, the working-class founder of the Katipunan. President Ferdinand Marcos, briefed by intelligence sources on the link between the Bonifacio tradition and the communist movement, responded by portraying himself as another Emilio Aguinaldo (who, we recall, had ordered the execution of Bonifacio in 1897). President Fidel Ramos, a former general, naturally identified with General and then President Aguinaldo. President Joseph Estrada, portraying himself as a latter-day Bonifacio, succeeded in drawing a massive following from the poorer classes despite his lack of sincerity in this identification. Obviously, these presidents succeeded by tapping the collective memory of the war against Spain.

The real battleground for Cold War memory makers, however, was the second great war. Few veterans of that Filipino-American War were left to remind the younger generation of their experiences. The government, largely consisting of politicians and bureaucrats educated under the Americans, persisted in its official forgetting of the Filipino-American War. Even during the recent centennial celebration of the revolution in 1998, there was hardly any official mention of the violent U.S. invasion. To remember the war with the Americans would harm the Cold War alliance, the military bases agreement, the special relationship as a whole—just as the edifice of the war on terror might begin to crumble if the public were allowed to remember freely the colonial and postcolonial wars in the Middle East that have led to the present blowback.

The official view was nevertheless challenged by a vocal group of activists who struggled to restore the memory of the Filipino-American War in the public consciousness. Among them were politicians and intellectuals Claro Recto, Teodoro Agoncillo, Leon Maria Guerrero, Renato Constantino, the Muslim Cesar Majul, and even wartime collaborator President José Laurel who founded the Lyceum School to promote a pro-Filipino rather than a neocolonial understanding of the past. Some of them had served the republic during the Japanese occupation. As a result of their reeducation campaigns in the 1950s and the 1960s, more and more educated Filipinos came to learn about the suppressed history of the Filipino-American War. By the end of the 1960s, a new, youthful generation had come to understand the first and second great wars as a single, continuous event—the unfinished revolution—in whose name a number of mass actions against the government were conducted beginning in January 1970. With the Philippine-American official construction of the past crumbling all around, President Marcos, with full U.S. backing, declared martial law in September 1972.

Our brief excursion into the politics of memory surrounding four past wars should help us understand how Filipinos have come to position themselves in the present war against terror. When U.S. soldiers returned to the Philippines in the early months of 2002 to help the government pursue the antiterror war, a significant portion of the populace, led by the president, welcomed them with open arms. Kindled in their minds were memories of the Americans as their allies, and even their liberators, in the war against Japan. Only a minority saw the return of the U.S. Army as a ghostly echo of their arrival in 1898 to occupy the Philippines by force.

Last October, President Bush cemented this perception by highlighting the common Filipino-American struggle against the Japanese as the precedent for the present war on terror. Most Filipinos, it seems, read about the wars in the Middle East and fail to see them as a mirror of their own country's experience in 1899. They have largely forgotten the Philippines' second great war—thus the enthusiastic applause that punctuated Bush's address to our politicians.

Bush told his Filipino audience to take sides in the war on terror, just as during the Cold War we had to take sides. "You are either with us or against us," he warned. Of course, the Philippines, being a poor country in need of aid, has been compelled to join the coalition of the willing. But it is not just poverty or pragmatism that has led to this. What we see are the effects of a century of manipulation or reshaping of collective memories about our past wars.

Having American troops fighting side-by-side with Filipino troops in the war on terror may bring back memories of the joint struggle against Japan, but it also entails forgetting the equally terrible Filipino-American War. Did Filipinos fight those past wars only to end up serving the empire of the day? When President Bush called on Filipinos to participate in waging war against what he termed the new totalitarian threat against civilization, he was reviving the Cold War call to all members of the "free world" to fight communism. But when in President Bush's speech Filipinos are asked to "defend ourselves, our civilization, and the peace of the world," isn't this thing called civilization a proxy for something else . . . like empire?

There is something more ominous, however, about Bush's framing of the current war in terms of civilization against terror. For he unintentionally alluded to a series of events—and a powerful sentiment informing them—that have bedeviled Philippine history ever since the Spaniards arrived in the sixteenth century. I am referring to the age-old attempts by the Spanish and American armies, the Philippine national government, and elements of the Filipino Christian population to place the Muslim areas in the south under their control and ownership, often using the trope of civilization to justify their acts. Responses from the Muslims—called *Moros* by the Spaniards—have taken such forms as the raiding of Christian towns to capture slaves, armed resistance to intrusions, an intensification of their own separate identity, and secessionism.

The Moros, in fact, figured as a kind of excess in the first and second great wars we have discussed above. Having suffered defeat at the hands of the Spaniards in the 1880s, the Moros saw in the Filipino revolution against Spain a chance to extricate themselves from control by the Christian north. They overthrew the revolutionary government at Cotabato, Mindanao, and refused to join the republic of 1898. After the American invasion and the defeat of the republic, some sultans and *datus* (chiefs) were persuaded to sign treaties accepting the U.S. military presence, but the U.S. forces soon came to be perceived as intruders by many local chiefs and Muslim clerics. A series of unequal battles were then fought between U.S. and Moro forces from 1902 to around 1910, producing legendary American heroes like Generals John Pershing and Leonard Wood. Likewise, the war—a jihad from the Moro perspective—featured some dramatic last stands of Moro forces, such as the massacres at Bud Dajo and Bud Bagsak, where hundreds of Muslims, including women and children, perished in heavy bombardment by U.S. artillery followed by ground troops storming in with their sophisticated weapons.

Like the Filipino-American War, the bloody suppression of Moro resistance to U.S. occupation suffered the same fate at the hands of official memory makers under American rule: it was not to be established in the collective memory. On the other hand, the narratives of collaboration, abolition of slavery, democratic tutelage, and steady incorporation of the Moros into the dominantly Christian nation-state would be celebrated. This has fostered the myth of the south's incorporation into, and belonging to, the body politic, to the extent that most Filipinos today see the eruption of violence there as a deviation from normalcy rather than as an irruption of a long tradition of resistance. All the easier it is, then, to plug the southern Philippines into the grid of America's war on terror.

The lengthy, ongoing war in the southern Philippines, collectively called the Moro Wars, constitutes the fifth great war in Philippine history whose significance the present war on terror particularly seeks to displace. Only by remembering their five historic wars and not just three, only by resurrecting those memories that are hidden away in the dark shadows of empire, will Filipinos begin to see that what they are being asked to do today is built upon a massive forgetting. The nation can only move forward if the Philippine Revolution, which continues to be the foundational event in nation-building discourse, is remembered in all its dimensions. This includes the pathbreaking though failed Filipino resistance from 1899 to 1902, to the establishment of today's global empire. This includes the failure of the revolution to incorporate the Muslim south.

The real ghost that haunts today's war is not General Douglas MacArthur's liberation of the Philippines in 1945. As I have argued in this paper, the real past in the present is the coming of the U.S. Army in 1898 led by General Arthur MacArthur in a "liberation" episode, followed shortly thereafter by the Filipino-American War, which in turn was followed by the Moro resistance to American occupation (which we might call the "Moro-American War"). The politics of remembering and forgetting these wars is what really constitutes the much-vaunted special relationship between the United States and the Philippines. At the most overt level, this relationship is manifested in such gestures as Bush's speech and the enthusiastic applause that punctuated almost every minute of it, in Filipino and American troops fighting side by side in counterterrorist operations in Mindanao, or even in a Filipino contingent being sent to Iraq.

I have since been told, however, that a number of Filipino lawmakers did not join in the applause, that many apparently clapped with one hand while extending the other in anticipation of the war funds that Bush had promised. Meanwhile, outside the heavily guarded congress building, protesters were demanding that the United States withdraw its troops from Iraq, Afghanistan, and the Philippines. One group, named Bayan, also called for "a public apology and reparation for war crimes committed by U.S. forces during the Philippine-American War."[6] Despite the power of the colonial state and its local progeny, suppressed memories of the second great war have always been just beneath the surface and will surely regain their potency as that old war's uncanny resemblance to the present war is recognized.

## Notes

The first version of this paper, titled "Wars in the Philippines: The Politics of Memory in the Shadow of Empire," was presented at a public forum in Fukuoka City, Japan, on September 21, 2003. Substantially revised after Bush's visit to the Philippines, it served as the keynote lecture at the annual convention of the Philippine Political Science Association, held in Davao City, Philippines, in October 2003. A third version was presented in February 2004 at a symposium in Seattle sponsored by the University of Washington's Southeast Asia Center.

1   The text of the Bush speech is available at usinfo.state.gov/xarchives/display.html?p= washfile-english&y=2003&m=October&x=20031018112610attocnicho.7477075&t=xarchives/ xarchitem.html.

2   Translation of the original Spanish document in John R. M. Taylor, *The Philippine Insurrection against the United States*, vol. 1 (Manila: Lopez Foundation, 1971,) 522.

3   *The Quirino Way: Collection of Speeches and Addresses of Elpidio Quirino* (Manila, 1955), 70–74.

4   Luis Taruc, *Born of the People* (New York: International, 1953), 208.

5   Ibid., 274.

6   The quote originally appeared in CyberDyaryo, www.cyberdyaryo.com/statements/ st2003_1009_01.html, which has since been removed from the Web. Another version can be found at www.inq7.net/brk/2003/oct/18/brkpol_7-1.htm.

## The Road to Hell Is Paved with Good Intentions:
## For a "Critique of Terrorism" to Come

Satoshi Ukai

### Terrorism—The Ultimate Political Concept

Let me begin with Carl Schmitt's *The Concept of the Political*, in which he says, "The political is the most intense and extreme antagonism" and "the substance of the political is contained in the context of a concrete antagonism."[1] This means that whatever term is used—totalitarianism, democracy, freedom—we cannot determine its concrete meaning in different contexts without taking into account that it is uttered at someone.

While Schmitt's proposition tends to dominate and regulate everything he says about the political in a self-referential fashion, I think, nonetheless, that the term *terrorism* provides a fine demonstration of what Schmitt calls the fundamental antagonism of the political concept. In this respect, might terrorism not be called the ultimate political concept?

*positions* 13:1 © 2005 by Duke University Press

Put differently, in another theoretical code, terrorism might be said to be a term whose operation is at once performative and constative (that is, in some sense, empirically verifiable), which is to say that one cannot determine if a certain phenomenon is terrorism without attending to its performative dimension. More than any other concept, with respect to the concept of terrorism, whenever and however it is debated, the constative cannot be thought of in isolation from the performative. This is what I would first like to clarify.

The term *terrorism* has been in use for some two hundred years, but it has not always been employed in the same context as it is currently used. It is necessary, then, to consider when the current sense of terrorism and its essential connotation appeared. Surely it is undeniable that it emerged from the historical and political conditions of the Middle East. In the following passage from *Prisoner of Love* (1986), Jean Genet recounts what a certain Palestinian said to him.

> Although you had your white, royalist terror in 1795, the word terror wasn't too terrible in French until lately. Jack the Ripper spread terror nicely enough in London, and so did Bonnot in Paris, but the word terrorist has metal teeth and the red jaws of a monster. The Shiites have inhuman jaws like that, it says in the papers this morning, and Israel must lash them to death with the poisonous tail of their army—the army that ran away from Lebanon. If you're against Israel you're not an enemy or an opponent—you're a terrorist. Terrorism is supposed to deal death indiscriminately, and must be destroyed wherever it appears.
>
> Very smart of Israel to carry the war right into the heart of vocabulary, and annex the words holocaust and genocide. The invasion of the Golan Heights didn't make Israel an intruder or predator. The destruction and massacres in Beirut weren't the work of terrorists armed by America and dropping tons of bombs day and night for three months on a capital with two million inhabitants: they were the act of an angry householder with the power to inflict heavy punishment on a troublesome neighbor. Words are terrible, and Israel is a terrifying manipulator of signs. Sentence doesn't necessarily precede execution; if an execution has already been carried out,

a sentence will gradually justify it. When it kills a Shiite and a Palestinian, Israel claims to have cleansed the world of two terrorists at once.[2]

Here, amid the Israel-Palestine conflict, the term *terrorism* makes an appearance in its contemporary sense. Moreover, it appears as a symbol of almost theological evil. Simply put a *d* in front of the *evil* in Bush's "axis of evil" and you have *devil*. How easy it is in English to shift from evil to the devil.

The term *terrorist* clearly entails a move to dehumanize the enemy. As Schmitt was keen to point out in *The Concept of the Political*, the enemy existed in essence as a "proper enemy" in European common law and was not thought to be evil simply for being an enemy.[3] Then, from a certain period, the enemy came to be dehumanized, criminalized, demonized. Schmitt saw this as arising from first the English, then the American destruction of the European order; but the transformation from terror to terrorism of which the Palestinian character in *Prisoner of Love* speaks suggests that it is a matter of introducing a sharp semiotic distinction between human and inhuman on the basis of a religious standard implicit in the term *terrorism*.

Another problem appears quite clearly and directly because we are dealing with Jean Genet. In his early works, Genet did not bring the political context to the surface; instead he focused on depictions of "pure" crime, of the world of general criminal offenses. Then, apparently, in his mid-to-late forties, Genet became politicized. Yet if one looks closely at the political struggles that concerned him in the 1960s, such as the Black Panthers' Black Liberation Army and the Palestinian Resistance Movement, it is not in the least irrelevant that in the 1980s the older Genet concerned himself with political phenomena whose nature situated them on the boundary between crime and politics. How are we to think of the violence at the intersection of pure crime and the pure political? In light of the current situation, such a task should include an examination of the debate between Carl Schmitt and Leo Strauss, as well as a new look at Schmitt's discussion of Hobbes.

Another point of intersection for Schmitt and Genet is their deep concern for the Middle East, but the problem is how to think about the relations between the terrorist and the refugee, these two figures who are forced to exist "outside" the world of human beings, omitted, eliminated, or otherwise excluded.

In fact, it was from refugee camps that the Palestinian Liberation Organization (PLO) emerged. Even though Genet has a great deal in common with the philosophical lineage from Hannah Arendt to Giorgio Agamben that defines twentieth-century human existence on the basis of the refugee, in a thoroughly different manner he considered how the Palestinian resistance movement was born from refugees.

The refugee is one who is subject to refuge. This is lived as an experience of profound shame. Oddly enough, possibilities spring up from this experience in the refugee's children's generation. Indeed, in Palestine, after the third Middle East war in 1967, some twenty years after the Nakba of 1948, guerrilla struggles started from within the scattered collective. The first intifada began in 1987, twenty years after the Israeli occupation of the Gaza Strip, the West Bank of the Jordan River, and East Jerusalem. In other words, resistance movements spring forth one generation after massive trauma. The resistance movement is also one of self-transformation.

Within the current system of aid for refugees, once one becomes a refugee, there are only two options: either abandonment without any refuge, or refuge if recognized as a refugee. It is never supposed that the refugee might become something other than a refugee. To be a refugee is to be outside the protective framework of national citizenship. When such people take a stand to determine their own destiny, they must, as a matter of course, act outside the law. The transformation of refugee into terrorist is thus inevitable.

In *Theory of Partisans* (1963), Schmitt says the following: "Those who fall outside the law seek the law within adversarial relations. In some instances, they fall outside the law because lawfulness and basic regulations break down. In other instances, they fall outside the law because of a disruption in the norms of justice that are hoped to bring law and legal protection. Those who thus lose the law discover the meaning of the law and of affairs through adversarial relations."[4]

Schmitt's insight provides the key to understanding why the PLO's guerrillas were the first type of terrorist to emerge in the Middle East. This was because they shaped themselves politically on the basis of falling outside the law, as refugees. This is how political actions outside the rule of law come to be called terrorism.

While I cannot go into details here, the actions of the PLO in the 1960s were fundamentally justifiable under the Geneva Conventions. The Geneva Conventions legally recognize armed resistance in occupied territories (those occupied by a foreign army). It was only natural for the PLO to claim that all of Israel constituted occupied territory. Such interpretations of the Geneva Conventions serve as a reminder that defining terrorism was a point of contention in international law at that time.

Previously, during World War II, a number of resistance movements developed in countries occupied by Germany, especially in France. Assassinations occurred, as did bombings on roadways and buildings held by the Nazis. Various kinds of violent resistance appeared, which the Geneva Conventions recognized retroactively. What is more, Nazi officials consistently called French resistance fighters terrorists.

In addition, when one looks at the writings of Louis Massignon on the founding of the nation of Israel, the term *Zionist terrorist* appears repeatedly. This is a direct reference to the military activity of right-wing Zionists who are today connected to the Likud political party. Generally, the violence that they exercised against Arabs and English settlers was called terrorism.

At the same time, I would like to make a basic point, which is that many of the phenemona called terrorism are not referred to as such by the people who practice them. One ought to recall that what today's Islamic fundamentalist groups call jihad might more objectively fall into another category, that of revolutionary violence or military resistance.

Clearly, at the very least, knowledge of the history of war over the past century, in as much detail as possible, is a precondition for theorizing about the problem of terrorism. Terrorism is exceedingly difficult to pursue as a concept, when one strives to do so simply and factually. Still, if we take a cursory look at the theoretical views of the past decades, how does our current horizon of thinking differ from that of intellectuals in the 1930s, for instance? At one time, in the midst of peril, culture was opposed to the barbarism of violence, and the schema of culture versus violence proved exceedingly powerful. Yet in course of the postwar era, what was called culture gradually showed itself to be a mere accomplice to all manner of violence, or another form of violence in itself. The binary opposition between culture as nonviolence and violence is now but an ideological tool. The fundamental task of the current era is how to evaluate the differences among violences. Or, to put it differently, if there is to be culture today, it should be directed toward the evaluation of different violences. Our era has largely moved away from binary oppositions toward thinking of difference. (I am, of course, generating a slogan, but I do not mean to construct a new binary opposition between today's philosophy of difference and yesterday's binary opposition [culture/violence].) The problem of the critique of violence, then, becomes one of how to think of the differences between violences without recourse to binary oppositions.

Inevitably, in the structure of any broadly political theater, site, or drama, binary oppositions return, and they act powerfully to imprint themselves on the brain as the ultimate binarisms beyond which nothing can go. As with Bush's proclamation of a "battle between good and evil," even though its absurdity has been exposed, it remains powerful. The fundamental task is to resist such binarisms and thus to practice a continual critique of violence.

When we look at the reality of what were called some decades ago revolutionary military struggles, we find that they turn out to be exceedingly diverse. Ways of exercising violence were quite diverse in liberation struggles in the third world. The spectacle is vast, from the practices of Nelson Mandela and the African National Congress (ANC) in South Africa to the communism of Cambodia to the Maoist Shining Path in Peru.

With violence that tends toward the revolutionary, there is first the problem of how to distinguish between people and things as objects of violence. The question that immediately follows is whether those who designate others as terrorists are ultimately able to sustain such a distinction. In 1964, when Mandela made his famous statement of protest at the Livonia trial, he insisted that the military section of the ANC called Spear of the Nation was designed to focus attacks on various sorts of material infrastructure in order to bring down apartheid without harming human lives. The goal of the military struggle was to drum up enthusiasm for the liberation of the African masses. From his younger years as a lawyer through his twenty-nine years in prison, Mandela consistently argued for the abolition of capital punishment. A single current, of respect for human life, runs through both his opposition to capital punishment and his call for military action.

This current of thought extends to the Zapatista in Mexico today. Military liberation struggles in the Third World make a clear distinction between violence to people and violence to things, which continues today. Yet in the context of actual conflict, the destruction of things is often called terrorism. It is essential to ask whether current definitions of terrorism make a distinction between people and things.

If one takes the instance of struggles that involved hijacking, members of the Popular Front for the Liberation of Palestine (PFLP) did not threaten human life when they began to practice hijacking in the 1970s. They did eventually blow up an Israeli plane as an act of military propaganda. But even in that instance, they landed the plane as soon as possible after hijacking it and got the passengers off, which served as political propaganda. By treating passengers humanely, they sought, in return, the release of members of their own group who had previously been captured. In the first wave of hijackings, the PFLP took hostages in order to open negotiations.

After the incident in Munich in 1972, the governments of Israel, various European countries, and America decided on a policy of no negotiation with terrorists. As a consequence, the tactic of taking hostages to use in negotiations broke down. Clearly, however, it was the establishment that first adopted the policy of extermination.

When one looks at the history of hijacking in very simple terms, there is a transformation with respect to the desired effects and tactical thinking related to it, especially today, especially in the use of time in the tug-of-war with the establishment. One result is the strategy adopted by those who acted on September 11, 2001—in hijackings that did not seek negotiation, hijackings in which the time until the desired effect approached zero, suicide attacks with airplanes. September 11 should be understood in light of this history of tactical struggle.

In other words, in the history of military struggles over the past decades around the world, someone like Nelson Mandela is the exception. There are many instances in which the use of violence has gone astray, and a great many groups resort to suicide as a consequence. Then, too, even in struggles that have succeeded politically, there have been many uses of military force that should never have been allowed. For instance, in the Algerian war of independence that began on November 1, 1954, the Front de Libération

Nationale (FLN) resorted to bombing residential areas and busy commercial districts. While Frantz Fanon gives a powerful description of it in *The Wretched of the Earth*, contemporary research has significantly changed the representation of this event. At that time, after 130 years of colonial occupation, the Arabs in Algeria had not formed a united group seeking liberation. The liberation front resorted to bombing colonial civilians, thus provoking an excessive response from the French colonial army, which forced the masses into a situation in which they had to risk their lives to gain independence.

Was such an exercise of violence right or not? The outbreak of civil war in Algeria in the 1990s shows without a doubt that the culture of violence there has not yet dissolved. The time has come for all of us, including the parties directly involved, to look closely at what sort of violence comes with the political phenomena that we have supported as an overall package. Here linger the questions about the use of words that I touched on at the outset: To what extent is such-and-such an act truly an act of terrorism? How and when do alleged terrorists differentiate themselves from terrorism? Under what circumstances shall we use the term *terrorism*? There is absolutely no constative, that is, empirically verifiable, definition of terrorism. While a critique of violence that is not a simple condemnation works through recollection of the past, it also nurtures discernment vis-à-vis violence in the present.

There is no clear-cut distinction between violence and nonviolence. It is not simply that we are generally caught between what is thought to be violence and what is thought to be nonviolence. Rather, we need to become discerning about differences in the operations of power in so-called nonviolent struggles or nonviolent movements. One example that I feel makes such differences palpable in an interesting manner is the activities of the group of volunteers in occupied Palestine who have come to be known in Japan by the acronym ISM, or the International Solidarity Movement. Members of this movement actively insert themselves between Israeli soldiers and Palestinian civilians to assure that the Israeli army cannot do anything violent. Israel believes that it has the right to punish all those associated in any way with suicide bombers by destroying the homes from which the suicide bombers came, utterly and immediately (which the Geneva Conventions clearly prohibit). The ISM keeps an eye on such activities, gathering around such homes in order to protect them. Needless to say, in light of conditions in Palestine today, members of the ISM take on a certain risk. They run the same risk as the relatives of the suicide bombers who today embody terrorism in its most representative form. In such a situation, violence and nonviolence live under the same roof, in symbolic terms. In order to establish a relationship of trust, the nonviolent group needs to not only speak out against the opponent but also abandon the very thinking that nonviolence is morally superior to violence. Otherwise there will be no collective action. Until now, the strength of what has come to be called nonviolent struggle follows from its moral superiority in comparison with violence. This notion has been dismantled. It is precisely by dismantling it that nonviolence proves itself inexhaustible. Frequently, when nonviolence is seen as a moral force, it has turned around and justified the use of violence. The best historical example of this is the transformation of the Christian philosophy of nonviolence into a theory that justifies the uncompromising exercise of violence, from the Crusades to contemporary America. When the activities of nonviolence by deliberately cutting off the possibility of moral superiority run a certain risk, one begins to see how different powers actually operate and intertwine, but not in binary opposition between violence and nonviolence.

Nonviolence actually comprises diverse kinds of movements. First in *The Politics of Nonviolent Action* (1973), and then in *Civilian-Based Defense: A Post-Military Weapons System* (1990), Gene Sharp delved into the history and legal theory behind civilian defense (that is, civilians defending themselves, not the state defending civilians).[5] Yet if one looks for a nonviolent form of movement appropriate to a specific situation, one cannot find any answers fixed in advance. In exercising popular resistance without arms, many factors are important: the kind of enemy confronted, the conditions under which the enemy is confronted, the management of everyday life amid resistance struggles. One ought to suspend judgment as much as possible, keeping in mind the diversity of so-called military struggles and direct nonviolent behavior. This is surely a condition for a critique of terrorism.

I have used the expression "critique of terrorism," which in fact derives from the theoretical tradition of the discourses of Marxism and especially Leninism. Prior usage of the term *terrorism* did not have to address practices as dehumanizing as those implicated by the term today. The contemporary use of *terrorism* establishes it as crime. For it submits that the terrorist is not one of us; the terrorist is a criminal. Once voices begin to clamor about the crimes of the terrorist in this way, we cannot help but adopt a similar stance against terrorism. If we do not, we are thought to approve of crime. What is crucial about the legacy of Lenin in the current context, then, is that Lenin clearly critiques terrorism in a dimension other than crime.

Judging is not the same as condemning. A certain kind of Christian thought distinguishes between judging and condemning, on the basis of forgiveness. Judging is not automatically condemnation because it is possible to judge and to forgive. Nevertheless, a history of terminology other than Christian judgment, condemnation, and forgiveness runs through the critique of terror.

The genealogy of revolutionary terror reached its apex in the Russian revolutionary movement with the assassination of Alexander II by the Narodnaia Volia. The Russian model supplied the standard image of the terrorist in the period before the start of the Palestinian liberation struggles in the 1960s. The Russian Socialist Party's introduction of Marxism to the Russian revolutionary movement inspired social movement based on concrete and scientific political views. Within the German Social Democrat Party (SDP), Eduard Bernstein attempted to show that Marx's predictions had proved false; Bernstein's revisionist views appeared in *Evolutionary Socialism* (1899). On the basis of this revisionism, Bernstein came to lead the right wing of the SDP. In the context of these revisionist debates, in 1901–2 Lenin wrote his famous series of articles called *What Is to Be Done?* In the article "Trade-Unionist Politics and Social-Democratic Politics," there is a famous section called "What Is There in Common between Economism and Terrorism?" Economism is a labor movement that tends to restrict itself to the improvement of the economic conditions of workers. It is a movement that does not make social revolution its principal objective. When Lenin looked at the two political stances, economism and terrorism (direct violent action against the government), he found that both shared a certain reverence for spontaneity. Let me cite a rather long but important passage.

At first sight, our assertion may appear paradoxical, so great is the difference between those who stress the "drab everyday struggle" and those who call for the most self-sacrificing struggle of individuals. But this is no paradox. The Economists and terrorists merely bow to different poles of spontaneity: the Economists bow to the spontaneity of the "pure" working-class movement, to form an integral whole. It is difficult indeed for those who have lost their belief, or who have never believed that this is possible to find some outlet for their indignation and revolutionary energy other than terror.[6]

With the subsequent systematization of Leninism, *What Is To Be Done?* has been read as providing a clear response to revisionism and economism: that response is a coherent political theory about how revolutionary organization injects political class consciousness into the labor movement from without, a sort of "external injection thesis." Today, however, when that kind of reading has lost almost all relevance, what can be learned from this critique of terrorism?

Political analyses that are in the broadest sense Hegelian tend to set forth an object to be criticized at both extremes. Then they show the essential unity of the polarized expressions, seeking a correct position through their sublation. Yet in the past decades, such analyses have not produced any sort of productive political culture. Still, even though Lenin may have been mistaken in his insistence that economism and terrorism share a reverence for spontaneity, there is something in his critique worth reconsidering. We need to consider the form that "spontaneity" takes today. Lenin wrote, "Political activity has its logic quite apart from the consciousness of those who, with the best intentions, call either for terror or for lending the economic struggle itself a political character. The road to hell is paved with good intentions."[7] I evoke this phrase "the road to hell" as a litmus test for those terrorism critiques that might actually enable terrorism crime today. It is crucial to recognize that those who are called terrorists arrived at such a point full of good intentions. Critique can only begin by recognizing the good intentions of these people, including Islamic fundamentalists. Yet at the same time, insofar as they are moved by good intentions, they open a path to hell. We return to this equivocity again and again.

There is no better time than today to undertake the work of rereading Lenin, in its original form, as a text, and to part with Carl Schmitt's *Concept of the Political* and his *Theory of Partisans*. (Schmitt, who formed his philosophy during the interwar period, cast a look full of admiration at Lenin as the enemy.)

I do not, of course, intend that we should return to what Lenin advocated. In the present context, Lenin allows us to problematize the redness of terror, or rather, what is today mistaken for red terror. We cannot continue to discuss terrorism as we do today, putting the actions of 9/11 in the same framework as Palestinian suicide bombers. The example of Palestine is, in the broadest sense, a variation on the struggle around territory that Schmitt problematized in his *Theory of Partisans*; it preserves a certain archaic quality. In a military organization like al Qaeda, territory or international rights do not provide political motivation. Therein lies the great difference. Rather twisted stances do arise, as with organizations that profess Leninism yet side with Osama bin Laden. Nonetheless, one point arises that a critique of terrorism cannot handle except through a return to Lenin: revolutionary terror is not the only problem; there is also the antirevolutionary terror that doubles it. This may seem obvious, but the contemporary political grammar makes it impossible to include right-wing terror that takes international capitalism as its target. I would not want to use Lenin to establish a strict opposition between "white" terror and "red" terror, but if 9/11 was the action of al Quaeda as alleged, we should acknowledge that it is not red terror, that is, revolutionary violence of the left, but a sort of right-wing antirevolutionary terror.

It is not clear what kind of philosophical discussion can happen between us and those who are far distant from us. But it is clear that we will have to pass through not only the question of Marxism or the modern revolutionary context but also the question of religion if there is to be some just critique. Lenin remains crucial but insufficient in this respect.

The most difficult point is the realities that we encounter when we reconsider the problem of sovereign terror, of sovereignty and terror. Certainly Schmitt is important. Yet more fundamentally, theories of sovereignty after Hobbes, Bodin, and Rousseau take the form of a secularization of political theology—in which case, it does not matter who grasps sovereign power, Marxists or secular revolutionaries.

I would like to turn to an excerpt published in *Le Monde diplomatique* from a 2003 work by Jacques Derrida called *Voyous* (*Rogues*), in which he writes of the "reason of the strong."[8] He cites the opening phrase from Lafontaine's fable "The Wolf and the Lamb," "La raison du plus fort est toujours la meilleure" (the reason of the strongest is always the best). While this is something of a truism in the context of U.S. unilateralism, Derrida emphasizes this phrase to indicate a fundamental abuse of power within sovereignty, an abuse of power that is at once terrorism. When one looks closely at what it means to be called a rogue state, it is not very difficult to see that those who coined the term and impose it on others are rogue states themselves.

Derrida's hypothesis opens a number of points for debate, which I would like to pursue here. According to Derrida, a certain national schema has been fundamental to the use of the terms *terrorism* and *rogue state*, with a tension between the nation-state and national sovereignty as its horizon. Now, with respect to the event of 9/11, Derrida insists that it was not a "major event" to the extent that it was more or less predictable. Insofar as 9/11 took a visible form, the operations that link rogue states to terrorism have a determinate limit. In such circumstances, in which no nation-state bears responsibility, the production and use of nuclear weapons becomes possible.

This means that human beings basically exist in a state of danger from each other, as Hobbes describes it in *Leviathan*. To cut through a rather difficult problem, in modern times the term *human beings* means citizens. If one asks what citizens are, they are those who are potentially soldiers. Those who are citizens are actually combatants. In *Theory of Partisans*, Schmitt follows this analogy, finding that all human beings are partisans. If one allows such an analogy, then one is only a step away from saying that all human beings are potentially terrorists. This becomes an immediate possibility.

A range of different explanatory schemata might be brought to bear on this situation, yet it seems to me that what is currently called terrorism is very close to the condition that Jacques Lacan touched on at the end of his essay "Logical Time."[9] A competition occurs in which each individual is to prove itself human. If you do not rush for the exit, you are not human. Lacan found in this a theory of assimilation. What happened after 9/11 is much the same. If you do not condemn the terrorist, you are not human. Clearly we are in a situation in which all are supposed to prove themselves human in a hurry.

Still, much as this sort of humanization of humanity reaches its limit, does not 9/11 as well? Is the harried sovereign ultimately human? The fact that American unilateralism appears inhuman to so many people reminds us that the so-called sovereign subject is not in the least human. While Hobbes compares the sovereign to a sea monster, the leviathan (Schmitt's account of Hobbes is largely an interpretation of the figure of the beast, the leviathan), he depicts the nation-state as a machine. In other words, his theory of the sovereign integrates these two figures, beast and machine.

As Paul Virilio recounts in detail in his essay "Revolutionary Resistance,"[10] Hobbes makes no distinction between terror and affect. Previously I noted that anyone is potentially a terrorist. Conversely, we all can become victims of terror. Currently there is every attempt to avoid discussing this, but under current global conditions there is absolutely no equality with respect to life. It is thus not in the least surprising that a powerful shock works to materialize our equality, but only in face of death and violence.

War always makes necessary a terror greater than possible death at the hands of the enemy. Soldiers will not fight unless they learn of a terror actually closer to death, that of their own national army saying, "If you don't fight, they'll strike you from behind." The same might be said of that politics of terror that strives to be revolutionary. In the case of revolutionary movements, in response to the aberration of terror being exercised against civilians, civilians—as revolutionaries—aim to establish another collective by overcoming the constant terror. In any event, when one strives to mobilize the masses coercively, the result is not people who are undone by terror. The result is people who are mobilized by terror.

The affect of fear is exceedingly subtle. Nietzsche regarded the person whose weakness allowed him to feel the subtlety of terror as one endowed with qualities that could give birth to the "overman." Also, at the opening of *The Pleasure of the Text*, Roland Barthes cites the words of Hobbes, "the one passion in my life was terror."[11] Even in the so-called experience of the text, this affect is irreducible.

So what is it that terrifies us today? Do we fear what truly should be feared? This matter demands ceaseless analysis. How to liberate oneself from fear, that is, terror? How to go beyond the framework of national protection? These are the sorts of questions that we should pursue, and Michel Foucault's discussion of biopolitics, or the politics of life, becomes germane. Once I am regulated as individual life and property, once I am made subject as an object of protection, I am inextricably enmeshed in the biopolitics of antiterror law. National defense currently is justified in the name of human security, while others call for public security. The question "How should we be liberated, and from what terror?" becomes a crucial, necessary condition for rethinking the horizon for a critique of terrorism, for liberating ourselves from this framework.

By way of conclusion, I would like to turn again to the problem of terminology. What especially merits attention is how broad interpretations of the term *terrorism* became rampant after 9/11. Of course, this word was subject to misuse from the start, but there are misuses and misuses. The political nature of this misuse is most evident in the "ism" of terrorism. The transformation of terror into terrorism constituted an attempt to categorize political violence as crime and thus to criminalize the enemy.

Has not terrorism come to signify the highest order of crime in order to break down the system of protections afforded on the basis of human rights and, by extension, to ignore the human rights of anyone suspected or convicted of terrorism (such as those currently imprisoned at Guantanamo Bay because they are said to be members of the Taliban or al Quaeda)? This is one consequence of the new tendency to refer to crime in general as terrorism.

Derrida has put forth the hypothesis that, historically, terrorism came to be used as a crucial framework insuring sovereign territory and political authority amid battles between allies and enemies. He feels that, contrary to appearances, such terms as *rogue state* and *terrorism* have a short lease on life. Soon they will vanish altogether. Naturally we don't yet know how things will turn out or whether this is truly what will happen. Nonetheless, it is likely that the rampant use of the term *terrorism* is already contributing to the weakening of its meaning. If *terrorism* is applied to all manner of brutal crimes, sooner or later the "ism" will wither away. Perhaps this is a sign that the term is entering into an auto-deconstructive phase.

Finally, I would like to conclude by touching on what might be called the history of slogans. An employee of the London branch of the Japan Broadcasting Corporation (NHK), Hiroshi Yamamoto, wrote a book of reportage on al Quaeda operatives called *Chain of Hatred* (*Nikushimi no rensa*).[12] The book consists of Yamamoto's energetic coverage of events during his long residence in Cairo as a correspondent. His observations are exceedingly instructive in understanding what kinds of people became involved in the illegitimate movement in the jihad lineage, such as Ayman al-Zawahiri, the philosophical ideologue of al Quaeda, and Ahmad Ibrahim al Sayyid al-Naggar, who was arrested long before 9/11 and sentenced to death in Egypt. The book opens with Osama bin Laden's slogan, which is to make a "Hiroshima in America." Some sections touch on Mohamed Atta, one of the executors of the 9/11 attacks, and some provide details of the various meanings given to the symbolism of the incident. In any event, the initial plan was to drop the planes onto nuclear power plants. But Ata himself ultimately renounced this plan, uncertain about the outcome of such an attack on nuclear plants. Instead of nuclear plants, they flew into the World Trade Center buildings. This tells us two things about the attacks. The goal was not simply to kill the greatest number of people. Nor was it simply that the World Trade Center garnered hatred as a symbol of American hegemony.

One possible outcome of an attack on nuclear plants would be a movement against nuclear energy. Derrida also called attention to this, for trauma is not simply a matter of the past. It also entails fear of worse things yet to come. Had bin Laden carried out his slogan of "Hiroshima in America," the target would have been nuclear plants.

The Bush regime has declared its right to engage in preemptive nuclear strikes. Now that there are nuclear weapons, we need to use them, and as a consequence, we need to make the enemy into an absolute criminal. It is much as Carl Schmitt predicted in *Theory of Partisans*. Frankly speaking, the current use of such terms as *terrorism* and *rogue states* is nothing more than a discursive strategy to enable the use of nuclear weapons. Moreover, the proper names in the slogan enact an analogy that is not an analogy, not exclusively. The slogan, in this sense, supposes the possibility of summoning friends. There is Che Guevara's famous statement, too: "America . . . will today have a task of much greater relevance: creating a second or third

Vietnam, or a second and third Vietnam of the world."[13] His was a statement uttered to friends throughout the world who might respond to it. One cannot help but feel that things have come full circle to see how the slogans and statements of the postwar era started with "no more Hiroshima" only to arrive at "Hiroshima in America."

As for antimilitarists in Japan who, as Japanese, have some sense of being the party concerned with this evocation of Hiroshima, how should they respond to its appearance? It seems that the Americans await one response. Or at least the stance of the Bush regime and the U.S. Department of Defense seems to imply a certain kind of response. In the wake of the attacks on the World Trade Center, various spokespeople made links between Vietnam and the so-called war on terror, which implied a perception of the second world, the third world, the whole world, as another Vietnam for the Americans. In its bid to counter bin Laden's slogan "Hiroshima in America," the slogan of an America that proclaims its right to the preemptive use of nuclear weapons can only create a second or third Hiroshima and Nagasaki, or a second or third Hiroshima and Nagasaki of the world. It is precisely in order to intervene in the automatic reflex between these two slogans, bin Laden's and Bush's, that we seek a critique of terrorism.

Translated by Thomas LaMarre

## Notes

This essay was originally a talk delivered in Japanese (" 'Jigoku e no michi wa zen'i de shikit-sumerarete iru'—kurubeki 'terorizumu hihan' no tame ni.") The phrase *kurubeki* expresses the notion *à venir*, which is often translated as "coming" or "to come." I opt for the latter here. The original transcription of the talk had no notes. The following notes have been added by the translator to refer the reader to Ukai's sources.

1 Carl Schmitt, *The Concept of the Political*, trans. George Schwab (New Brunswick, NJ: Rutgers University Press, 1976), 29–30.

2 Jean Genet, *Un captif amoureux* (Paris: Éditions Gallimard, 1986), 439. Translation modified from Jean Genet, *Prisoner of Love*, trans. Barbara Bray (Hanover, NH: Wesleyan University Press, 1992), 325–26.

3 Schmitt, *The Concept of the Political*, 54.

4   Carl Schmitt, *Partisan no riron* (*Theory of Partisans*), trans. Kunio Nitta (Tokyo: Chikuma Shobo, 1995), 189.

5   Gene Sharp, *The Politics of Nonviolent Action* (Boston: P. Sargent, 1973); Sharp, *Civilian-Based Defense: A Post-Military Weapons System* (Princeton, NJ: Princeton University Press, 1990).

6   Vladmir Il'itch Lenin, *What Is To Be Done? Burning Questions of Our Movement* (Beijing: Foreign Language Press, 1975), 92–93.

7   Ibid., 93.

8   Jacques Derrida, "La raison du plus fort" ("The Reason of the Strongest"), *Le Monde diplomatique* (January 2003), 10. The essay is an excerpt from *Voyous* (*Rogues*) (Paris: Éditions Galilée, 2003).

9   Jacques Lacan, "Le temps logique et l'assertion de certitude anticipée" ("Logical Time and the Assertion of Anticipated Certitude"), in *Écrits* (Paris: Seuil, 1966), 197–213.

10  Paul Virilio, "Revolutionary Resistance," in *Popular Defense and Ecological Struggles* (New York: Semiotext(e), 1990).

11  Roland Barthes, *The Pleasure of the Text*, trans. Richard Miller (New York: Hill and Wang, 1975).

12  Hiroshi Yamamoto, *Nikushimi no rensa* (*Chain of Hatred*) (Tokyo: Nihon Hôsô Shuppan Kyôkai, 2002).

13  Che Guevara, "Message to the Tricontinental," April 16, 1967.

# Life during Wartime

Josh Brown

*positions* 13:1 © 2005 by Duke University Press

Balanced Coverage...

Traveling abroad and
denying you're American.

Trying to locate information
on triumph-all-the-time TV.

Breaking News - Justification
for Iraqi War discovered on
Long Island!

THERE ARE SOME WHO WOULD LIKE TO REWRITE HISTORY— REVISIONIST HISTORIANS IS WHAT I LIKE TO CALL THEM.

Lie,
And then lie again,
And then lie about lying.

Bring them on!

THERE WAS NO SMOKING GUN — BUT THERE **COULD'VE** BEEN A SMOKING GUN — SO THERE PROBABLY **WAS** A SMOKING GUN — ONLY YOU COULDN'T **SEE** IT...

The Fugue (State) of War.

MONDAY, FEBRUARY 16, 2004

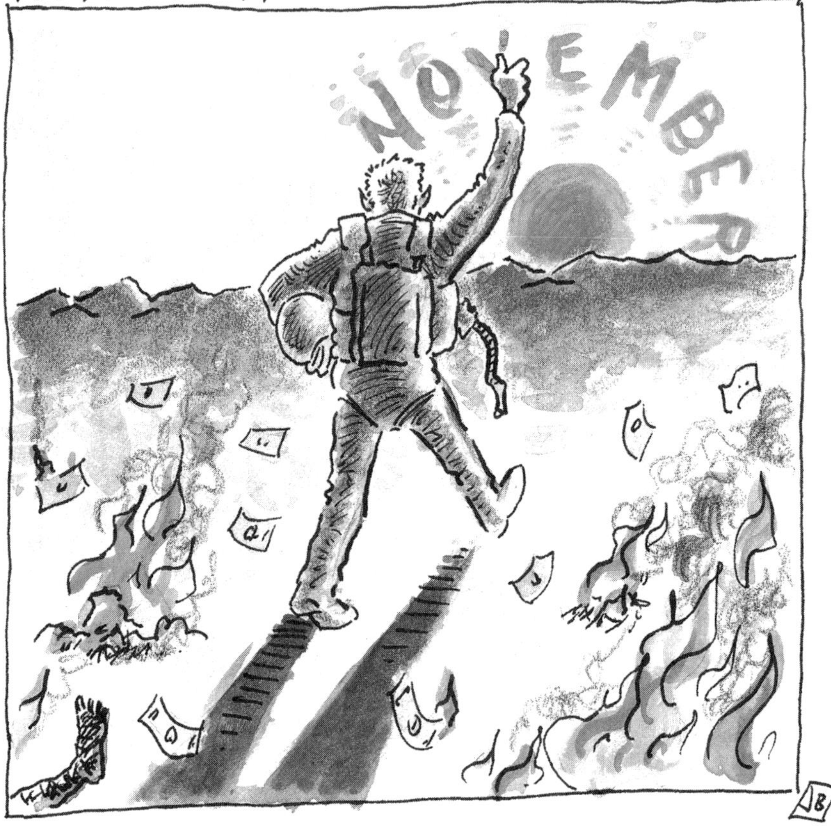

# Raw(hide): World War IV, Part 3, the Sequel

Sue Golding (johnny de philo)

> Where do we draw the line here between logic and experience?
> —Ludwig Wittgenstein

**rehearsal (mid-game-as-end-game-as-opening-play-of-the-game).** The art of warfare is a delicate business, but what it produces is not. We might wish to call this art (of warfare) a kind of game, one whose rules are located precisely in the material rupture of systematized sense-certainties—shot through with the instant fleeting of its come. (It's a deeply sticky business after all.)

**playing the game (opening moves).** Like bombs before the drop, memory, movement, indeed politics itself nowadays condense into a proliferation of singular, zap-instants: rootless (say, rhizomatic) event-horizons, nodal points, gestures, signatures, "looks" that make their sting or stake their claim "in passing." Foot soldier moves to pawn; pawn takes queen (and

*positions* 13:1 © 2005 by Duke University Press

indeed, becomes queen). En passant: This has little or nothing to do with spectacle as such; it has even less to do with morals or ethics or God (except in as much as spectacle, morals, God can condense into singular zip-instants). Rather, today's warfare arts have a whole lot more to do with the ability (or not) to capture one's prey while on the move; more bizarrely still, to do so at the very moment when speed eclipses time, duration eclipses space and netiquette eclipses content. We could call this a matter of *installation*, one whose opening play repeats the middle over and over again—not because of some direction from on high or center or singular leadership—but as the embeddedness of pluralized pawny-ness, replete with all the real-time expressions this pawn-power play might produce: a kind of rhizomatics of rule making, a kind of viral load where the uninvited keep reshaping the entire play of the game, chess pieces notwithstanding.

**employer.** To whom or to what does this ability/restriction to move one way or another owe its allegiance? I want to be all postmodern and say: to the destruction of Grand Narratives! Or to long-range Strategy! Or even to the immediacy of Tactics! (In defeatist, self-deprecating mode I might say: to the primacy of Tradition! Opinion! Money! Religion!) But whatever analytic boat or mood swing comes to mind, in the final analysis, or even (and especially) in the middle of it, there seems to be an equally determined move to repeat ad nauseam the age-old Machiavellian instruction to the Prince—binaric to its core, sophomoric in its zero-sum logic, and crucial to the building of any modern industrialized state (and quite a few feudalistic ones); the phrase every young student, soldier, statesman, and street militant alike learns by rote and takes to heart; to wit: there will always be "leaders and led," "friends and enemies," "axes of evil and good" in order to sustain or create new power regimes, and, indeed, in order to create the very stuffing of politics/movement itself.

I want to say: No! That's not exactly right! (Though it's not exactly wrong, either.)

**rhetorical echoes.** *Senegal after Radiohead after (Kant after Duchamp) after Nietzsche after Turing after Kierkegaard after Adorno after Marx after Hegel . . .*

*or how I learned to dream in technicolor and not just black and white. Remarks on Science as a new Color* (or Vico after Wittgenstein). Should the very fact that we are caught in the wild drama of a (not quite fully embedded) structural shift brought on by the death of metaphysics and the birth of singular pluralities and curved time-space mathematics matter when speaking of power? Or is it only appropriate in certain fields of art, certain fields of relativity, certain fields of quantum physics, certain fields of sexuality, media, psychology, grammar, literature, politics, identity, philosophy, medical science, history, secularism—i.e., in those areas where "black and white" as analytic tools no longer fit—and possibly never did fit?

**a bad smell.** Wouldn't this (either-or) create a kind of "brain-dead but still alive" moralism rooted in a time (not so) long past—and in some places, not past at all—that we might wish to call oppressive?

**irony.** The demands of credit-card credit and the slippery economies to which those demands give birth means that in the end (or in the middle of the end), the only people who will have money in their pockets will be: the poor. Power will have long since evacuated that domain.

**quick thinking.** That the status quo's status manages to reproduce itself in a seemingly infinite series of discrete (or otherwise) power plays, discussions, media blitzes, clever advertisements, "smart" bombs, and other bizarre/cruel experiments (like growing human ears onto mouse heads)—and yet remains intimately knotted to a political nostalgia, and not to the very multiply dimensional structures to which this rapid obsolescence is tied—is not a big mystery.

**musical chairs.** Picture this: a child's game, well known in its immediate sense of dysfunctionality writ large—the game of musical chairs. For purposes of establishing a common memory databank, I shall recap the game as follows: a series of chairs are set in a line with one too many participants for the number of given chairs. A gun goes off, the music begins, and the children run around the chairs frantically attempting to be near this or that chair so that when the music stops—suddenly, and on the wrong beat—they must grab and sit on said chair (Rule #1). The game is already skewed; we all know this from the start: one player will always-already be caught without a chair. The one caught out when silence descends, well, that one must exit, stay at the sidelines, or go somewhere else. (Get lost: Rule #2.) The game is repeated until there are only two participants and one isolated chair left. I never liked this game, whether or not I managed to be victorious with the one remaining trophy chair. Who cares about the chairs anyway? I was always more curious about the play of the game. (This curiosity meant that I always played to the bitter end of this silly little game.)

**"Everyone evacuate the premises immediately."** Not an unusual statement these days; plausibly announced by bomb-squad police or other suitable candidates, say: market mechanisms, imminent bad weather, morality gate-keepers, losers at musical chairs; forget the existential questions of life (why? why me? and so on) for, quite remarkably, the natty, bitty practical every-day problems of translocation, displacement, and other forms of decay will suddenly flash before you, with only microseconds to spare, microseconds in which a decision must be taken and enacted. This flash/decision/enactment can be broken down by way of the following set of interrogations: What would you *grab* at the very moment of decisive indecision and chaos? That which is close at hand or that which holds the most sentimental/memory value? Or that which is lightest (or all three)? Some kind of technical equip-ment, say, a mobile phone or your computer laptop (should you have one); extra batteries? A strong pair of shoes? Water? Second set of questions: Where do you go? Do you run ahead as a herdsman? asks Nietzsche, or turn into a pillar of salt, as did Lot's wife? Third set of questions: How would you get to where you wish to go (assuming there is no direct gun to your head or cattle car waiting)? How do you get to where you want to go, especially if you are not certain where you wish to go or for some other reason cannot get there, say, because you may be suffering from a certain degree of shortsight-edness? (Because in that case, you cannot say to yourself, says Wittgenstein, "Look at the church tower ten miles away and go in that direction."[1])

**twenty-four hours.** A small question, then, about mobility and its impli-cations: why is it that one can only go back or forward twenty-four hours in (our) bio-time and space? No matter the speed or the curvature of the movement, the uncertainty of the destiny; even if one leaps thousands of light years forward and speeds through the wormholes of the galaxies with greater agility than even the inventors of Star Trek could imagine; even if one floats in a balloon, is delayed endlessly in airports, or flies by the seat of one's pants; even if one is gay or straight, Muslim or Jew, a witch or a warlock, transgendered or binarically split into male or female; even if one comes from or surges toward the East or the West; even if one is the target of a racist attack or becomes its perpetrator; even if one is adorned in leather, piercing, and tattoo; even if one is engaged in peculiar sex acts or none at all; still, at the moment—this very instantaneous moment of our contemporary moment—one gains or loses only twenty-four hours of bio-time, a twenty-four-hour micromemory slice of time at the best of times. It does not matter if it is a corrosive, nuclear, toxic time, twenty-four hours is the limit to the forward or backward movement and mobility of time, at any given time.

**putting bread on the table:** How will you be able to read/interpret the rules of the game, if and when you "arrive" (wherever that "arrival point" may be)?—regardless of whether the language spoken appears to be (or even is) the "same" language, say, "international/exchange English" or even "art," for example. What codes of identity or identities must you somehow embody or occupy, or be seen to occupy, in order to "communicate"? What will be lost in translation? Or found—by way of Rosetta stone hieroglyphics? How will the differences already encumbering your life surface as explanatory nodal points or clusters of meanings (say, around race, sex, class, age, nationality, eating habits, drug use, or varying dislocations within and between these islands of identity and difference)? Which battlegrounds will you choose to stand upon, or be forced to stand upon? How will you "fit in"? By bowing and scraping, cap in hand, hoping the "flaws" won't be noticed or by boldly going where angels dare not tread? Will you fall prey to the assumption that "people are the same everywhere" whereby we return to the Eternal twenty-four-hour relay race of mobility, blood, and death compelling your every move? Or will you fall prey to the loop of musical chairs, trophies notwithstanding?

Where will you buy your milk? Pleasure your body? Rest your eye? Get dental and medical? Share your joke?

**i want to go home (there is no home).** Shall we say for the sake of brevity, romanticism, and truth that "home" is a place wherein one can be bored (without having to give account); that it is a place to relax; a place to laugh; a place steeped in promise-fulfilled comfort zones or rough-riding nights (with willing players at hand); a place to be perfectly and completely ill; a place to read a book (or write one); a place to wander; a place to fuck; a place to hide, regroup, bathe, play drums, remember the "I" of me or the "you" of they without penalty of death, unwanted humiliation, or shame? A place to be completely incomplete and unconditionally conditional? A secret place where one can move without having to go anywhere (nasty) at all?

**the people's dream.** Close your eyes and picture yourself in the dream home of your dreams! Or perhaps you are worried you will never get there! Or perhaps you are already in it! Is your household dream vision a foreseeable expression of your own hard work and sweat, a collective effort, or just a roll of the dice? Maybe it is all three. In a fit of depression, I should like to say "only the roll of the dice"; in collective wolf mode, I should prefer to say "the pack's own doing"; in being the bold and the beautiful, I should like to say "a good architect."

**lying (on the carpet).** So let us dream it! as a kind of sumptuous, generous portable fire! this home! this moveable feast! this banquet! Let it leap from our brains, and skins, and pleasures, and wants into some kind of permanent structure, some kind of perimeter, ready and able to hide, contain, reframe that fire, that ice, wind, drought, that crazy kind of nourishment. (Perhaps this is what Lyotard meant when he so quietly wrote: "Who knows not how to hide, knows not how to love."[2])

**fluid dynamics.** It's been a long, hard day at (a) work; (b) play; (c) fill in the blank. Tiredness starts at the back of the neck, life being rather a grind, repetitive, monotonous, and a little bit grey. As I enter my house, I realize I'm entering the home of my youth, a kind of neo-suburban-military split-level affair, snug, uniformed, sometimes green, and tucked away in a ticky-tacky county as part of a ticky-tacky city, surrounded by a series of ticky-tacky Confederate states, just a few miles south of the Mason-Dixon line. It is here where I learn what it means to be a Yankee and how not to fit in. It is here where I learn how to skateboard, my finest achievement being able to go downhill at top speed: on my head. It is here where I learn how to play "doctor" and where I start my very first period. It is here where I open the door to this house, all red walled and blue carpeted, with my mother sitting at a table or on the couch. I am always shocked to see her—as she is dead—nevertheless, we have the same conversation, time after time, door after door: "My God! You're alive!" I shout in (a) joy; (b) grief; (c) horror. I run to her, hugging her, alternatively as a grown adult, alternatively as a child, hugging her, hugging her! "It's okay, dear," she gently responds, running her fingers through my hair. "When realized I was alive, I simply opened the casket and came home."

**postmodern romanticism.** Housing-as-hiding-as-home: mutant knowledge, shape-shifting to fit the needs of its inhabitants.

**rehearsal  [mid-game-as-end-game-as-opening-play-of-the-game].**  Perhaps this notion of movement—a kind of muscular Eternal Return relay race back and forth against (and buttressed by) the twenty-four-hour festival of life and clocks—is the not-so-secret telos of modernity itself, the seemingly "real" basis, the biological scientistic, rational choice-within-a-small-parenthesis-of-choice, "enlightened" basis for certain commonly held views. In particular, it underwrites a few claims about equality and has similar implications for the commonality or universality of experience itself; to wit, this twenty-four-hour rule is applicable to all and sundry, regardless of nationality, ethnic origin, sexual orientation, religious belief, or aesthetic inclination. You might prefer the shorter variant, which goes something like this: at the end of the day, as it were, we all *die*, regardless of any other consideration. Later version: If I cut myself, do I not bleed?

And yet I want to say: this does not make "being human" or its suffering "universal" (though there is something about this blood and limit of death thing not to be ignored).

**slippery amputations.** "But to learn all about these recondite matters," Melville recommends,

> your best way is at once to descend into the blubber-room, and have a long talk with its inmates. . . . When the proper time arrives for cutting up its contents, this apartment is a scene of terror to all tyros, especially by night. On one side, lit by a dull lantern, a space has been left clear for the workmen. They generally go in pairs, a pike-and-gaff man and a spade-man. The whaling-pike is similar to a frigates' boarding-weapon of the same name. The gaff is something like a boat-hook. With his gaff, the gaffman hooks on to a sheet of blubber, and strives to hold it from slipping, as the ship pitches and lurches about. Meanwhile, the spade-man stands on the sheet itself, perpendicularly chopping it into the portable horse-pieces. This spade is sharp as hone can make it; the spade-man's feet are shoeless; the thing he stands on will sometimes irresistibly slide away from him, like a sledge. If he cuts off one of his own toes, or one of his assistants', would you be very much astonished? Toes are scarce among veteran blubber-room men.[3]

Well, supposing that the "this" is located somewhere in the blubber-room of life. Or, better yet, that it *is* the blubber-room of life. What difference does its *location* matter to *us*? Or whether it is shoeless or not? To experiment with space and time and numbers and slipperiness and speed—simultaneously— as an amputation or a style, or a color, a code, a system, a weapon, a poetics, or a ship of fools, merely underscores, at least in the first instance, a curious feature: its integrity.

**reassuring doubt.** Integrity comes in several varieties: the word, the promise, the friendship, the [blood] relation, and, for the more spiritually afflicted, the soul. (This list does not exhaust the list.) Interestingly enough, it also doubles as the vehicle to carry out or maintain the aforementioned list. So it would not be unfair to say that integrity elicits a paradox: despite the odds (or perhaps because of them), there is something of a "given-ness," a sturdiness, an unchangeability about integrity (as in the promise—if you do such and such, I, Moses, will, despite bad weather or river conditions, deliver you to the promised land), while at the same time sneaking in a kind of unstated *probability* or *capability* or *reliability* to do so. Now, integrity as capability; capability as a repeatable gesture; the repeatability of a gesture as eliciting the predictability of a "what is to come next"; the what is to come next as probability (and not just possibility); the probable-possibility as some kind of sturdiness; sturdiness as some kind of reliability—surely must count for *something*. But that the sun goes up and the sun goes down, more or less on a regular basis, twenty-four hours a day, every day (or at least does not go dancing around the buildings at all hours of day and night according to some whim) is not, really, what is meant here by integrity.

**the giving of a gift (or impropriety and whether pigs can fly).** Let's say that the word *integrity* is to become the proper name we give to a certain kind of coherence, a certain kind of multiplicity/dimensionality of rhythms, rifts, light waves or beats. Still, the condition for its execution and deliverance seems to rely on a "something else" or a "something other": say, for example, the projected *intention* of the promise giver to the promise receiver (and vice versa). But if this is true, then a whole series of problematic assumptions around who or what is giving and receiving promises when and how surely must infect our otherwise perfect games of truth. It might even touch on that nebulous terrain called memory or faith or even the more superstitious (and attractive) glow spheres of a spell! Nevertheless, it underscores the not-so-problematic "fact" that intention (or anyway, its conditions) is not only—like the integrity from which it springs—multiple, slippery, cruel, paradoxical in a probability kind of way, but also sensuous, bitter, sometimes wrong, sweaty, alive, human (also in a probability kind of way). This makes intention itself both a part of and, at the very same time, quite separate from its word, promise, friendship, viewer relation, soul. Rather similar to an instant (of time/timings)—or a fragment without edge, weight, or volume—or a surface economy of sorts, it remains separate from the very entity of which it is a part. For, like its cousin integrity, intention can shape-shift while retaining its recognizability as an authoritative "this is (it)," or "I mean what I say" (and in so declaring, makes it have weight, volume, edge). Strangely, though, intention/integrity becomes neither the form (but it is the form!), nor the structure (but it is the structure!), nor the nodal point (but it is the nodal point!), nor the gap between two "opposing" points or edges (but it is also the gap!). A ticklish situation, to be sure.

> [interlude] **on the dark side (of the moon); sense-certainty as vicious circle [I].** Our doubts form systems, and systems form our horizons; horizons form our paths; paths, our goals; goals form our experiences; experiences, our doubts; doubts form our systems; systems form our horizons . . . Stuck in that vicious circle? Don't go blaming your tools (or other logics of instrumental reason).

> [interlude] **on the dark side (of the moon); sense-certainty as vicious circle (II).** Perhaps what propels your every move is a certain sense of discipline, a certain sense of lust, a certain sense of ambition, but the kind rooted in neither love nor money. A certain kind of (bureaucratic) intelligence, this certain sense of discipline and order: a certain kind of fear, a certain kind of cruelty. A certain kind of paranoia we so nonchalantly call: management.

**light switch.** First, the mathematical problem of certainty: Did you know that the square root of any positive number after zero is eventually—I mean, after a while (that is, at least to nine digits, sometimes rounded up or down)—always and without fail equal to 1? Peculiar, though not fascinating, except to the very few. Indeed, probably only to those with calculators and extra time on their hands, bored with some other administrational task (say, figuring out the law of averages). But with the aid of light-avoidance techniques—blank stares, self-abuse, whimsy, for example—surprising things can be accomplished! And even with the most simple of calculators! Like pressing the magic $\sqrt{\phantom{x}}$ (square root) button enough times until a one (1) emerges from any (positive) anonymous chaos.

**lighter switch.** Second, the mathematical problem of uncertainty, that nagging little problem presented by irrational numbers and their friends (Möbius strips, string theories, relativity, fragmented infinities, surface structure circuitries, quanta, and other tidal waves-dots-webs, 3D game boards and their ilk). Despite the aging fact that Einstein and others show, unrelentingly, how uncertainty is neither void nor Other nor imaginary friend nor utopian option of the Real, the consequences of their work still elude our grasp. On the other hand, perhaps we should just run back to our nice little calculators and avoid trespassing onto these mathematically peculiar swamplands of tension and delight: I should like to say: No! (but without so much certainty).

**lightest switch. A theory of the ordinary (as easy as 1, 2, 3).** Forget about fractions or fragments of a whole and the itty bitty in-between betweennesses of the either/ors in life. Let us inhabit, for the moment, the ordinary, seemingly basic comfort zones admitted, say, in the phrase: whatever+1. In this zone, let us allow the "whatever" be any whole number, including zero, between nought and infinity. Now, according to Gödel's infamous theorem, any ordinary (that is to say: whole) number within any ordinary calculus (as in addition or multiplication) or their related ordinary systems is always-already "undecidable"; that is to say, is always-already neither provable nor unprovable within that system.[4] This may seem counterintuitive: for have we not been taught that n+1 is always n+1 (or 1+1 is always 2), no matter where or how or when? A scandalous irritation to normality and ordinariness, to be sure.

The erstwhile Mr. Braithwaite, friend of Gödel, drew out the first of many weird implications of this "undecidability/unprovability" within any system:

> Gödel was the first to prove any unprovability theorem for arithmetic, and his way of proof was subtler and deeper than the metamathematical methods previously employed. Either of these facts would have ranked this paper high in the development of metamathematics. But it was the fact that it was a proposition of whole-number arithmetic which created such a scandal.[5]

**it gets worse.** The delicate, but inescapable, conclusion that even in simple maths, undecidability was the primary feature of all (dynamic) systems meant also, both logically and practically speaking, that all dynamic systems, even and especially the most simple, would also always-already (and, paradoxically) be: incomplete. Now this by itself was not really enough, despite its stunning simplicity, to rock the very foundation of philosophic, aesthetic, and scientific "uncertainty" propositions heretofore untouchable when it came to the very notion of "systems," not to mention logic, reason, and indeed the art of warfare itself. This was because before his "incompleteness theorem," the very concept of uncertainty tended to be tied to the concept of totality, wholeness, enframing, etc. (and its ability or not to escape that totality, wholeness, enframing, etc.). What was now on offer, instead, and more bizarrely, drew up a kind of logic that not only proved the unprovability of any simple system and the logic of "totality" or "wholeness" that the very concept of "system" emitted; but that wholeness and the certainty/uncertainty to which that wholeness gave weight was at its core "differently whole," a kind of differently wholeness that depended on something else or something other to make its cohesiveness "stick together" (i.e., become whole). It meant more oddly still that this differently whole entity was sutured by discrete fragments that were themselves neither fully formed (neither, say, as atoms or molecular/cellular entities) nor "abstract concepts" (neither, say, as thesis or anti-thesis before being strapped into their synthesized grounds or goals).

**i want the whole truth and nothing but the truth so help me God (there is no whole truth and nothing but the truth so help you God).** In a superficial sense, then, this "incompleteness" move echoed the not-too-dissimilar methodological wisdom set out by Marx, who constantly reminded us that "the whole is always greater than the sum of its parts." But for Marx (as well as for other strategic and tactical dialecticians, metaphysical or otherwise), there had to be some kind of telos or unfolding to which this "greater sum" owed its allegiance. This then implied that meaning, in order to be meaningful, accessible, and "real," had always and also to express or inhabit some kind of transcendental "becoming" or "immanence" or "negation" or "excluded middle" or other kind of quasi-messianistic/theological garment. But now, if it were true that wholeness itself no longer entailed boundaries, or rather, that discrete entities (like whole number integers, say the number $1$ or $5$ or $n+1$) could no longer be conceptualized as entailing structural paths, be they continuously formed or even discontinuously formed linear trajectories, then it also meant that "difference" ceased to fall outside the system, the logic, or the not fully formed concept/abstract sense of, say, the terms *thesis* and *anti-thesis* but instead was wholly constitutive of it (that is to say: of the system, the logic, or the abstract concept).

To be blunt: Gödel's incompleteness theorem underscored the fact that whatever sense or truth emitted from those whatever+1 or whatever−1 comfort zones had more to do with mimetic viral assemblages and respectively linked recursive logics than with the semiotics of representation, sign, signifier, signified. Or to say this slightly differently (and therewith say something perhaps very different): it meant that a fragment was not always or only a "portion" of the whole, say, a slice of the pie or a piece of the puzzle. Sometimes a fragment just "was." Or to put it again, slightly more clearly and yet more damning still: there was (and is) no "outside" or "inside" or "in between" to reality and its creatures, including, for example, the whole of the universe, despite its ever-expanding or shrinking state.

**i'm my own grandma.** To restate this remarkable move, one last time and in a slightly aestheticized-political form: the most ordinary of truths could only (and did only) inhabit its functionality as truth by way of a viral—that is to say strangely fragmented or "differently totalized"—logic, where meaning could only (and did only) "make" sense (in the strongest terms of the infinitive phrase: to make [something happen] by, say, putting 2+2 together in an ever-expanding, recursively designed system, with no inside or outside or boundary or God). Moreover, or more to the point, this "putting together" did not necessarily entail intentionality or consciousness or indeed any form of subjectivity as such; it was subtler, some might say more meaningful and closer to the logics of sound and sense rather than knowledge per se; a kind of "intuitive" logic; closer to networking an event (of appropriation) or the techne of poesis; where meaning is generated by resorting to its own recursive birthing process, recursive geneaology, recursive systematizing. "This syntactical fact," according to most metamathematicians, but particularly to the now breathless and excited Braithwaite, meant that Gödel's discovery of this incompleteness and the recursivity to which it was attached remained "one of the greatest and most surprising of the intellectual achievements of this [the twentieth] century."[6]

**how to tell time after Gödel (after Einstein after Bergson after Bachelard)— or (recycled) tales from the crypt.** Deleuze had a particularly useful phrase for this pluralized event of incompleteness and recursivity. He called it, simply enough: cinema-time; and he christened its recursive requirements as "the powers of the false." Or, as our friend would say, and I quote at length:

> The cinema is always narrative, and more and more narrative; but it is dysnarrative in so far as narration is affected by repetitions, permutations and transformations which are explicable in detail by the new structure. However [as he also insisted], a pure semiotics is unable to follow the tracks of this semiology, because there is no narration (nor description) which is as "given" of images. The diversity of narrations cannot be explained by the avatars of the signifier, by the states of a linguistic structure which is assumed to underlie images in general. . . . It is in this sense that falsifying narration depends directly on the time-image, on *opsigns* and *chronosigns*, whilst traditional narration relates to forms of the movement-image and sensory-motor signs. . . .[7]
>
> In Nietzsche's phrase, "with the real world we have also abolished the apparent world." What remains? [asks Deleuze. Answer:] There remain bodies, which are forces, nothing but forces. But force no longer refers to a centre, any more than it confronts a setting or obstacles. It only confronts other forces, it refers to other forces that it affects or that affect it. Power (what Nietzsche calls "will to power" and Welles, "character") is this power to affect and be affected, this relation between one force and others. This power is always fulfilled, and this relation is necessarily carried out, even if in a variable manner according to the forces, which are present. . . . The whole cinema becomes a free, indirect discourse, operating in reality. . . . [We then have a] *series of time*, which brings together the before and the after in a becoming, instead of separating them; its paradox is to introduce an enduring interval in the moment itself [and] also shatter the empirical continuation of time, the chronological succession, the separation of the before and after.[8]

**spitting on the curve-ball rhizomatics of the pitch.** Einstein was not the first, and certainly not the last, but he was perhaps the most effective challenger not only to the legend of the chronos as empirical succession/linear logic or circular repetition of time (picture a round clock, tick-tick-ticking away), but also a challenger to its corollary, i.e., to the tidy and rather clean injunction that forbids the comingling of time with space and vice versa, space with time.[9] Pre-(special) relativity theory, and for many folks, post-relativity theory, too, demanded that time stay on its side of the fence, and indeed, that space make room by staying far away or, better yet, remain rooted to a ground (any ground). There were times, of course (say in story telling, as in "once upon a time"), that time was allowed special dispensation and could occupy the very fence from which it was supposed to stay detached; and there were places (say in physics or urban geographies) where space could loose its groove and take on the garments of text or place or shape. But it was only when speed and light and distance and the relativity of those variables to each other entered the picture (any picture) that our time(s) and our space(s) were free at last. Free, that is to say, to make way for plural logics; that is to say, cohabiting multiple dimensionalities, morphed continuities, wormhole aesthetics.

One might wish to say that space + time as "space-time" becomes the ground-less/rootless and utterly surface curveball rhizomatics of the pitch.

Some might call this stretching of the dimensions a kind of constellation, a shape-shifting where distance and speed overtake time (and become it); where folds take on rhythm and therewith become its beat; where force has a materiality, indeed an end-game as mid-game that is not seen or smelled or tasted or touched but is toxic and mean and playful and erotic nonethe-less. (Mental note: Maybe we should just call it "all that jazz"—a kind of "pluralized event," this surface circuitry dynamic curveball rhizomatics of the pitch: a poetics; that is to say, the poetics of the visual-acoustic [cinema] time as speed-time as sense/sensuous-time; as our times.)

**eye of newt; tongue of frog.** Darwin simply called it: the origin of the species, or in a word: evolution. (Mental note: Might we then now understand, against all those creationist busybodies, that evolution is itself—albeit "con-tinuous" and to use the present vernacular: morphed/ "mutationism"—no longer "linear" [if ever it was] or chronological or transcendent? I'd like to say: yes, but without too much certainty.)[10]

**private culture/public nature (Cheshire cat and the question of national se-curity).** Have you noticed that privacy has gone all postmodern? Slipping and sliding through the public sphere rather than in opposition to it; secretly but overtly adorned now in one outfit, now in another; sometimes wearing the all-too-fashionable axes of evil garments (truth and will and God Is on Our Side outfits); sometimes wearing only the Emperor's new clothes? Dialectics be damned! Diverse cultural memories take flight and scatter into the void, and in their sacred places: the resurrection of homogeneous memory, a singular public memory, and a unilateral laugh. A funny kind of security, this inverse resurrection of the age-old nature/culture divide; an odd kind of historical clarity; a peculiar kind of nationalism, this newborn oxymoron "public nature": simultaneously itself, its Other, and its synthesized brand-name namings, which, in turn, form the groundless grounds and heightless heights for both its lacks and its excesses. One might just think it's a recycled fascism, though this time sans the need for national borders or ethnic sovereignties.

[interlude] **in between engagements.** Access to washing machines can be a luxury for some, especially for those who find themselves walking the streets—with no cover against all that pigeon shit.

**a few questions and answers.**

Question: When is a curve no longer a line or a point?

Answer: When it morphs into an imaginary number (where n is part real, part make-believe).

Question: When is an imaginary number no longer a vectored curve?

Answer: When its rhizomatic spreadsheet is conditioned by its molecular regime.

Question: When is the condition of a molecular regime problematic?

Answer: When that molecular regime is able (just because it can) to install the *war machine*, as Deleuze would call it, into every available hole and niche and quadrant.

Question: When is a war machine able to "install" itself everywhere at anytime without too much (or any) awareness or resistance that a microfascism is starting to implant and grow? That is to say, when can the war machine install itself "just because it can"?

Answer: When the morphed continuum recursivity's viral load paradoxically subsumes the dividing lines while simultaneously resurrecting segmented strata. Translation: It has nothing to do with "false consciousness" and even less to do (at least in the beginning) with identity politics, nationalisms, and ethnicities. It is rather a particular kind of bureaucracy, a rather particular kind of managerialism, a particular kind of art/school mutation, sweeping over Europe (old and new) at this very moment, as we speak. It is a paradoxically situated "situation": both binarically coded and deeply "open-ended." "The masses certainly do not passively submit to power," observes the Deleuze and Guattarian eye, "nor do they 'want' to be repressed, in a kind of masochistic hysteria; nor are they tricked by an ideological lure. Desire is never separable from complex assemblages that necessarily tie into molecular levels, from microformations already shaping postures, attitudes, perceptions, expectations, energy, but itself results from a highly developed, engineered setup rich in interactions: a whole supple segmentarity that processes molecular energies and potentially gives desire a fascist determination. Leftist organizations will not be the last to secret microfascisms."[11]

**the tired man speaks.** (The tired man speaks. . . . In the last milliseconds of the "what does it matter," the tired man speaks, wears, brandishes his/her last speck of individuality, possession, dignity.) Haven't we heard this somewhere before, say in some famous man's remarks about the ability or not to write poetry after the genocidal stamping out of human identities, as so many singular beings (identified, too, with the individual group identity of Jew, Christian, Muslim, gay, mad, whore, gypsy, Other) were condemned to endure? A collective headstone of black ash, smoke, and dust, which, as Adorno so morbid-eloquently put it: wriggled ever skyward from the ovens of Auschwitz and elsewhere.[12] I want to say, by saying this: that to want, and to know that one wants, should not be forgotten or thrown away, as if "unimportant," "begging the question." For those honest enough to admit it, this remains at the very basis of a new being, poetics, and, indeed, politics.

**microfascism/macrofascism and the problems of everyday life (I want to go home [there is no home]).** Ordinary fear, according to our friend Mr.

Freud, is quite distinct from anxiety or fright. "Anxiety," he writes in his *Transitions and Revisions*, "describes a particular state of expecting the danger or preparing for it, even though it may be an unknown one."[13] Or, as the old phrase used to go: "just because you're paranoid doesn't mean they're not after you." With fear, one knows precisely the object of their worry; that is to say, they know the "what" or the "that"; they just do not know the when or the how or the where. Fright, on the other hand, is the name we give to the state a person gets into when he (or she) has run into danger without being prepared for it; it emphasizes the factor of surprise.[14] Terror, we might tidily conclude, is the name we give when all three (anxiety, fear, fright) condense to form the condition of the unconditional (freedom, law, hope, love), en passant.

**microfascism/macrofascism and the problems of everyday life (I want to go home [what's become of my home?]).** What, then, is fascism and its accompanying terror(ism)s? From the point of view of the fascist, it is nothing more or less than the embedded trajectory where, as Deleuze and Guattari detail, "the barriers between offices cease to be 'a definitive dividing line' and are immersed in a molecular medium (milieu) that dissolves them and simultaneously makes the office management proliferate into microfigures impossible to recognize or identify, discernible only when they are central-izable: another regime, coexistent with the separation *and* totalization of the rigid segments."[15] What, then, is fascism and its accompanying terror(ism)? From the point of view of the anti-fascist: it is the horror and disgust of being witness to, participant in, and host-body for this molecular-political cancer. Deleuze and Guattari, again:

> Rural fascism and city or neighbourhood fascism, youth fascism and war veteran's fascism, fascism of the Left and fascism of the Right, fascism of the couple, family, school, and office: every fascism is defined by a micro-black hole that stands on its own and communicates with the others, before resonating in a great, generalised central black hole. There is fascism when a *war machine* is installed in each hole, in every niche.... If Hitler *took power*, rather than taking over the German State administration, it was because from the beginning he had at his disposal micro-organizations

giving him "an unequalled, irreplaceable ability to penetrate every cell of society," in other words, a molecular and supple segmentarity flows capable of suffusing every kind of cell. . . . What makes fascism dangerous is its molecular or micropolitical power, for it is a mass movement: a cancerous body rather than a totalitarian organism.[16]

In the searing scream that each being shouts at the moment of this "event," the secret (and not-so-secret) event-rebuilding of the binaric codes; in that searing scream: "Oh God! Why hast thou abandoned me?!" the silence can be—and always has been—deafening.

OH! This putrid skin! Would it not have been so alive!

**covering a multiplicity of sins (perhaps).** So, how did you begin your journey? With eyes aglow and tail a-wagging? Or were you forced by great gulfs of war, famine, gangland terror? Curiosity? Fear? Trembling? Perhaps it was a family life not quite up to scratch? Or perhaps you were a wolf running hungry with the pack? Maybe you saw yourself as a freedom fighter or an artist or a deserter or all three? Perhaps your bravery, cowardice, complicity makes you think you are: Invincible. Then again, perhaps you were just terribly frightened (or not frightened enough)? Whatever is compelling your every move, hindsight is not just 20/20 vision, and romanticism is not just for fools and horses.

**word of warning.** "Anyone who does not understand why we must speak of these things must feel what we say to be mere trifling."[17]

## Notes

This article contains sections from my *Games of Truth (A Blood Poetic in Seven Part Harmony)*, (London: University of Greenwich Press, 2003) and from *Housing* by L. de Boeck (Maastricht: Jan Van Eyck Press, 2004), 5, 7–8, 123–35, 150–54, 170. The mathematical sections in this piece were presented at the Deleuzian (n–1) symposium, July 7, 2004 (The Philosophicum: University of Cologne) and were done entirely in pitch darkness, save for a tiny torchlight.

1   Ludwig Wittgenstein, *Culture and Value*, ed. G. H. Von Wright in collaboration with Heikki Nyman, trans. Peter Winch (Oxford: Basil Blackwell, 1980), 33.

2  Jean-François Lyotard, *Libidinal Economy*, trans. Iain Hamilton Grant (London: Athlone, 1993), frontispiece dedication.

3  Herman Melville, "A Squeeze of the Hand," in *Moby Dick* (Hertfordshire: Wordsworth Editions, 1992), 429.

4  Kurt Gödel, *On Formally Undecidable Propositions of* Principa Mathematica *and Related Systems*, trans. B. Meltzer, introduction R. B. Braithwaite (New York: Dover, 1992 [Basic Books: 1962 (first publication: 1931)]), 38.

5  R. B. Braithwaite, "Introduction," in *On Formally Undecidable Propositions*, 4.

6  R. B. Braithwaite, "Introduction," in *On Formally Undecidable Propositions*, 32. Of interest: "I'm My Own Grandma" is a country-twanged Americana song, whose refrain and the first stanza go something like this: "I'm my own Grandma—It's the darndest mix-up; I'm my own Grandma (and it can't be fixed up). Funny I know, but it really is so: I'm my own Grandma. Many many years ago when I was 23, I was married to a widower as grand as he could be. The widower had a grown-up daughter who had hair of red; my father fell in love with her and soon those two were wed! OH! I'm my own Grandma, it's the darndest mix-up. . . ."

7  Gilles Deleuze, "The Powers of the False," in *The Time-Image*, Cinema no. 2 (London: Athlone, 1989 [1985]), chap. 6, 137.

8  Deleuze, *The Time-Image*, 139, 155. The other two time-images to which Deleuze refers in this quotation and that he develops in "The Crystals of Time" and "Peaks of Present and Sheets of Past: Fourth Commentary on Bergson" (chaps. 4 and 5, 68–97 and 98–125, respectively) deal with, as he puts it, "the order of time, that is, the coexistence of relations or the simultaneity of the elements internal to time" (155).

9  See, in particular, Henri Bergson's *Duration and Simultaneity: Bergson and the Einsteinian Universe* (Manchester: Clinamen Press, 1999 [1922]), especially the letters between Einstein and Bergson, in which the former gently chastises the latter for not allowing relativity itself to enter the discussion on its own terms. Bergson wrongly requires an "objective"—that is to say "outside"—entity to "ground" the duration and simultaneity of time, distance, space, speed, whereas Einstein requires the relation to act as ground. In a certain sense, Bergson is at least attempting to rid philosophy of its dialectical obsessions without falling into liberalist or empiricist stratagems, but he does so at a rather high price—a point Gaston Bachelard makes with glaring precision in his book-length attack on Bergson, titled *Dialectic of Duration* (New York: Clinamen, 2000).

10  See Charles Darwin, *The (Illustrated) Origin of the Species* (London: Faber and Faber, 1979 [1859/1860]). See especially the discussion on the eye and its links to, among other things, the worm, in "Organs of Extreme Perfection and Complication," 111–16.

11  Gilles Deleuze and Felix Guattari, "Micro Politics and Segmentarity," in *a thousand plateaus: capitalism and schizophrenia* (London: Athlone, 1988/1999), 215.

12  Paraphrased from Theodor W. Adorno, "Meditations on Metaphysics: After Auschwitz," in his *Negative Dialectics*, trans. E. B. Ashton (London: Routledge, 1973), 363.

13  Sigmund Freud, "Transitions and Revisions," *Beyond the Pleasure Principle*, in *The Freud Reader*, ed. Peter Gay (London: Norton, 1989), 598.

14  Ibid.

15  Deleuze and Guattari, *a thousand plateaus*, 214.

16  Deleuze and Guattari, *a thousand plateaus*, 215.

17  Ludwig Wittgenstein, *Philosophical Grammar*, 125 (London: Basil Blackwell, 1974), 174.

**Totalitarian Democracy: A New Poem**

Lawrence Ferlinghetti

> The first fine dawn of life on earth
> The first light of the first morning
> The first evening star
> The first man on the moon seen from afar
> The first voyage of Ulysses westward
> The first fence on the last frontier
> The first tick of the atomic clock of fear
> The first Home Sweet Home so dear
> The sweet smell of honeysuckle at midnight
> The first free black man free of fright
> The sweet taste of freedom
> The first good orgasm
> The first Noble Savage
> The first Pale Face settler on the first frontier

*positions* 13:1 © 2005 by Duke University Press

The last Armenian and the last Ojibway in Fresno
The first ballpark hotdog with mustard
The first home run in Yankee Stadium
The first song of love and forty cries of despair
The first pure woman passing fair
The sweet smell of success
The first erection and the first Resurrection
The first darling buds of May
The last covered wagon through the Donner Pass
The first green sprouts of new grass
The last cry of Mark Twain! on the Mississippi
The First and Last Chance Saloon
The ghostly galleon of the half-moon
The first cry of pure joy in morning light
The distant howl of trains lost in book of night
The first morning after the night before thinking
The last new moon sinking
The last of the Mohicans and the last buffalo
The last sweet chariot swinging low
The first hippie heading for the hills
The last bohemian in a beret
The last beatnik in North Beach with something to say
The last true love to come your way
The last Wobbly and the last Catholic Anarchist
The last paranoid Lefty
The last Nazi
The first bought vote in the first election
The last hand caught in the last cookie jar
The last cowboy on the last frontier
The last bald eagle with nothing to fear
The last buffalo-head nickel
The last living member of the Abraham Lincoln Brigade
The last Mom and Pop grocery
The last firefly flickering in the night

The first plane to hit the first Twin Tower
The last plane to hit the last Twin Tower
The only plane to ever hit the Pentagon
The birth of a vast national paranoia
The beginning of the Third World War
(the War Against the Third World)

The first trip abroad by an ignorant president
The last free-running river
The last gas and oil on earth
The last general strike
The last Fidelista the last Sandinista the last Zapatista
The last political prisoner
The last virgin and the last of the champagne
The last train to leave the station
The last and only great nation
The last Great Depression
The last will & testament
The last welfare check for rent
The end of the old New Deal
The new Committee on Unamerican Activities
The last politician with honest proclivities
The last independent newspaper
printing the news and raising hell
The last word and the last laugh and the Last Hurrah
The last picture show and the last waltz
The last Unknown Soldier
The last innocent American
The last Ugly American
The last Great Lover and the last New Yorker
The last home-fries with ketchup-to-go
The last train home at midnight
The last syllable of recorded time
The last long careless rapture
The last independent bookstore with its own mind

The last best hope of mankind
The lost chord and the lost leader
The last drop of likker
The cup that runneth over quicker
The last time I saw Paris, Texas
The last peace treaty and the Last Supper
The first sweet signs of spring
The first sweet bird of youth
The first baby tooth and the last wisdom tooth
The last honest election
The last freedom of information
The last free Internet
The last free speech radio
The last unbought television network
The last homespun politician
The last Jeffersonian
The last Luddite in Berkeley
The last Bottom Line and the last of Social Security
The first fine evening calm and free
The beach at sunset with reclining nudes
The lovers wrapped in each other
The last meeting of the Board
The last gay sailor to come aboard
The first White Paper written in blood
The last terrorist born of hate and poverty
The last citizen who bothered to vote
The first President picked by a Supreme Court
The end of the Time of Useful Consciousness
The unfinished flag of the United States
The ocean's long withdrawing roar

The birth of a nation of sheep
The deep deep sleep of the booboisie
The underground wave of feel-good fascism
The uneasy rule of the super-rich

The total triumph of imperial America
The final proof of our Manifest Destiny
The first loud cry of America über alles
Echoing in freedom's alleys
The last lament for lost democracy
The total triumph of
totalitarian plutocracy

**CODA**

Cut down cut down cut down
Cut down the grassroots
Cut down those too wild weeds
in our great agri-fields and golf courses
Cut down cut down those wild sprouts
Cut down cut down those rank weeds
Pull down your vanity, man, pull down
the too wild buds the too wild shoots
Cut down the wild unruly vines & voices
the hardy volunteers and pioneers
Cut down cut down the alien corn
Cut down the crazy introverts
Tongue-tied lovers of the subjective
Cut down cut down the wild ones the wild spirits
The desert rats and monkey wrenchers
Easy riders and midnight cowboys in narco nirvanas
Cut down the wild alienated loners
fiddling with their moustaches
plotting revolution in hopeless cellars
Cut down cut down all those freaks and free thinkers
Wild-eyed poets with wandering minds
Soapbox agitators and curbstone philosophers
Far out weirdos and rappers
Stoned-out visionaries and peaceniks

Exiles in their own land!
O melting pot America!

# Contributors

**Bei Dao** is the Mackey Poet at Beloit College. His book *Midnight's Gate* will be available in 2005.

**Jim Bonk** is a graduate student in East Asian studies at McGill University, specializing in the literary history of Republican China.

**Joshua Brown,** a professor at the Center for Media and Learning, CUNY Graduate Center, is the author of *Beyond the Lines: Pictorial Reporting, Everyday Life, and the Crisis of Gilded Age America* (2002).

**Carolyn Eisenberg** is a professor of history at Hofstra University and the author of *Drawing the Line: The American Decision to Divide Germany* (1996).

**Lawrence Ferlinghetti,** the poet and author, is the founder of City Lights Books in San Francisco.

**Matthew Fryslie** presently resides in Taipei.

**Sue Golding** (johnny de philo) is chair and professor of philosophy in the visual arts and communication technologies at the University of Greenwich, London. She is also director of the postgraduate Critical Studies, New Media Arts program. Her latest book, *Dirty Theory*

(2005), concentrates on the muscular sensualities of poetics in visual-acoustic culture, ethics, and art.

**Freda Guttman,** a Canadian peace activist and installation artist, is a member of the Jewish Alliance against the Occupation and of the Montreal chapter of the International Solidarity Movement.

**Harry Harootunian** is a professor of East Asian studies and history at New York University. His most recent publication is *The Empire's New Clothes: Paradigm Lost, and Regained* (2004).

**Sharon Hayashi,** a lecturer in Japanese cinema at the Center for International Studies, Rikkyo University, Tokyo, is codirecting a documentary on Japan's pink film industry.

**Reynaldo Ileto** is a professor of history and the coordinator of the Southeast Asian Studies Program at the National University of Singapore. His latest book, *Knowledge and Pacification: Essays on the U.S. Conquest and the Writing of Philippine History*, will be published in 2005.

**Joy Kogawa** is a Canadian novelist, author of *The Rain Ascends* (1995). She lives in Toronto and Vancouver.

**Kuang Xinnian** teaches modern Chinese literature at Tsinghua University, Beijing, where he is currently specializing in modern Taiwan literature. He is the author of *1928: Geming wenxue* (*1928: Revolutionary Literature*) (1998).

**Thomas LaMarre,** a professor of East Asian studies at McGill University, is the author of *Shadows on the Screen: Tanizaki Jun'ichirô on Cinema and Oriental Aesthetics* (2005).

**Sumit K. Mandal,** a research fellow at the Institute of Malaysian and International Studies (IKMAS), Universiti Kebangsaan Malaysia, is working on a manuscript on Arabs and Islam in Java in the nineteenth and twentieth centuries.

**Edoarda Masi,** author of *Storie del bosco letterario* (2002), has retired from the Istituto Universitario Orientale Napoli.

**Brian Massumi,** a professor in the Département de Communication, L'Université de Montréal, is the author of *Parables of the Virtual* (2002).

**Anne McKnight,** an assistant professor of East Asian studies at McGill University, specializes in film noir and Cold War cultural studies in Japan.

**Carel Moiseiwitsch** is a Vancouver artist and longtime social activist. She taught for more than ten years at the Emily Carr Institute of Art and Design and currently works with IV drug users living with HIV/AIDS in Vancouver's downtown Eastside.

**Alberto Moreiras** is a professor of romance studies at Duke University and is the author of *The Exhaustion of Difference* (2001).

**Claudia Pozzana,** a researcher in the Department of Linguistic and Oriental Studies, University of Bologna, is working on a manuscript titled "Thinking Poetry: The Contemporary Chinese Poetic Configuration."

**Alessandro Russo,** an associate professor of sociology, School of Education, University of Bologna, is working on China's Cultural Revolution.

**Laurie Sears,** a professor of history at the University of Washington, is working on a manuscript titled "Trauma, Haunting, and Memory in Indonesian and Dutch Indies Literatures."

**Satoshi Ukai** is a professor of language and society at Hitotsubashi University in Japan. He is the author of *Responsibilities* (2003) and is currently working in the field of contemporary French literature and ideas.

**Marilyn Young** is a professor of history at New York University. She is the coeditor, with Lloyd Gardner, of *The New American Empire* (2005).

# Amerasia Journal

*Amerasia Journal*—the frontrunner on Asian American history, social issues, immigration, politics, economy, literature, and community studies for 30 years. Thoughtful, informative, in-depth—*Amerasia Journal* offers viewpoints that challenge conventional assumptions, superficial analyses, and media distortions that shortchange our understanding of Asian Americans and Pacific Islanders.

MAILING ADDRESS: UCLA Asian American Studies Center Press
3230 Campbell Hall • Box 951546 • Los Angeles, CA 90095-1546
(310) 825-2968 • FAX: (310) 206-9844 • E-mail: aascpress@aasc.ucla.edu

I would like a 1-year subscription (3 issues) to *Amerasia Journal*
(includes a free subscription to *CrossCurrents*, newsmagazine of the
UCLA Asian American Studies Center):

☐ $35.00*/individual   ☐ $55.00*/institution
Make checks payable to **UC REGENTS**
*CA residents, add 8.25% sales tax

No shipping charges on *Amerasia Journal* subscriptions in U.S.
Foreign subscriptions to *Amerasia Journal*, add $12.00 per year.

Name _____

Address _____

State _____   Zip _____

Card Number   VISA/MASTERCARD/DISCOVER accepted        Expiration Date

Signature _____   Phone Number _____   Total _____